A JOURNAL OF CONTEMPORARY WRITING

IRISH PAGES

DUILLÍ ÉIREANN

IRISH PAGES is a biannual journal (Spring-Summer, Autumn-Winter), edited in Belfast and publishing, in equal measure, writing from Ireland and overseas. It appears at the end of each six-month period.

Its policy is to publish poetry, short fiction, essays, creative non-fiction, memoir, essay reviews, nature-writing, translated work, literary journalism, and other autobiographical, historical, religious and scientific writing of literary distinction. There are no standard reviews or narrowly academic articles. Irish-language and Scots writing are published in the original, with English translations or glosses. IRISH PAGES is a non-partisan, non-sectarian, culturally ecumenical, and wholly independent journal. It endorses no political outlook or cultural tradition, and has no editorial position on the constitutional question. Its title refers to the island of Ireland in a purely apolitical and geographic sense, in the same manner of The Church of Ireland or the Irish Sea.

The sole criteria for inclusion in the journal are the distinction of the writing and the integrity of the individual voice. Equal editorial attention will be given to established, emergent and new writers.

The views expressed in IRISH PAGES are not necessarily those of the Editors. The journal is published by Irish Pages Ltd, a non-profit organization.

Submissions are welcome but must be accompanied by return postage or an international reply coupon. No self-addressed envelope is required. Reporting time is nine months. If work is accepted, a copy on disk may be requested.

Your subscription is essential to the independence and survival of the journal. Subscription rates are £16stg/€26/$45 for one year. Visit our website at www.irishpages.org for a subscription form or to order online. Credit cards are welcome.

IRISH PAGES
129 Ormeau Road
Belfast BT7 1SH

Supported by **The National Lottery®** through the Arts Council of Northern Ireland

Legal Advice: Elliott Duffy Garrett, Belfast

IRISH PAGES is designed by Alicia McAuley Publishing Services and set in 12/14.5 Monotype Perpetua. It is printed in Belfast by Nicholson & Bass.

This issue has been generously asssisted by Foras na Gaeilge and the Arts Councils of Northern and Southern Ireland.

Foras na Gaeilge

ISBN 978-0-9561046-4-9

Ulster-Scots Agency
Boord o Ulstèr-Scotch

IRISH PAGES

CHRIS AGEE, *Editor*

CATHAL Ó SEARCAIGH, *Irish Language Editor*

ANDREW PHILIP (Scotland) *and* STEPHEN DORNAN (Ulster), *Scots Language Editors*

SEÁN MAC AINDREASA, *Managing Editor*

AONGHAS MACLEÒID, STEPHEN ELLIOTT *and* JACOB AGEE, *Editorial Assistants*

EDITED IN BELFAST
VOLUME 9, NUMBER 1

IRISH PAGES
DUILLÍ ÉIREANN

VOLUME 9, NUMBER 1

CONTENTS

After Heaney

Tinteán an Ghabha
(*The Smith's Hearth*)
By Eoin Mac Lochlainn
2014

THE VIEW FROM THE LAGAN

Omphalos and globe.

Several things struck me, firstly, as I compiled the previous issue of this journal ("Heaney", Vol 8, No 2) – and then, subsequently, after it was published. Whenever I spoke to anyone on this island at all familiar with Seamus Heaney, I noticed that this person could almost always recollect vividly the exact moment that he or she heard the news of the great poet's death. I found myself thinking that only once before had I experienced such a collective *frisson* of national loss: the death of JFK in the United States, where I grew up. Heaney, this seemed to suggest, was (and was felt to be) the greatest living Irish person at the time of his ill-fated death – a thought I frequently had, in fact, when he was alive.

So many people in Ireland and overseas read, admired, and watched him. The extraordinary degree to which "Heaney" was a creative and ethical exemplar, shaper, mentor, influence, and generous friend for his fellow poets and writers came through especially powerfully in that issue, with its 54 contributors from Ireland, Britain, the United States and further afield (many of them among the most distinguished writing now). When the issue was finally released to our subscribers and announced in our electronic newsletter, it came as no real surprise, then, that we immediately received an inundation of interest and orders through our office, online on our website (www.irishpages.org), and from the book trade. But what *was* surprising was that this interest went way beyond the borders of the *soi-disant* "literary world", with its usual associations rooted in urban, cultural, intellectual, and institutional milieux. He had, in addition – as this interest dramatically demonstrated – a wholly unique reach into what the poet Eoghan Ó Tuairisc once affirmed as "daoine cothroma na hÉireann" (the plain people of Ireland). No wonder orders were arriving not just from conurbations, literati, and universities, but also from parishes and remote townlands, in virtually every county on the island.

In reflecting on the *why* of all this, I am drawn yet again, almost against myself, to another idea about Heaney I have carried around for a good while: that in Seamus (whom I knew well) we come as close as we are likely to come in a modern context to the shaping and enlightening role, both contemporaneous and enduring, of the early "Irish saints" *vis-à-vis* their surrounding communities. These figures were not always clerics or anchorites, like Colmcille or St Kevin of Glendalough, and frequently not even "saintly" in our usual sense; they were often communal leaders or others of social, ethical, or imaginative "power" whom the church converted later to its own hagiographical purposes, to its succession of "spiritual laureates."They are remembered even now, all over Ireland, when their sociological origins have long vanished, for the informing closeness to their home place of their ethical example, personal charisma, and/or (in certain cases) written testaments of succinct beauty. Heaney, of course, belongs to the historiographical rather than the hagiographical, and indeed was a most modern Nobel laureate who never stopped travelling outwards from the always-close *omphalos* of County Derry; nonetheless, for all that bigger world, aka "Heaney's Globe", no less important to his poetry, I daresay that he will be remembered and read, with especial power, for centuries and centuries, by the people of this island.

The Editor

VARIETIES OF IRISHNESS

—

Seamus Heaney

In the element of his genius.

Editor's Note: The following uncollected address was delivered at the Annual Conference of the Ireland Funds, held on 24–25 June 1989, at Fitzpatrick's Silver Springs Hotel, Cork.

I am honoured to have been asked to give the keynote address here this evening and I knew I should have refused straight away. However, if I might use just a small verse not written by myself – I regret to say – but my very good friend Bill Cole, who has written a great series of verses called "River Rhymes" … This one isn't about a river. It's about the Gulf of Oman:

> Sailing on the Gulf of Oman I got to thinking about Onan.
> I knew the Bible had forbid it, but anyhow I went and did it.

I should have refused.

"The keynote address" is a deeply pacifying phrase. It has all the steadying effect of a word like "keel" or "anchor" or "bedrock." It prepares you to feel reassured and confident. The very words "keynote address" operate like a booster shot to all your confidence systems. You settle down and prepare to be reinforced, which is all very well for you. But it has been a puzzle to me as a person of literary interests without the barest rudiments of economics, without any worthwhile historical knowledge or political insight. It has been a puzzle what such a person can say in a keynote address to a conference specifically geared to those very economical, historical, and political matters. Indeed, in the last couple of days, thanks to my dread illness, which Dr O'Reilly cured for me – this turned into a panic, this *puzzle*.

Nevertheless, self-pity is never an edifying spectacle, and self-deprecation is always a suspect rhetorical mode, so let me say straight away that I intend to speak here as a writer – that is to say, to speak personally and exploratively, trying to come at the truth from traces of it that might be inside, rather than from evidence of it that I might methodically gain from the outside.

Speaking as a writer involves following the sixth sense and proceeding on the off-chance. It involves testing the ground by throwing a shape and generally advancing by the roundabout path of intuition rather than the direct and, alas, often earnest, path of logic. For as W.B. Yeats once said (and then wrote apparently thousands of times in the fly-leaves of books of his own), "For wisdom is a butterfly, and not a gloomy bird of prey."

I am talking about *impulse discovering direction*, about *potential discovering structure*, about *chance becoming intention*. This is the movement I depend on in all my other doings and writings – the only process that I trust, really. The only process that gives what I say, or you say, any biological right to exist, as it were. And I believe it is the same process as that which the Ireland Funds must be eager to identify in the multitude of projects which come to their attention and compete for their admirable and indispensable patronage. Creative work – whether it happens in the emergence of a lyric poem out of language, or in the development of a community project out of local resources – is like any other work.

Work involves the moving of a certain force through a certain distance, as far as I remember from school. It involves the identification of an origin of energy, then the creation of conditions in which that energy can exult freely in itself, in order to multiply and transform itself and the conditions into something new. And not just into something new, but rather into something which is actually renovated.

So what renovating thing can we find to say for ourselves, to ourselves, this evening? What note can we key in to? Renovation, after all, implies a certain amount of return to the old resources and a certain *reprise* of old motifs. "We are earthworms of the earth", as the poet said, "and what has gone through us is what will be our trace." In my end is my beginning. Or to express the notion in a less mystifying line from the poet Yeats, "What can I do but enumerate old themes?"

One old theme of my own, which is by no means original to me, is the doubleness of our focus in Ireland. The way we have a capacity for living in two places at one time and in two times at one place.

That philosopher and prodigy Richard Kearney has thrillingly denominated this as one of the marks of what he is bold to have called "The Irish Mind." This capacity shared by all traditions upon the island to acknowledge the claims of two contradictory truths at one time without having to reach for the guillotine and decide between the head truth and the rump truth. Without having to decide *either or*, preferring instead the more generous and realistic approach of *both and*.

Perhaps this approach arises out of the persistence upon the island of what we call "Varieties of Irishness." It certainly survives in a multitude of ways from the veteran's advice to young reporters in Belfast – i.e., "If you are not confused, son, you don't understand the problem" – to my late mother-in-law's completely logical rebuke to one of her children who has taken more than her fair share of cookies or biscuits – there we are, two places in one line – anyway, my mother-in-law said to these kids taking more than their fair share, "If everybody takes two, there won't be one each."

All of us can acknowledge the justice of this, even if all of us sense that there is something slippery at the centre that we want to actually escape from. And that intellectual unease matches perfectly the social unease I felt when confronted with the doubleness of my own life 20 years ago in Belfast, when I was in a fish-and-chip shop on Tate's Avenue at a particularly tense moment in 1969, in the newly politically disrupted life of that predominantly Protestant suburb.

I happened to have collapsed already in that time. I had been on television the night before in some kind of literary context, highly unpolitical, and one of the lassies in this chip shop was a young girl from England who didn't know the danger she was walking through. So she said: "Oh, you're the Irish poet." The chip-shop owner folded her arms and looked at me over the steam and said, "Not at all dear, he is a British subject living in Ulster." "Wouldn't it sicken ye?" she said to me. Of course, I nodded at her.

Well, as I say, I have been well used to living in two places at one time for as long as I can remember. So for all the people here from north of the border, it would be superfluous, and it could be folksy, to overstate and over-insist on that.

Varieties of Irishness are where it's at, no doubt, and the various people involved are dab hands at keeping the "both and" way of life going, at full tilt. Apparently there is a phrase in Cork – I don't know how true this is – but Sean O'Reilly once told me an account of the Cork equivalent of living in two places at one time, which was a phrase which always intrigued me: "Yes too." I don't know if that is a real phrase or not.

South of the border also has its doubleness. Its two-timing in the one place. We may indeed live in a country of conference hotels, computer printouts, property deals, electioneering, fish-kills and stereophonic discos. But we also to a greater or lesser extent continue to inhabit an imagined island, a mythologically grounded and imaginatively contoured island that belongs in, shall we say, art-time and in story time, in a continuous present of our own thinking memory-life. Only in Ireland, perhaps, could we have evolved a quasi-national holiday based upon a fictional character and dated it to coincide with the art-time of a work of pure imagination set in Dublin on 16 June 1904.

Joyce wrote in his diary 20 years later, and two years after the completion of *Ulysses*, "Will anyone remember this day?" But he needn't have worried, of course. The national inclination to live by a time that is eternally reoccurring, rather than chronologically hurrying past, would stand him in good stead.

"Bloomsday" is a modern manifestation, and a consciously Joycean exploitation, of a way of being in the world that has been second nature to all Irish people from time immemorial. "We like to think," says Hugh O'Donnell in Brian Friel's play *Translations*, "We like to think that we dwell around truths immemorially posited."

And although the schoolmaster is being ironical in his perception, the irony is his only defence against the helpless realization of the truth of the perception itself – namely, that people's myths of themselves and their worlds are stronger and more influential upon their conduct than any reasonable, rational, prudent estimate of the conditions pertaining in the actual world where they live.

I'll illustrate this tendency to dwell in the out-of-time time in all kinds of ways. But perhaps the most personal and vivid occasion was in the mid-1960s when Marie and I were travelling from Belfast to Waterford. On our way through Wexford, we saw a sign for the "Historical District of Boolavogue", famous as the site of a spontaneous pocket of resistance, one might say, in the rebellion of 1798.

A song about that event commemorates Father Murphy spurring up the rocks with a warning cry and a rebel hand setting the heather blazing. And since this was always one of my mother's favourite shut-eyed ones, some part of myself dwelt around that name immemorially posited in the Wexford landscape. So, I turned off the main road to follow what was not so much a Wexford by-road as the road also taken by Thomas the Rhymer in the Old English Ballad, where the road was given its full romantic title, "The Road to Fairyland."

I was driving not towards any administrative diocesan unit or any ecclesiastical building called Boolavogue. I was driving, rather, towards the eternally receding centre of yearning in a musical cadence. I was following a signpost into the acoustic of a song rather than into the geography of a parish.

At any rate, I had already gone more than the two miles that the signpost had indicated and had seen nothing significant, when I met an old man on a bicycle. I pulled up and he slowed down. I screwed down my windscreen and he screwed up his eyes. We gazed across the immense distances that intervened in the six inches or so between our faces.

"I am looking for Boolavogue", I said, explaining myself, but I regret also insinuating that, although I had a Northern accent, there was nothing to fear by my variety of Irishness.

"Ole oh, you've passed Boolavogue. You'll have to turn and go back and keep your eye opened for a church on your right-hand side at the corner."

"Oh", says I, insinuating again, "is that the church where Father Murphy was?"

"Oh, it is", he says, "but there's a different priest there now."

This was a fine example of poetic time being brought down into actual history. I came to a farcical *reprise* of what we might call the Oisín motif. In a manner of speaking, I grew to a hundred years old in a split second. My illustration, though, is less important than the psychic phenomena which it is intended to illustrate, which are the doubleness of the world we inhabit and, by extension, its bilingual nature. For there is a language proper to the internal world that lies at that still previous point of our lives – and a language for the busy efficient world that occupies the more hurried usual hours of our mornings, evenings, and afternoons.

Professor Proinsias Mac Cana has drawn attention to one delightful instance of these two languages in an account of a famous scribal tail-piece which was appended to a twelfth-century manuscript of the *Táin Bó Cúailnge* and I shall come to that presently. But since we are in Cork, I think it is proper to offer as well a local instance of the kinds of psychic phenomena we are dealing with in this context.

This involves the story of the Cork schoolmaster who was certain that two of his pupils were copying. But the schoolmaster was uncertain as to which was the *copyist,* as it were, and which was the *copyee.* So he kept the two kids in at lunchtime one day, sat them together at a double desk, and set them a composition on "The Swallow."

And after they got started and had written the first sentence or so, he separated them to different corners of the room, let them sit a few minutes, and then took up the exercise books. He knew his culprit immediately when he read the following two sentences.

The first sentence read, "The swallow is a migratory bird." The second sentence read, "He have a roundy head." This tale was told to me by John Cronin, who speaks the two languages. He is from Cork but he is also a professor of English. At any rate, when John Cronin told me the tale, I realized that it was a two-sentence history of Anglo-Irish literature.

First comes a correct, stilted school-book English which obliterates all natural personality, a kind of zombie speech that walks in the evacuated space where the living Irish language displays itself naturally and distinctively: "The swallow is a migratory bird."

Then comes the breakthrough of the afterlife of Irish into the underfed English, and something eerie happens. The grammar goes wonky and contact is re-established and all personality, all reservoirs of assuredness and impulsiveness are located: "He have a roundy head." In the second sentence we recognize an intelligence working in its element; in the first we recognize an intelligence working out of its element.

To work too innocently within your element may be to dwell in a disabling way within the circle of unconsciousness. But to work too insidiously beyond your element may be to inhabit, in a differently disabling way, the circle of self-consciousness. But that is another story, and you are all intelligent people and you can draw all the morals you want from it.

For the moment, I am simply interested in noting another example of the Irish psyche flitting like a bat between the light of a practical idiom and the twilight of a previously remembered sure place.

So we go on to what that twelfth-century scribe wrote at the conclusion of the long tale of the *Táin Bó Cúailnge*, *The Cattle Raid of Cooley*, described repeatedly in the Irish language, which was his mother language and the language of the story. He described the conventional conclusion to such labours, a kind of grace after transcribing thousands of pages, which went in Irish translation like this: "A blessing on everyone who shall faithfully memorize the time as it is written here and shall not add any other form to it."

Professor Mac Cana, writing about this inscription in Richard Kearney's collection of essays, *The Irish Mind*, takes up the story as follows – that is, after having written the blessing, and everyone shall faithfully memorize this, *et cetera*:

But then, as if this abbreviated invocation of the story's magic potency had reminded him of its rank paganism, the scribe immediately deferred to Christian orthodoxy by adding another codicil, this time in Latin, a pedantically formal dis-including of any personal interest in, or responsibility for, the narrative which he had so faithfully transcribed – and it went like this: "But I who have written this story or rather this fable give no credence to the various incidents related in it. For some things in it are the deceptions of demons, others are poetic figments. Some are probable, others improbable, while others are intended for the delectation of fools."

Mac Cana goes on:

This nice instance of medieval diglossia neatly epitomizes the disparity between the cultural context of the two languages, Irish and Latin. On the one hand, we have to do with the culture which is coeval with the Irish language and received its verbal expression through it, first orally and then from the late 6th century, both orally and in writing. It is a mythopoeic culture, innocent of secular chronology and relating people and events in the past by reference to genealogical affiliation or to the reigns of famous kings legendary or historical.

On the other hand, there is the Roman and international culture which was introduced to Ireland with Christianity and the Latin language and which extended its influence from the first half of the 6th century onwards. It is the creation of a church rooted in finite time by the central fact of incarnation and by its inheritance from Imperial Rome. And in consequence it brought with it to Ireland a view of time and history – of secular and sacred, of artistic and religious, categories – that was radically at variance with native Irish society.

What Mac Cana is identifying as a crisis in the Irish conscience in the twelfth century has obviously been repeated in traumatic ways since – and in none more traumatic than in the shift from Irish to the English language. But in the last 50 years, the collision between an international culture and commerce and a native tradition and conservatism matches very intriguingly the pattern which Mac Cana traces home in his treatment of his chosen bilingual text.

For the old Irish emotion in the phantasmagoria of myth, read the demure, frugal, admirably visionary, yet intellectually obscurantist, world of de Valera's Ireland: pastoral, pure, and papist. For the Latin moralism and ecclesiastical organization of the twelfth-century church, read the rational programmatic spirit of Sean Lemass, Dr Whitaker, the First Economic Plan, etc. Need I go on? Of course not.

The analogy supplies itself – and the complication which I insisted on in the beginning has to be remembered because it's not very long ago since I was in the room where Dr Ken Whitaker, who was always held up as the prophet of modernism and internationalism, stood and sang "The Lark in the Clear Air"; and in another context, his pupil and master of International Latin, as it were, Dr Tony O'Reilly, played on the piano the timeless airs and heart-tugging tunes of Thomas Moore. Nothing simple. But, as Ben Kiely says, "Nevertheless."

To return to the conclusion of the *Táin*: it seems to me that the Latin disclaimer after the Irish blessing represents the same kind of disjunction and doubleness of values that we recognize when we hear the ghettoblaster going full blast on the bog bank and when we see the Dallas architecture of the Connemara bungalow. We acknowledge the inevitability of the thing, but recognize that spiritual and aesthetic violence is being done.

Obviously it would be sentimental to pretend that the old traditional world of season and custom and site and rite has survived in any real way. As Liam de Paor pointed out in an article in *The Crane Bag* over ten years ago, "Even the best traditional musicians are now professionals." The tradition itself has entered the realm of the commercial. Aran sweaters on the whole are not for people in Ireland. Computers rather than *caubeens* are what you are going to expect in Mayo.

The old world has been unfocused, literally un*focus*ed. Indeed, this Latin word *focus* for *hearth* provides us with one single, central, physical, and etymological instance for reading the big shift from the old Ireland to the new. That was a shift from the undifferentiated world of storytime and seasonal recurrence, settled values, absorbed rhythms, the world of sacred, common, impersonal modes of behaviour. A shift from that to the new world of individuated freedom, economic independence, emotional self-direction, unsanctioned behaviour almost, and a secular, almost relativist permissiveness.

The very word *hearth* seems like an anachronism or a nostalgia in this new world. In fact, those who are old enough to remember first the closing-up of open hearths in countries and their occlusion and replacement by the little bandy-legged iron stoves – and then the removal of the stoves altogether and the indiscriminate placing of radiators – those who remember this have already, in the memory bank of their bodies, a record of the almost physical modulation which one's being suffered in the modernization process.

The hearth had indeed been the *focus*, the centre, the heat and heart of the house's meaning. It admitted daydream as well as providing service. Any hearth was all the hearth that had ever been in one hearth. Every morning the fact of fire was wonderful all over again; the primal flame was apprehended with gratitude and rekindled.

Flash forward – *run forward* as they say in the video business – to the central heating system and then you have a levelling out of wonder, if you like; you have the insulation of your being from the actual sensation of flame. You have the neutralization of space by the grid of pipe and radiator. You have comfort, but you have unfocused a part of your being.

In some dumb part of yourself you have left the world of roundy heads and entered the world of migratory birds. You are speaking international Latin rather than hearth Irish. You are a secular modern inhabitant with a sort of lacuna in your midriff. You are capable, comfortable, and a little displaced. You are a little in exile from your first self and your first place but you don't quite know how – and you, of course, you are not alone.

You are the usual, professional, urban, eighties, Irish success story. You may even be London Irish or American Irish or Canadian Irish, but certainly you feel this vestigial capacity to focus around some old field of force that somehow is neither marked on the map nor written into the schedule.

But then, by accident, you get back into some ancient familiar location, somewhere with a sort of prenatal purchase on you. An old house, say, like the one I found myself in recently, where I lifted a latch for the first time in years; and there, in that instantly cold metal touch, in the pleasing slackness and scissor and slap of the latch mechanism, something unpredictably invigorating happened.

My body awakened in its very capillaries to innumerable and unnameable rivulets of affection and energy. The moment that latch made its harsh old noise, a whole ancestral world came flooding up. And that inundation persuades me that in all of us (the lacuna in the midriff notwithstanding) there is a supply of dammed-up energy waiting to be released.

In other words, a connection is possible between your present self and your intuited previousness, between your inchoate dailiness and your imagined identity. Your *Irishness*, to put it in yet another way, constitutes a big unconscious voltage derived from memory and place and attachment to place and to people and all it needs is some transformer to make it current in a new significant and renovative way.

I am now proceeding, as I promised, by intuition and by indirection from the inside, on the wing of metaphor and suggestion. But I still believe I am proceeding towards the kind of truth we would want to key in to. For it seems we have here an analogy for the emotional structure of a modern, creative, patriotic action. A correspondence could be posited between the inner unsatisfied and unspecified excitements that my latch set off in me and the sharp desire that all of us occasionally experience to pay into an effort that would have renovative effects upon the unfocused, yet beloved, Ireland of the present, North and South.

And, just as one can find an energy source in the ghost-life of the lifting latch, so one can base an intellectual and philanthropical project upon fidelity to some absent but intuited original Ireland of the affections and the imagination. And the more *varieties of that Ireland* there are, the better and the healthier the whole thing will turn out.

So, please understand that all my talk of bog banks and latches and hearths and visits to Boolavogue and my relish of folk speech in Cork and loyal speech in Belfast are not sighs for a lost Ireland. They are not, I hope, simply the usual cry "God, but aren't they a great ould crowd." I intend them as little points of recognition and affection – but I want to suggest that it is upon exactly such chancy manifestations of affection and connection that we must build a work of meaning.

Creative work, as I said in the beginning, is a matter of *impulse discovering direction, of potential discovering structure, of chance becoming design.* And what is exemplary about the members of the Ireland Funds and the work they do is the way they have combined their impulse to drive off the main road and enter the acoustic of the song world. They have combined that capacity with the capacity to plot the coordinates of the journey by employing the most advanced technology. They have the capacity to find Boolavogue by the exercise of technological navigational aids. The Ireland Fund and, before it, the American Irish Foundation, successfully found ways of allowing its members simultaneously to live in dream-time and to keep abreast of the historical moment.

I know, from long association with many of you, that your impulse is affectionate, ancestral, local and – blessedly at times – whimsical. But I also know and applaud the fact that your affection does not exhaust itself in self-satisfaction. On the contrary, you have made that impulse exalt and multiply and transform itself (and the Irish conditions) into something *renovated*. You have applied, as it were, the enabling power of your international equipment to boost and transform the operations of the Irish vernacular.

And I might say, in particular, I am aware of your long attentive interest in the work of the Field Day Theatre Company and of how valuable that has been to us over the years. There have been happy personal commitments among your members that have kept this connection vital. But there has been also a more general and benign concern, which has helped us in our renovative design.

The financial grants are, of course, a crucial part of the support that you give; but in enterprises like Field Day, and many others that you support –which, in our enterprise anyway, involves the touring of plays and next year the publication of a two-volume synoptic *Field Day Anthology of Irish Writing* from the fifth to the twentieth centuries – a kind of bible of the whole thing – in such an enterprise, the amplification of our note through having you as both a sounding board and a transmitter has been of vital importance.

But, if self-deprecation is no way to begin a keynote address, flattery may be a tactless way to end it. Much as I would like to pour the oil of eloquence upon the greatly deserving heroic head of A.J.F. O'Reilly and play the bard to his *ard rí*, I will leave you instead with some lines by T.S. Eliot, lines which encompass very chastely and very beautifully much of what I have been stumbling crookedly in pursuit of. They are lines which apply with particular force to Dr O'Reilly's epoch-making service to Ireland and service in the world. They apply also to the purposes and functions of the Ireland Funds generally and they apply to all emigrants and inner-exiles of whatever variety of Irishness.

They come from T.S. Eliot's *Four Quartets*, from the section called "Little Gidding", and they address with classic succinctness the core of the matter which I too have been considering. Let us call it finally the use of memory.

This is the use of memory;
For liberation – not less of love but expanding
Of love beyond desire, and so liberation
From the future as well as the past. Thus, love of a country
Begins as attachment to our own field of action
And comes to find that action of little importance
Though never indifferent. History may be servitude,
History may be freedom. See, now they vanish,
The faces and places, with the self which, as it could, loved them
To become renewed, transfigured, in another pattern.

The transcription of this address is published courtesy of the Ireland Funds and the Estate of Seamus Heaney.

Seamus Heaney was awarded the Nobel Prize for Literature in 1995. His twelfth collection of poems, Human Chain *(Faber), was published in 2010. He died in Blackrock Clinic, Dublin, at 7.30 am on 30 August 2013 and is buried in the family plot in Bellaghy Cemetery, Bellaghy, Co Derry. He is survived by his wife, Marie; his children, Michael, Catherine Ann and Christopher; and his granddaughters, Aoibheann and Anna Rose Heaney.*

BARDIC VOICE

—

Robert Crawford

Literary risk.

No poet should feel obliged to engage with politics. All poets should be free to do so. A poet who wants to write politically hears two voices. One, the bardic voice, urges him or her to speak on behalf of a community, a tribe, a gender, a nation; the other insists only on truth to the individual self, an unstable self which may elude communal, tribal, gender or national definition. In Scotland, as in Ireland, and many other countries, bardic voice is a strong presence (even in fiction). It's clearly there in Gaelic poetry. When Lachlann Mór MacMhuirich (here in my translation) incites his clansmen,

> Be belters, be brandishers,
> Be bonny, be batterers

he's speaking to and for the tribe; differently inflected, that bardic impulse is there in the public poetry of that Gaelic-speaking Latinist George Buchanan whose Renaissance Latin epithalamium for the marriage of Mary, Queen of Scots to the French dauphin includes a paean to Scotland in which Buchanan operates as a proto-poet laureate; in Scots and English, our starriest bard is Burns – "Caledonia's Bard, brother Burns", as he was called, masonically, in this city; signing himself "Yours for Scotland" and identifying with the heart-breaking "Little White Rose", Hugh MacDiarmid, too, like Sorley MacLean, sought out a bardic role, which was for him at times, as it had been on occasion for Burns, a political one.

Yet there are other great Scottish poets for whom this bardic voice has been something to eschew, or at least to modify vigorously; Dunbar can deploy bardic voice, including stinging, satirical bardic voice (for surely flyting is the flipside of bardic encomium), but in that phrase "Ersche brybour baird", the word "baird" (bard) is a Lowland insult; in his *Lament for the Makaris* Dunbar's truest tribe is simply poets, and not absolutely all those makars in that poem are Scottish; William Drummond of Hawthornden, the first Scottish poet to write English with complete fluency, was more of a recluse than a bard in his faction-ridden land; more recently, Norman MacCaig seemed eager to renounce the bardic in one of his most political poems, "Patriot", in which he declares slyly and with vehement individualism,

My only country
is six feet high
and whether I love it or not
I'll die
for its independence.

The quarrel with himself out of which Yeats made poetry was principally an argument between individual (often erotic) lyric voice and bardic voice. There is a related quarrel within the poetries of Seamus Heaney, Eavan Boland, and many other recent Irish poets, including Paul Muldoon, that most influential English-language poet of his generation. The phrase "bardic voice" sounds old-fashioned; it seems to belong, perhaps, to medieval Gaelic chieftains or to that world of declamation set out by Catherine Robson, whose book *Heart Beats: Everyday Life and the Memorized Poem* (Princeton University Press, 2012) centres on the nineteenth century and has on its cover a kilted schoolboy reciting Robert Burns. Maybe instead of using the term "bardic voice" I should be referring to poetry that is fitted with its own effective public-address system, but I want to stick with the term "bardic voice" not least because it emphasizes the longevity of poetry as an archaic and abiding as well as a modern art form. "Bardic voice" is a sound system, both because of the way it orders a system of sounds and because its sense of attunement or attack is an attempt to articulate, however indirectly, something of a sound system of government.

I admit that the phrase "bardic voice" still makes us awkward here in the land of James Macpherson; it risks sounding too antique, too bound to the norms of Romantic lastness, too Ossianic. Yet the term "bardic voice" is worth using because it not only signals poetry's access to the power of public address, but also reminds us how important such access has been in Scotland, Ireland, and elsewhere. Ironically, and perhaps because whetted by their long residence in England, there may be more Scottish bardic voice in the English-based Scottish poets W.N. Herbert and Jackie Kay than in some of the best known Scottish-based poets of my generation. In their poetic practice John Burnside and Don Paterson have refused to bring bardic voice to issues of national identity and the politics of British unionism or Scottish independence. On rare occasions Kathleen Jamie (perhaps like Meg Bateman) has adopted bardic voice only to unshackle herself from it, whether in "The Queen of Sheba" or in "Mr and Mrs Scotland are Dead."

Bardic voice can be a temptation, even an off-the-peg uniform, for Scottish poets. The temptation is grandiosity, egotism, and reductivism: the illusion that the nation and the self, the "I", are pompously, even bumptiously, at one. I recognize that temptation; but I remain committed to risking at times elements of bardic voice. Since my first collection of poems, A Scottish Assembly, published in 1990, I've felt an attraction to the possibilities not just of so-called private voice but also of kinds of bardic or public voice, of poetry that can articulate aspects of a national community with a subtle but unashamed political inflection. Like many – probably most – poets of my generation and the preceding generation, I lived outside Scotland for a considerable time in my twenties, and my decision to return here was an act of deliberate commitment. It was during six years in England, and not least as the result of a relationship with a refugee, that I came to realize what it meant to me to be Scottish and some of the things that being Scottish might mean in and for poetry. I chose for my first book an epigraph from Margaret Atwood:

> Some people think that the word Nationalism means "let's all put on jackboots and kill everybody else", but our cultural nationalism has a very modest mandate – namely that we exist. It seems to threaten some people.

But, though A Scottish Assembly is by no means all political, its poems, like some of the poems in my more recent collections, go beyond mere cultural nationalism to point in the direction of political independence. Though my favourite poet remains T.S. Eliot (who once wrote that "History is now and England") and my orientation is both instinctively and deliberately Scottish-international, my biography of Burns is clearly titled The Bard, and I do believe in the possibilities for Scottish poets of a bardic stance, but not a simplistic one; much of what I've written in poetry and in prose has been geared to articulating a sense of Scottish identities as complex, and of our poetic traditions as multiple; hence the title of the early 1990s magazine Scotlands, and the design of the Penguin Book of Scottish Verse which Mick Imlah and I edited, and which begins with that Latin masterwork the "Altus

Prosator" along with my old teacher Edwin Morgan's striking facing translation; hence the resolutely polylingual argument to my history of Scottish literature, *Scotland's Books*; and when I say resolutely polylingual, I don't mean simply the mantra of English, Scots, and Gaelic – I mean also Latin, Old English, Old French, Old Norse, and Old Welsh, as well as more recent immigrant tongues: the whole hybrid and gloriously impure caboodle.

I admire the way that Morgan for Scots and English, and, more recently, Meg Bateman for Gaelic, have acted not just as poets but also as wardens and sharers of the hoard – anthologizing, criticizing, writing literary history, and translating the poetry of the past without compromising the creative gift. Bateman and Morgan have fused to a risky yet commendable extent the professorial and the bardic. Let me repeat that poets don't have to speak for the nation, the gender, the sexual orientation, the tribe, but they can try at times to do so; and at times such as the 2014 independence referendum, I think that (though I do understand why some of the poets I've mentioned resisted doing so in their work) bardic voice – whether it was Liz Lochhead channelling Burns in the Portrait Gallery or young poets reading in village halls – was often the appropriate thing to risk.

Perhaps now, though, in the period after our independence referendum, we've become even more wary of yoking – as some of us did during the political campaign – poetry and politics. And, yes, in the decades since the heyday of Hugh MacDiarmid, many have argued that the two should be kept apart. In 2014 I published a sequence of political poems that were part of my collection, *Testament*, and also a prose book: *Bannockburns: Scottish Independence and Literary Imagination, 1314–2014.* Neither of these books is simply propagandistic. Yet it would be hard to read either without realizing that I support Scottish independence. Now, in 2015, it is hard not to feel a shiver of failure. Whatever poets did to back "the cause", it was not enough. All those readings, those would-be bardic songs, those discussions, those attempts to sing a new Scotland into being, were almost, but not quite, enough.

It wisnae us, of course. It was the economists, the politicians, the rest. They didn't quite get their act together. The months after the referendum, for those among the 45 per cent at least, were months of "if only." If only there had been a six-percent swing in the right direction. If only the currency question had been more deftly addressed. If only culture had been debated as much as oil. Yet, let's face it, o fellow bookish ones here in the

National Library, nobody really issues the lament, "If only there had been some better sonnets." "Poetry", W.H. Auden so famously said in his elegy for W.B. Yeats, "makes nothing happen."

Yeats didn't seem to believe that, though. When, close to the end of his life, his poem "The Man and the Echo" posed the question, "Did that play of mine send out / Certain men the English shot?" The implied answer is not entirely clear; but the anxiety that poetry does indeed have the power to make things happen is evident. In his book *Poetry, Poets, Readers: Making Things Happen* (Oxford University Press, 2002) the English poet and critic Peter Robinson has devoted much intellectual energy to the issue of whether or not poetry makes things happen, and it's a question that poets and readers – including those in Scotland now – shouldn't shirk. Scotland is neither Ireland nor America; to start with, it is one of the unusual glories of modern Scottish nationalism that no man, nor woman, nor child has been shot as a result of it. Yet we can and do learn from aligning ourselves with Irish, American, Australian, and other poetries. In her book *Songs of Ourselves: The Uses of Poetry in America* (2007) the historian Joan Shelley Rubin shows how one of the jobs American poetry has done is to say, "I am an American." Yeats – some of whose finest poems clearly and conflictedly say "I am Irish" – gives the lie to any assertion that poetry cannot or should not be political and cannot take on a bardic, national voice with aplomb. Yet Yeats also vigorously asserts the poet's impulse to cut away from the political, and follow the (sometimes lustful) lyric impulse. His late poem "Politics" begins:

> How can I, that girl standing there,
> My attention fix
> On Roman or on Russian
> Or on Spanish politics?

and this poem concludes with the simple, and lamenting exclamation,

> But O that I were young again
> And held her in my arms!

I salute Yeats's wandering eye: there is poetry in it, as there was in his hopeless, intrepid pursuit of Maud Gonne decades earlier. But I honour, too, his continuing engagement, however difficult, with politics; and I think we should reflect on that here in Edinburgh in 2015.

For if Yeats is emblematic of the great political poet, then he is also an emblem of long and sometimes anguished bardic waiting, and waiting is certainly the situation in which we find ourselves in today's Scotland. No sooner was our referendum narrowly lost – a swing of six per cent would have made all the difference – than it seemed in the most recent UK general election that the cause of Scottish independence, as if on the rebound, was on a winning streak. For those of us who want to see an independent Scotland, the issue now is how best to wait, how to endure waiting, and how to sustain that waiting.

Well, Yeats waited, and poetry is good at sustaining, at keeping open long lines of communication. Yeats the poet of urgency was also a great poet of committed resilience, his sustaining lines of communication running to Indian and Japanese and ancient Greek culture as well as to London, Oxford, Stone Cottage, Dublin, and Sligo. It was in the early 1890s, *three decades* before the founding of an Irish Free State, that he addressed himself "To Ireland in the Coming Times" and wanted to be "brother of a company" of distinctively Irish nationalist poets. It was over twenty years later that the "terrible beauty" was "born", and it was almost another twenty years before Yeats the parliamentary Senator would assert with regard to vague Utopianism that it could produce as an "image of such politics" a "withered old and skeleton-gaunt" humanity. Yeats is an inspiration: his resilient and lyrical waiting paid off; but Yeats is also a sounder of warnings against making the heart a stone – against poetry simply and solely as propaganda.

Poetry, including bardic poetry (and perhaps no successful poetry is purely "bardic" in the most reductive sense of that word), must be something subtler and more oblique than propaganda, while still asserting a public voice. Most of Yeats's poetry is not political, even if he could rise on key occasions to being a great political poet. Yeats's bardic example may be set beside Burns's bardic example as a magnificent instance of a poet who can be political without renouncing his gift. Burns's bardic humour is glorious, and sets him apart from Yeats; but Burns is also a serious political poet. The song that begins "Scots wha hae" is clearly a song of Scottish independence, but also a song of the Enlightenment; it is attuned to the French Revolution as well as to Bannockburn. Yet most of Burns's work is not so directly political. The bulk of MacDiarmid's best poems are not political either, or at least not narrowly political. And the same goes for Neruda, and for Seferis, that poet-translator-diplomat true not just to the Greek past but also to the uncanny and universal "secrets of the sea" that are "forgotten on the shore." Who in their right mind would choose to represent MacDiarmid by one of the "Hymns to Lenin" rather than by "Empty Vessel" or "The Bonnie Broukit Bairn"?

It's good to think here in the National Library about poetry and politics, not just in the immediate arena of 2015, but also in much wider contexts. Whatever else they need to be, all poets must, at times, be bookish; that is, they need to read deeply and love their art not just in their own country and community, but across space and time. That is what nourishes us. Poems need to live on the breath and in the moment; but they need, too, to be able to last, to move across boundaries of chronology and culture. Good poetry doesn't belong exclusively to one generation, either living or dead. Each of us, if we write verse, must find our own way of articulating that; since the referendum I have been working on a series of poems asserting the resilient *quidditas* of Glasgow, Edinburgh, Greenock, Dundee, Aberdeen – poems of Scottish cities; but also on a book in Scots called *Chinese Makars*, where the poems have absolutely nothing to do with Scottish politics. I hope that to work like this, like writing about T.S. Eliot, is a way of keeping open those long lines of communication which poetry offers and which too narrow adherence to any "party line" of political cause can threaten to atrophy. Whatever else it is, 2015 is a time to assert and reassert internationalism in this country; which need not mean forgetting about locality or independence.

One of the most arresting questions asked about art and the referendum came from our greatest composer, James MacMillan, when he asked where was the great art that came out of all the referendum "Yes" campaigning. You can bounce the question back, of course: what was the great art of "No"? Yet, instead of doing that, and just to induce even more cultural anxiety, one might ask, where is the great art that's appeared *since* the referendum vote – but to think that way is misguided. Again, it's important to stand back and take a wider perspective. In terms of Scottish poetry, it does seem hard to ignore that so many of the poets of recent times, from MacDiarmid and MacCaig to Lochhead and Jamie, have been supporters of independence; yet, though it may be valid to do so at certain times, there are dangers in looking at their work or public pronouncements *only* in search of political commitment. To do so may be valid but short-sighted. If we take a longer, larger view of the politics of poetry, then what is more striking is the absence of support for British unionism in modern poetry from these islands. It is as easy to find great poetry that articulates a sense of England ("History is now and England") in the poetry of the last century as it is to locate poetry that attempts (often successfully) to articulate kinds of Scottishness or Irishness; yet the poetry of Britishness (as distinct from jingoistic verse) is very hard to find.

That fact tells its own story, and it is a story replicated in fiction. If you remove from literary history the powerful Scottish unionist articulations of some supposed Britishness voiced in the eighteenth and nineteenth centuries by such novelist-poets as Smollett and Scott, then it is stunning how little articulation of Britishness there is in English fiction. No major English novel is set in Scotland, for instance, with the questionable exception of Woolf's *To the Lighthouse*, which may be nominally located on the Isle of Skye, but whose *milieu* smacks very much of the beautiful south-west English environment of Woolf's childhood summers. Ultimately, this failure to articulate positive ideals of Britishness is a striking aspect of literature from England, and, though eighteenth and nineteenth-century Scottish writers attempted to remedy it by championing in "Rule, Britannia" and elsewhere an ideal of a united Britain which included "Caledonia stern and wild", it is hard to discern this British strain in Scottish literature beyond John Buchan. So, what I am arguing is that taking a wider-scale view of Scottish, English, and British literature strengthens, rather than in any sense compromises, the view that the auguries of writing in poetry as in fiction continue to point in the direction of Scottish independence. Taking such a view sustains our waiting.

We should not expect masterworks to appear every other Wednesday. We should not beat ourselves up unduly if even in 2014 no clear masterwork was published to articulate the dream of Scottish independence in poetry. Instead, while taking into account the textual evidence of such immediate productions as Christopher Silver's 2014 anthology *Inspired by Independence: Artists and Writers Imagine a Better Scotland* (to which I, like many others, was delighted to contribute), we should realize too that such a book and other literary gatherings are part of a greater, carrying stream that certainly does include impressive individual works and bodies of writing from the recent and more distant past. Among these, surely, and now sifted by time, are the work of Alasdair Gray and Edwin Morgan; and, sustainingly, though Morgan died in 2010 and Gray is now seriously ill, 2015 has brought significant signs that the work of each continues to inform and underpin debates about literary politics. In Gray's case David Greig's striking theatrical adaptation of *Lanark* now presents a stage version (made by an important dramatist vehement in his support for the Yes campaign in 2014) of the most famous novel by a Scottish novelist celebrated for his commitment to the cause of Scottish independence; while *Lanark* (Canongate, 1981) is certainly not the same book as Gray's *Why Scots Should Rule Scotland* (Canongate, 1992), nonetheless, as I argue in *Bannockburns*, Gray's perennial theme of the individual who seeks independence from a situation of entrapment can be seen as having a political dimension, and one that persists in the context of today's Scotland.

For readers of Edwin Morgan, the publication of his large selected correspondence in *The Midnight Letterbox* (Carcanet, 2015) serves to emphasize that most of Morgan's literary interests were *not* political. Indeed, it can be amusing to see Morgan in 1968 wondering if people may react to a poet's politics simply in terms of "Oh, I see old MacDiarmid's at it again … meaning that it is a sort of poet's privilege to be interested in politics but nevertheless to be fairly likely to be foolish." Morgan was wary of the too narrowly "Scottish" and, though his imaginative fascination with metamorphosis does have a political dimension, one detects surprisingly little interest in Scottish politics in this particular selection of his letters, and what there is comes relatively late: in 1987 he writes how "Alan Brownjohn of the Poetry Society in London is collecting poets' voting intentions, plus reasons for choice; I said SNP since I saw Scotland as 'a frustrated republic and would like to help it to become a real one.'"This is the Morgan who had published *Sonnets from Scotland* in 1984 with its "Respublica Scotorum", and who, later, in 1990, the year that saw the publication of his enlarged *Collected Poems*, thought that politically,

> It is a very strange moment, when almost everyone believes some constitutional and/or other change is standing at the door, and necessarily so, yet a combination of nervous and nerveless hands seems unable to grasp the knob and open up.

Soon afterwards, in 1992, Morgan complained how "we are up against a government that not only means to preserve the Union but is searching for ways to *strengthen* it, and one can only hope it overreaches itself in this, and thereby precipitates a broader discontent than manifests itself at the moment." "I don't believe 'poetry makes nothing happen'", Morgan wrote in a letter of 1998, and six years later he was invited by Jack McConnell to become the inaugural Scottish Makar, going on to produce his poem "For the Opening of the Scottish Parliament" on 9 October 2004. Morgan was too ill to read his poem (it was read by Liz Lochhead, who would succeed him as Makar), but it stands as a signally successful piece of bardic oratory, a public poem of which Scotland remains proud:

> Open the doors! Light of the day, shine in; light of the mind, shine
> out!

Let me acknowledge again that the danger with the phrase "bardic voice" is that it sounds old-fashioned, linked inextricably to Yeatsian "last Romantics." In Scotland, however, Morgan gave the lie to that, while still managing to draw on what he called the poetic "resources of Scotland" as well as on an astonishingly wide range of poetic sustenance – from Gilgamesh to Ginsberg; and it was Morgan who in the penultimate dictated email of *The Midnight Letterbox* produced a tellingly astute statement on the public role of the poet as laureate; never a party hack (Morgan was not a joiner of political parties), he did attempt with grace a bardic voice, conscious of writing as a national poet at a time when

> the people of Scotland … are, I think, quite certain of a movement in politics and society that is developing towards a very different way of looking at things – a Scottish as compared to an English way. The two nations (if we want to use that term) are still closely attached, but moving from that towards some kind of separation, although there may be argument about what degree of separation there should ultimately be.

Morgan's thoughts here are too long to quote in full, but are worth reading in *The Midnight Letterbox*. There he goes on to invoke the Hungarian national poet Petőfi and his "National Song", before concluding that this work

> was a reminder that a national poetry should not be involved in clinging to any particular political idea, or writing for money, and it is certainly not to be seen as a passing gift (whether granted by a queen or anyone else). Rather, poetry at this level should remind people that if they want to achieve something in the world, and to really be taken seriously, then they need to show the world what they stand for. And surely those who are best equipped to articulate this are good writers, and this includes poets.

Though he certainly did not use the term, and though (as a gay man who had kept his sexuality secret for decades, and in other ways) he certainly understood the need for private voice, what Morgan is articulating here is the case for what I am calling "bardic voice" in poetry. Bardic voice needs to be a crafted, sometimes unfashionably rhetorical tone of address; it should not be stuffy; it is present in Dunbar, in Burns, and in many other poets; and it remains a valid and urgent – though not the only valid and urgent – kind of voice to be heard in 2015 as it was in 2014 and has been for centuries before. To be a poet in Scotland now means, on occasion, to take the risk of bardic voice, not because we can be sure the work will last, but because of a deep desire to risk articulating something that matters. That's what led to some of us risking "bardic voice" in 2014, and leads me still to stand by and voice, both personally and inclusively, that risk.

This essay was delivered at the National Library of Scotland on 23 September 2015 as part of the "Poetic Politics" conference marking the first anniversary of the Scottish Independence Referendum.

Born in Lanarkshire, Scotland, Robert Crawford studied and taught at the Universities of Glasgow and Oxford, moving to St Andrews in 1989. A Fellow of the Royal Society of Edinburgh and of the British Academy, he has published six collections of poetry and over two dozen other books, most recently Testament *(Cape Poetry, 2014) and* Bannockburns: Scottish Independence and Literary Imagination 1314–2014 *(Edinburgh University Press, 2014). His* Young Eliot *(Cape), the first volume of his two-volume biography of T. S. Eliot, appeared in 2015.*

RECOLLECTIONS OF AN EMIGRÉ
(variations on Antonio Machado)

Ciaran O'Rourke

Tonight I'm thinking of the war again,
its shatter and spin of eyes and limbs
on the rooftops, bridges, sun-bare hills;

and thinking of the song it shreds
in wheatfields, cities; and the breath it steals
from quiet streets, to scatter as death

on the burning farms – death, which I see
has time, tonight, to pause here, too,

to pluck a lemon from the hanging bough,
which quivered in the wind, as the sun withdrew.

———

From the earth, from visions,
from the gravel roads,

from dust in the breeze,
from bones, from blood,

from the risen flame
as the morning sings,

from the half-heard voice
from the flooding verge,

from the pummelled gut
when the rifles bark,

from the clear-eyed heat
of the corpse's gaze,

raise hymns, raise anthems
to the man the bullets buried ...

Lorca, as the bombs chant on
to hunt your elegy,

Grenada's chorus
will lift its fists

and call the city yours.

———

Did you see the sky today,
the rainbow spilling
from its gash of cloud?

Or, as I did, the bell-jar
of sky-refracting light and rain,
globed above the compact fields?

Something woke and sent me to it,
flinging the windows, un-
battening the heart!

There among the cypresses,
in the lemoned haze of garden and summer,
you stood, as if returned

from a rain-lit morning, the whole air
wet around us, and your face a-gleam ...

I felt it all come back today,
as if no longer vanished, nor a dream.

———

In my country, to live
is to want to live

between a Spain that rots
and a Spain that yawns.

You, who are new
to the world, and fresh:
look to your God, or run quick,

for one Spain or the other
will cause your heart
to icen up, and break.

———

It's time to fashion songs
the world might share,

as if to sing were knowing
knowledge impotent
on the seas we all go under, in the end.

Or as if the key we needed
was the one we lack, and every lock a whimper
in the blood and brain.

So sing, you songsters! Though no beam
of light can thud the earth
but the lines evaporate, or fade …

What is it words say, after all?
And what the water, from the fluent rock?

———

These days death
goes on, and life abides.

And our part, too,
is partly death:

to die, but
to die building

our paths across the sea.

———

That swarm bedamned,
of poets cricketing love-tunes
to an empty moon.

I'll keep company instead
with this one who walks
beside me in the dark.

For he says that those
who speak in solitude, like him,
hope also, in their way,
to talk to God.

———

Would you lead me again
down the white track,
my hand in yours, our voices
free and undulating
in the noon-deep air?

As I cross and re-cross
the shattered plazas now,
the shadows vivid,
the cart-wheels splintered
by their load,

I turn from the broken vista
to that place in sight
of mountains,
where your heartbeats still
are whispering, like wings.

———

When we were sleeping, maybe,
the hand hummed near once more,

which once sowed darkness
with the seeds of stars,

and this time
sent a music through it:

a strum-note echo
on the sea's guitar,

which reached and rippled
through us, as a sound

or two, a single word,
that trembled on our lips

and spoke the truth.

———

I loved you once, old shack.

She lived in you
      like spring
in the air a plane tree makes.

Now the stone's
wind-wickered
      at your side,
and to look
into your heart

is like blowing breath
into a cage:

the dust rubbles
round itself
in the breeze.

But up, see:
cold moons
      touch
in the windowpane ...

And there am I,
going out again,
naked and unhappy,
      to roam
the ancient street.

Ciarán O'Rourke was born in 1991 and studied English and History at Trinity College, Dublin. He received a Masters in English and American Studies from Oxford in 2014. His poems have appeared in a number of publications, including Poetry Ireland Review, Poetry Review, The Irish Times, The London Magazine, New Welsh Review, The Spectator, *and* The SHOp. *His pocket-pamphlet* Some Poems *was published as a Moth Edition in 2011.*

THE GENIE'S OOT THE BOTTLE

Neal Ascherson

Already independent.

In a long, shallow article published recently in *The Financial Times*, the historian Simon Schama accused Yes supporters of betraying their own past. The great names of the Scottish Enlightenment, he wrote, had treasured the union for its universalism, for rising above petty things like national boundaries.

True, the Enlightenment in Scotland, England, and continental Europe sought universal principles. But one of the principles was equality, and another was the right of human beings to govern themselves in freedom. Denis Diderot, revered by his Scottish contemporaries, wrote: "Every colony whose authority rests in one country and whose obedience is in another, is in principle a vicious establishment."

Scotland was never a colony, unlike Ireland or Van Diemen's Land. But, having once been a partner in the union, Scotland in the course of the twentieth century became a dependency. You all know why and how: the end of Empire with its opportunities, Scotland's industrial and urban decay, the long Cold War peace after 1945, the postwar expansion of the centralized British state, the decisive political divergence as voting patterns in Scotland and the rest of Ukania separated after about 1950. The outcome was a situation in which authority rested in London and obedience rested in Scotland – Diderot's "vicious establishment."

Devolution has mitigated that a little. It moved some authority to Scotland. But its unintended consequence has been to undermine what remains of obedience. You see, the 1707 Treaty of Union is already over – it's dead. It was soundlessly blown up like a *Red Road* tower block, at the moment in 1999 when Winnie Ewing said: "The Scottish Parliament is hereby reconvened." For the last 15 years, we have been living in an informal, low-rise, lower-case union, its ever-changing skyline made up by Westminster and Holyrood as they go along. The sweep of transformation, now become a torrent since the referendum campaign began, heads towards the completion of self-government.

Like so many others, I used to want just that complete self-government – I wanted Scotland to run its own affairs as other small, normal nations do.

Only that. Independence seemed a high green fruit, ripe maybe in the far future but not yet. But two things changed my mind.

The first was what Tony Blair showed us in 2003. There's an affliction called Reynaud's phenomenon – you lose feeling in your fingers. I got Blair-Bush phenomenon. I found I had lost the feeling of living in an independent country. That's a horrible numbness. But where unless in Scotland could I get that feeling back?

The second thing was David Cameron's decision to strike the devo-max option off the referendum paper. The choice was to be simply independence: yes or no. Everything or nothing. How can you wish nothing for your country?

The argument for Scotland's return to independence has a pull and a push. Of all the Yes opinions I heard on an eight-day "bus-party" referendum journey this May, only a handful were about "push" – about perceived threats to Scotland in the next few years if we remained in the union. Instead, people talked about the "pull": about "what sort of Scotland do we want?", the better, fairer country they hoped to construct. More generous and powerful local self-government, openness to more immigrants, an outward-looking Scotland active in the world, "a listening Scotland where my son can grow up and have prospects …" And so on.

Few of them were committed SNP types. But strikingly, none of them assumed that their hopes could be realized within the union. They weren't always right about that. Some of their ideas, at least, could be carried through by a determined Holyrood parliament under current devolution. But their assumption confirmed the almost terrifying failure of the Better Together campaign to make an attractive, positive case for the union – as opposed to its shaming and sometimes farcical "Project Fear."

Why terrifying? Why shaming? Because I want everyone who votes a serious No out of love for their country, because they have a different vision for its future, to get the respect they deserve. Not to be dismissed as just one more Project Feartie.

The Yes may well not win the vote in September. But it has already, overwhelmingly, won the campaign. In the long term, that may come to matter more.

In the dark years before the Velvet Revolution in Czechoslovakia, Vaclav Havel used to say: "We don't need to wait for it. Let's start living in truth now – right now. Let's live 'as if'." And the Polish workers, before there was Solidarity, said: "Let's create spaces – authentic spaces in which a real

Poland exists, in which we talk openly, wait for no permission, design our own future."

We can learn from that. I have never seen Scotland in such a mood of creative doubt, of opening locked minds and changing opinions, of self-questioning, of new faith. I'm thinking of a woman in Dalmuir trying to live on £71 a week, who cried out to us: "We can do it, we can do it! The genie's oot the bottle; and there's no getting it back in."

So we shouldn't wait either. Never mind what happens on referendum day. We should be saying: "Wake up, we are independent already, now, today. And from today we shall start to act as if we were citizens of an independent country." And don't worry – history will catch up with us.

This essay was written for "Scotland on the Cusp: A Reading for Independence", 6 July 2014 at Òran Mór, Byres Road, Glasgow.

Scotland voted No in the Scottish Independence Referendum on 18 September 2014.

Neal Ascherson, a native of Edinburgh, was born in 1932 and has spent most of his life as a journalist, much of it as a correspondent in Central and Eastern Europe, and later as a columnist for The Observer, The Scotsman *and* The Independent on Sunday. *He is the author of eight books of non-fiction beginning in 1963, most recently* Black Sea: The Birthplace of Civilisation and Barbarism *(Jonathan Cape, 1995) and* Stone Voices: The Search for Scotland *(Granta, 2002). He lives in London.*

THE KILLING

Malachy Tallack

Back damoarn.

He was breathing, that was the first thing. The heavy reflex of air in his lungs. He was a body, waking. Then the sounds came. Those same breaths, and the stirring of the sheets. The room itself, becoming itself. The shape of the air around him. Downstairs, a clock was ticking in the kitchen. An American clock, with a ship painted on the front. Once it belonged to Sandy's grandfather, and now it belonged to Sandy. He liked to hear it as he wakened, to focus himself. And sometimes, when his thoughts were elsewhere and the sound had been erased, he would stop and listen just to hear it again, as though it were new.

Outside, starlings squabbled on the telephone wire and in the fuchsia bush at the end of the garden. Somewhere in the valley, sheep gossiped among themselves, and a cockerel was crowing. It was Annie's cockerel, perched on the wooden henhouse beside her shed, at the very end of the road. Or perhaps it was standing on the square of lawn beside her gate, where the grass was ragged from hens scratching and dogs pissing. Further still, beyond Annie's croft, the sea gasped against the stones on the beach. There was little wind, so the ocean was hardly more than a whisper. A car came up the road, rattling. The exhaust needed fixed, so it was Michael's car, with Michael driving. That meant it was 8.15 a.m., or perhaps a little earlier.

Sandy still hadn't opened his eyes, though he could see the room around him now, and the house and the road and the valley. He could see it all as it was, and as he knew it would be. And everything was much as it always was, except that Emma was not there. She was gone, and he was lying on her side of the bed, his face against her pillow, and his body held beneath the weight of her absence.

The night before, she had left, as she said she would, taking two bags and promising to come back soon for more. The move was not a surprise. They had talked about it for weeks, and agreed, and decided. She was ready to go, and he was ready to let her; but still the first night alone was hard. For three years they had filled this house together. Now he had to fill it alone, and he didn't yet know how. There was no liberation in her leaving; he just felt smaller than he had before.

After packing her bags, Emma had driven the few hundred yards to her parent's house to tell them she was going. She had not wanted to worry them before, and Sandy could only imagine how that conversation had gone. Lying in bed, awake now, he did imagine. She would have given them the facts: it's not working; it can't work; I'm going to stay with a friend in town for a few weeks, till things are sorted, then I'm going south again, at least for a while. Her parents would have said little, but nodded and expressed concern, regret, sadness. She would have gone to the car and sobbed. Perhaps they would have cried, too, he wasn't sure.

———

Today, Sandy was meant to help Emma's father with the killing. His lambs were in from the hill, and had been on grass for a month. It was cold enough now to hang them, and they were ready. Sandy had promised to help, as he had the past two years, but he hadn't expected the timing to be like this. On the morning it was to happen he could hardly pull out, but the thought of the day ahead made him feel weak. He opened his eyes and let a long breath slide from his lips into the cold room. For a second it appeared above him – a tiny cloud – and then was gone.

There was no point in a shower; he would need one later. Clean, old clothes, dragged from the bottom drawer. A jumper, jeans, a hat. Sandy poured a bowl of cereal and set coffee on the hob to boil. He ate, looking from the window, then stood up to drink the coffee. He shifted his back and tried to loosen his shoulders. A walk up the road would make him feel more awake, he thought. It would make him feel more ready. He set the mug on the draining board and took a coat from the back of the door. Outside, the day was more still than he had thought. It was one of those days when you could hear someone talking from the other side of the valley, had there been someone there to talk. Sandy's boots clopped on the tarmac as he walked up the road, the sheathed knife in his pocket rubbing against his leg with every stride.

"This is home", Emma had said, the first time she brought him here to meet her parents. Her arm swooped from left to right, taking in everything they could see, and she laughed. She had meant her home, of course, for this is the place she was brought up, the place she knew best, and the place she wanted to come back to, though she hadn't told him that yet. But that first time, as they stood together in front of the house, with the smell of her mother's cooking spilling through the doorway, he knew it could be his home, too. More so than the council house in town, where his father slept and drank and watched television. More so than the city flat he shared on the mainland. More so than anywhere he had been before. The view that her arm had encompassed – the heathered contours of the hill, the patched green of the valley, and the sea beyond – seemed bigger, then, than all of those other places.

She was not his childhood sweetheart, though sometimes it felt that way. In fact, they had never met before university. Or if they had, neither of them remembered the occasion. They had gone to different schools, in different year groups, and had different friends. He knew her name, and her father's name, but not much more than that. They met in the city, among mutual acquaintances, first at a party, then in the pub, where they sat together and spoke to almost no one else for the entire evening. Sometimes it was a chore to meet somebody from home, but that night it was a revelation. It was like finding a person with the same books on their shelf, or the same music in their head. She knew him already. She understood the part of him that no one else could understand: the part that was always here.

"We're tied to the islands by elastic", Emma told him once. "You just have to decide how you live with it. Either you go away, and stretch the elastic – gradually it will slacken off, and you'll feel relaxed, freer maybe – or else you give in to it, and there's no shame in that. Just close your eyes and let it pull you back. Let it carry you home." A year after that first visit, they had been carried back here together, and this had become his home. For three years it had been their home. And now she was gone.

———

David was standing at the entrance to the byre, a basin of hot, soapy water in his hands. Setting it down on the work bench he turned and nodded at Sandy.

"I wis up early daday, so I got da lambs in afore brakfast."

"Dat's fine", Sandy said. "How many have we to do?"

"Joost eight daday. I hae tings ta be gittin on wi laeter. We can dae da rest damoarn if du's able. Else I can dae dem mesel tru da week."

In the stock box, the animals shuffled restlessly.

"Is du ready to start then?"

"Aye", said David, walking towards the trailer. He paused beside Sandy, and laid a hand on his shoulder. "A'm sorry, boy", he said, and nodded again. "A'm really sorry." Turning, he undid the catch on the trailer and lowered the ramp to the ground. "A'm ready when du's ready."

David stood aside as Sandy pulled open the gate and stepped into the box. The lambs pressed against the back wall, then separated as he came towards them. One tried to squeeze past him and he grabbed it around the shoulders, then passed it out through the gate. Taking a front leg in each hand, David walked the animal towards the byre, and Sandy turned round for another. The trailer was parked at a slight angle to the byre door, but he stepped out then with the second lamb held tight between his knees, and closed the gate behind him. Somehow it felt wrong not to watch, as though by looking away he would be dodging the guilt that was rightly his.

There was a carefulness to David's actions – a deliberate regard for what he was doing. Everything was laid out where he needed it, and everything was ready. He had done this hundreds of times before, but he never did it automatically. He was mindful, always, of each step along the way. Leaning over, he picked up the bolt gun and held the lamb tight against himself. Sandy turned the head of the animal he was holding and covered one eye with his palm, as David had told him to do. *Du niver keens*, he'd said. *Du niver keens.*

There was no hesitation. The trigger was squeezed and the gun popped. It was oddly unstartling. His own lamb never flinched, but the other one shook hard as its nerves spasmed, the back legs flailing and kicking the air together. David picked up his knife, drew it deep across the animal's throat, then pulled the head back and let it bleed. Sandy realized he'd been holding his breath, and he relaxed as he watched the blood pour out onto the concrete. When the shuddering had stopped, David removed the head and laid it in front of him. He lifted the body and turned it upside down, out of the mess.

"Okay, A'm ready fir da neest een."

When both lambs were lying dead, side by side, the men picked up one each and carried them into the byre – front legs gripped in one hand, back legs in the other. They set them down on the curved, slatted benches by the doorway, feet pointing at the roof. David shook his knife in the basin of water, then wiped the blade and washed his hands. Sandy removed his own knife, and turned it over, inspecting it.

"Is he sharp enoff?" asked David, looking over.

"Should be. I'll gie it a go."

"Is du wantin da radio on?"

"No, thanks. Leave it aff."

Though he'd done this job several times before, Sandy did not feel confident. There was a lot to remember, and he waited until David had begun before he started himself, looking over and watching the older man's movements. He removed the feet first, splitting the second joints, then washed the blade. He lifted the skin around the breastbone and made an incision, slicing a straight line – first one way, towards the neck, and then the other, towards the belly. Lifting the flap of pelt that faced towards him, he pressed the knife underneath, helping the skin to separate from the flesh, like a label from a parcel. He laid the blade down, then put his knuckles into the space he'd created, running them up and down against the joining line, pushing it back, widening it, until his whole hand could fit inside. *Du haes tae be forceful an gentle at wance tae no tear da skin*, he reminded himself. *Don't use dy fingertips.*

As the body began to emerge, Sandy felt the shape of the ribs on his hand, the firm curve of the flesh. It was hot and clammy, and as he reached his fist further, towards the bumps of the spine, he tried hard not to be distracted, to think only of what he was doing. One side complete, he walked around and began from the other, loosening the lamb from itself until his hand met the space he'd already made underneath. His knuckles were stinging with the effort, and he paused a moment before continuing – slicing and lifting and stripping, until the cloak of fleece-lined skin had been completely unwrapped. The animal lay naked on the bench.

Sandy looked over at David, watching the quick, perfect movement of his hands. He followed what was being done, and copied, lifting the thin membrane that covered the stomach cavity, slicing it carefully, keeping his blade away from the bulging gut below. A fatty, fetid smell erupted from within, and the coiled mess emerged, delicate and horrific. *This is where it can go wrong*, he thought. *Everything you don't want to break is here: a full bladder, bowel, stomachs.* He cut a line from the groin up to the sternum, then cut deeper up towards the neck, splitting the rib cage.

Last time they had done this together, David must have felt he was passing something on. Emma was his only child and he had never taught her how to kill a lamb, how to turn it into food. He was not a traditionalist in every way, but he was in this one. Men taught their sons, and so he taught

Sandy. Sometimes, perhaps, he had imagined that knowledge being passed on further, to his own future grandson, though he never spoke the thought out loud. But now, today, the severing of that thought was apparent to both men. Today they were only neighbours. The understanding of that change stood between them as they turned around their tables in silence, like lonely dancers.

"Is du feenished?" asked David.

"Almost. I'll be wi dee in a second."

David walked to the cupboard on the side wall and fetched a handful of metal hooks. He punctured the hind-leg tendons of his lamb and pushed one through each. Sandy stood beside him, and took hold of the hooks, then lifted the lamb as high as he could manage. David put his hand in and cut away the liver and the heart, setting them aside. He sliced the diaphragm and cut the windpipe and oesophagus, then pulled the insides out, flopping the guts into a plastic bucket at his feet. Finally, the kidneys were removed, with a white clump of fat congealed around them.

"Okay, hang him up", David said, "and we'll dae da idder een."

———

Eight bodies were suspended from the rail that ran along the front wall of the byre, marbled pink and purple and white. All warmth had gone from them now, and all hints of the life so recently ended. They were solid and stiff and alien. The two men cleaned the mess – bundling skins and guts into black bags, scraping the jellied pool of blood from outside, piling the heads behind the trailer and brushing detergent over the red-blotched floor. Then they stood together in the doorway, looking out over the croft and the valley.

"Is du wantin ta tak een o yon heeds heem?" asked David. "Fir company, lik."

Sandy paused, letting the joke hang between them for a moment, enjoying the awkwardness of it. Then he laughed.

"No, I'll likely be alright, thank you."

David nodded, solemnly. "If du says so."

Sandy noticed a splatter of blood on the older man's face, and he felt an urge to tell him, or to wipe it off with the sleeve of his jumper. Except that it didn't matter at all.

"Will du be back damoarn?" David asked. "I cud dae wi dy haelp ageen."

"Okay, yes. I'll be back tomorrow."

"Gid. A'll aks Mary to mak mer maet fir denner. Du can eat wi wis. Come alang aboot teyn, if dat suits dee."

Sandy smiled, and picked up a polythene bag with two livers inside, the clear plastic clinging to his greasy hands.

"See you tomorrow", he said, then turned and walked back up the driveway, and out onto the road, towards the house where Emma no longer lived.

A writer, editor and singer-songwriter, Malachy Tallack was born in 1980 on Shetland. His first book, 60 Degrees North *(Polygon, 2015), about the circumpolar regions of the world, was a BBC "Book of the Week" choice. He was the editor of* Shetland Life *for five years, and is the editor and founder of the online magazine* The Island Review. *He is currently based in Glasgow.*

ANTRIM CONVERSATION

Moya Cannon

Pain and suffering are like false currency
passed from hand to hand
until they meet the one
who does not pass them on

(Simone Weil)

Chalk is stained brown near the waterfall.
It crumbles away easily,
as flint nodules are prised out;
the flint itself is poised
to split into slivers,
a suggestion of blades,
a memory of the trade which this
sharp wealth engendered.

The small, tidy man who paused on his stick
to talk to us in the lane,
on this Sunday of rose-hips and blackberries,
had a voice soft as chalk.
He spoke first of weather and houses and sheep,
of a life working *to put wee shoes on wee feet*
and we talked on and on in the September sunshine
until nodules of hurt washed out
in the stream of his words.

He spoke of being woken at home as a child
by the bark of uniformed men with guns;
of his own young son being beaten up;
of prison, of *not knuckling under*
and then, of his satisfaction on hearing
that a man's head had been blown off
in a neighbouring town.

(This poem continues after Portfolio.)

PORTFOLIO: IN THE AEGEAN

Enri Canaj

No possession but hope.

Sailing from Turkey
Mytilini, Greece
June 2015

Enri Canaj was born in Tirana, Albania, in 1980. He spent his early childhood there and moved with his family to Greece in 1991 after the fall of communism. He studied photography at the Leica Academy in Athens and participated in 2007 in a British Council project on migration, attending a year-long workshop with Magnum photographer Nikos Economopoulos. Since 2008, he has worked as a freelance photographer, with his images appearing in Time, New York Magazine, Newsweek, Paris Match, Le Monde Diplomatique, *among many others. His work has also been exhibited in Turkey, Kosova, Belgium, Poland, and India, as well as in Greece. He is based in Athens and works throughout the Balkans.*

Prompted by his own experience as a child, Canaj began photographing the migration crisis as a personal project in 2014, when the first large waves of refugees began. He has written of the experience:

> *When I photograph I'm 100% there: watching people, hearing their voices, their screams, the sounds of the sea, the boat-engines, living all that ... Every single minute they have to deal with smugglers, money, the sea, the sun, the rain, the hunger ... but I have also experienced the huge power people have to survive – a power that comes only from hope ..."*

Greek Coast Guard
Near Chios, Greece
September 2014

Father and daughter after Coast Guard rescue
Mytilini, Greece
June 2015

On an uninhabited island
Inousa, Greece
September 2014

Syrian refugees
Inousa, Greece
September 2014

Skala Sikamias beach
Lesbos, Greece
September 2015

Skala Sikamias beach
Lesbos, Greece
August 2015

Molivos Beach, arriving from Turkey
Lesbos, Greece
October 2015

Koraks beach
Lesbos, Greece
September 2015

Molivos beach
Lesbos, Greece
October 2015

A boy from Syria, just arrived from Turkey
Lesbos, Greece
August 2015

Molivos beach
Lesbos, Greece
October 2015

Moyra refugee camp, queuing for papers
Lesbos, Greece
October 2015

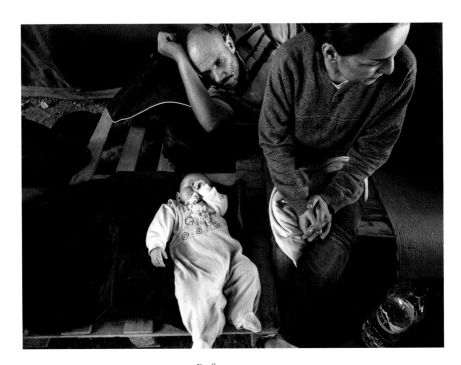

Refugee camp
Chios, Greece
September 2014

Moyra refugee camp, queuing for papers
Lesbos, Greece
June 2015

Lost sisters, Shahat (6) and Syria (10), from Syria
on the Greek-Macedonian border
Idomeni, Greece
August 2015

Atakudin (15) from Afghanistan, under an olive net
Moyra refugee camp, Lesbos, Greece
August 2015

Omar from Eritrea
Chios, Greece
September 2014

Afghan boys at a refugee camp, under olive nets
Lesbos, Greece
August 2015

Hiding from the police, near the Greek-Macedonian border
Euzoni, Greece
June 2015

Hiding from the police, near the Greek-Macedonian border
Idomeni, Greece
October 2015

Greek-Macedonian border
Idomeni, Greece
May 2015

Greek-Macedonian border
Idomeni, Greece
August 2015

Greek-Macedonian border
Idomeni, Greece
June 2015

PORTFOLIO

is generously supported by Nicholson & Bass Ltd, Belfast.

History's hard cart rattled on
as flint nodules shattered
into narrow weapons
as we wondered, dumbly,
what shift of bedrock,
what metamorphosis,
might heal such wounded,
wounding ground.

What do we know of the chalk,
the flint, of other's souls
or of our own,
or of what might break in us,
if history's weight
pressed heavily down?

How do we know
that we could hold the pain
and not pass on
the false and brutal coin?

Moya Cannon was born in Dunfanaghy, Co Donegal, and now lives in Galway. Her fourth collection of poems, Hands, *was published by Carcanet Press in 2011. She is a member of Aosdána.*

MARY ANN & DOROTHY

Ruth Carr

Author's Note: The following poems (part of a larger sequence) explore various parallels, real and imagined, between the lives of Mary Ann McCracken (1770–1866) and Dorothy Wordsworth (1771–1855).

BUT FOR THEIR DIPPING PENS

In truth,
they both preferred the tongue,
the swirl of words in the mouth,
their northern twang;
the to-and-fro
between friends – well water
shared on the road – a sojourner's story;
the surge of argument pounding on stubborn rock.

That said,
without the flow of thought crammed onto paper,
we'd never grasp that foxglove feel for things
from inside out, that Dorothy way
of seeing;
never trace the grit of Mary Ann working
a crack, scratch by scratch, to let the light
break through on things kept dark.

But for their dipping pens,
we could not dip beneath the selfless surface,
could not begin to fathom how they held.

ROSEMARY STREET, BELFAST

The street remembers when it was a lane
remembers the spark of her heels,

times when silent tears salted a cup
of ale in old White's Tavern.

The church still stands in stone
a meeting ground for the hopeful

and the hopeless: for any soul the old
embrace of human-kindness.

Walk its historied cracks. Read the words
carved deep in a doorway:

Faithful to the last, mindful of
the lamp-oil burning late across the street

where Mary Ann wrote letter after letter
pleading, cajoling, pressing the case

for humane action – all in her slight,
unshakable hand, holding her own.

This place is crying out for her; waiting
for that quickening step again.

THE LIBERATING ART

it is late in the darkening house

from a simmering well
the stroke of the quill
as it charts the pull of resistance

of unbound thought

in the grace of the candle
you conjure
your own unsinkable craft

to cover the criminal distance from north to south

spluttering wax brings you back
to the table, the chair, these walls
this mooring of light

it is late
about two in the morning
bid god speed and goodnight

WEPT BY HER BROTHER'S SCAFFOLD

do not be deceived by the words inscribed
mind when they were penned
how politic, how purblind
to narrow her to that heart-pour of tears
that cost her dear
barred from the closing moments of his life –
the dying male
the weeping female
a frame of words completely missing out
her head, her hands
the years and years and years
she practised what he died for
díleas go héag

Note: *Díleas go héag*: Faithful unto death (Irish).

A LIFE

Drawn to kindred, half-lost souls, you listened
to them, wrote them into the landscape that

you walked and loved and breathed, keeping
old Fisher busy stitching leather.

Hoofed it to Ambleside and back, sometimes
by moonlight in hope of a letter.

Dried still-fragrant leaves for a second brew,
the third for the neighbours.

Speared as many stitches as words, shirt after shirt,
stocking after stocking.

Papered the walls with newsprint above the buttery
to line little lungs against damp.

These were the patterns that cut and pinned your life.
For years the walking worked its balm,

the robin's "slender" song, the light on Rydal
letting you belong, for a while –

the wind in your weathering face,
the seeds of wild white foxglove wrapped

in a docken to take home and plant
in your mutual "slip of mountain" at Town End.

A POSTSCRIPT FOR DOROTHY

And how the moon might have cracked
and birthed anew
filled with ink in whole eclipse
had you walked your own wild gait
instead of reining in to serve his rhyme.
Or might you never have taken a step
beyond the parsonage gate
without that certainty
instilled in him
by you?

Mary Ann McCracken (1770–1866), political activist and social reformer, was the daughter of a prominent Belfast Presbyterian shipowner and sister of Henry Joy McCracken, one of the leaders of the United Irishmen Rebellion of 1798, with whom she shared an interest in radical politics and the oral music tradition. For his part in the 1798 Rebellion, Henry Joy McCracken was court-martialled and hanged at Cornmarket, Belfast, on land given to the city by his grandfather, after refusing to testify against his comrades-in-arms. After the death of her brother, whom she had doctors attempt to resuscitate, Mary Ann McCracken became one of the foremost Abolitionists in Belfast and remained so for many decades.

Dorothy Wordsworth (1771–1855) was an English author, poet, diarist, and avid naturalist. She was the sister of the poet William Wordsworth, and the two were close all their lives. Wordsworth had no explicit ambitions to be a public author, but her posthumous writings consist of journals, letters, poems, and children's short stories.

———

Ruth Carr was born in Belfast in 1953 and attended Queen's University Belfast. She is the author of two collections of poetry, There Is a House *(1999) and* The Airing Cupboard *(2008), both from Summer Palace Press. She recently received a bursary from the Arts Council of Northern Ireland to explore poetically the lives of Mary Ann McCracken and Dorothy Wordsworth. She works in community education and continues to live in Belfast.*

TIME AWAY

Juliana Roth

Grown by the sea.

November is on its way, Carol thought as she walked around the yard, adding the last of their Halloween decorations to the large, red chokeberry bushes and whitening dogwoods. They wove together to hide the house from Small Point Road, an asphalt stretch an hour outside of Portland. Her knee-high green gardening boots kept fallen rose branches from cutting her calves as she bent down to weed beneath them. It was getting harder for her to get down on her own, so she really only wore them out of habit.

Cotton spiderwebs laced themselves between her fingers, and she scraped them off against the face of the mailbox, like shedding a layer of her chapped skin. The box was empty; nothing to be brought inside except for a few leaves of basil from the pot next to the door. They chopped up nicely on the counter, sizzling and curling up into themselves as they met the hot olive oil in the skillet. The crackling filled the lonely kitchen around her. She turned the flame down and dropped slices of tomato and sausage into the pan.

Bill was out in the shed. He worried the growls from his electric saw would make their way into the kitchen, annoying Carol as she cooked. He put down the saw, still on. The door to the shed no longer fit the frame, and it flew open. Bill pulled a cement block out of the corner, wedging it against the door to keep it shut. The saw's buzzing moved the machine along the worktable, as though it were alive. A screech let out as the blade cut fruitlessly at the head of a hammer. Bill pulled the plug from the wall, quickly, hoping to hide the mistake, hoping that Carol hadn't heard.

He knew there was a box of his old tools somewhere in the shed, ones used to make the fence that ran along the property so the hunters would stay off, out of sight. Ansel had gotten him an electric saw years ago for Father's Day, saying it was safer and easier to handle. It took a while for Bill to agree, but he eventually did. Lately, the vibrations it sent through his hands were disorientating, making his birdhouses crooked.

The toolbox was under some tarps and most of the saws inside of it had rusted. Bill was making wooden faces for when Janey came to visit, ones he'd attached to the trees for her laughter, her wonder. They were almost done. He wiped the old saw against his jeans and began to work again. It was a difficult cut to do, one that grooved through the wood to make curves smooth as lips. The dip came out too deep. Bill worked faster, knowing that Carol would be calling out to him soon. When she finally did, he waved it off. *Five minutes.*

———

Bill went back out early the next morning and packed the wood pieces into one of the canvas shopping bags Carol used when she went to Hannaford. He liked the drawing on it, a crow riding on the hood of a tractor. It reminded him of their dream, why they'd moved here. Pulling from the bag as he walked down the trail, Bill arranged the wood pieces perfectly together on the neck of the trees to form faces: one with owlish eyes and a small mouth made of bark, another whose chestnut grin showed teeth underneath a fat, knobby nose. He wrapped the back of his hammer around any nailhead that went askew. They came out quick and landed at Bill's feet in a pile of brown leaves. Again, he centered the nail on the red dot drawn with the pen kept tucked behind his ear. *Bang.* The nail was perfect, dead-on like the pupil of an eye made of a light oak. Such ease had become rare for him.

After the final tree, a willow, Bill kept down the trail to where the dirt started to mix with sand, ending at a rocky beach. This was the walk he would take Janey on that weekend. She would ask him about the house overlooking the shore, and Bill would look down at her and tell her that it was empty. A couple had bought it for the summers, but hadn't been down in two years. Or was it three? Bill found a spot on a boulder by the waterline where he could watch the waves roll into each other. Not even ten years ago, he could recite the first and last names of his past five years of students, sometimes their parents, too.

As the water covered the sand around him, then pulled away, back to where it had come, Bill held tight to the smooth surface of the rock face, afraid to be pulled along with it. It seemed that for most of his life, he had let the water's force take his body. When the produce stand went under, he'd floated. When Carol mourned her body's unwillingness for a second child, he'd splashed. Now, Bill let the tip of his shoe dip into the cold water as his fingers fought for his grip on the smooth surface of the rock. He would not go again, not easily.

"You can try all you want", Bill yelled out, challenging the waves like an old fisherman who refused to put an engine on his rusting rowboat. "I'm not coming with you."

Looking past the wooden counter to their yard, almost vacant of blossom, Carol watched the trailhead. When Ansel was younger, she used to send him down to hide in the bushes and spook Bill as he came up the path. It was all staged, of course, Ansel not being any good at staying silent during the wait. But Bill convinced the boy he had some sort of special power, faking a stumble and yell when Ansel popped out at him. That's what Bill was good at as a teacher, convincing the children they'd been the first to come up with an answer, that they were little investigators that could find newness in the world. It's what made Bill well known at the elementary school in Woolwich. New mothers with husbands who were pulling away as the kids grew from being toddlers, men who started taking more shifts at work, picking up golf, locking themselves away in the basement with videotapes. These women clung to Bill as some proof that their husbands could one day become something else.

A glimpse of a neon orange beanie came up the hill, then Bill's sweaty face appeared. Carol felt the small relief of a jealous ache, like when he used to drive off to work, and she knew there'd be children and mothers waiting for him to excite and satisfy. Often, he'd come home with little left. Carol would try to distract herself by sorting their extra seeds into small plastic bags that the gardening shop down the road would pay her for, by making big dinners and telling Ansel to save some homework questions for Daddy. Now, there wasn't much left for her to do that soothed the wait. His breath was heavy as he reached the back steps. She filled a mason jar with water and met him at the screen door.

"The sun's almost set. I don't want you getting lost out there", she said, pushing the door along its track. "Remember what happened with Jeffrey?"

"A walk can't be *too* long. I know my way out of there. Jeffrey was over eighty, plus", he said, entering, "I was setting things up for Janey."

"Oh, what is it?" Carol asked, hopeful. Usually it would be days before Bill showed her a finished project, as if he wanted the newness to wear off before she got to see, like she might ruin it before it had a chance to settle in.

"A surprise." Bill pulled out a chair from the glass table and sat down. The wrinkles around his mouth pulsed as he chugged the water down.

"Can't you trust me with it?" Carol joined him. She looked hard at him, deciding if he'd describe the faces to her, the ones she'd seen on his work table that morning while he was taking a shower. Each was made of varying wood pieces, their grain and color popping out against each other, except for the eyes that sat on top, happy pairs. She'd studied the eyes, jumping from the ones that were in a frozen wink to the egg-shaped ones that reminded her of Mr Potato Head. If she stayed long enough, maybe the faces would wake up from the trance Bill had put them in and talk to her.

"Sure", Bill said. He placed the hammer on the table. It smelled of salt and seaweed. Carol rubbed at the wet handle.

"You down at the water too?" she asked, nervous.

"For a bit. Washed some dirt off the hammer."

"Bill." The bottom of his pants were wet up to the knees.

"It was dirty", Bill said as he packed the hammer away into his bag again.

"Won't the salt rust it?"

"I guess so, forgot about—"

"Look at your pants. Did you drop it?" Carol looked as though she might cry.

"No. And it wouldn't mean anything if I did. A thirty year old could drop a hammer. Most do." He got up to run his hands under the sink. Carol watched as the warm water soothed their shaking.

"Think of what happened with Jeffrey", she said, wanting to be near him, to stand behind him with her arms around his waist, to steady him. "Remember how close he got when he was out there?"

"Jeffrey had a bad heart. I'm not at risk for that. If anything, I'd just get lost." The water started to spurt. Something was caught in the faucet.

"But isn't that worse?" Carol asked. Bill turned off the sink, staring at the drain.

"I built that trail."

———

The next afternoon, Janey came. She sat tall, riding in the front seat of Ansel's Terrain as they drove up the dirt driveway. Bill checked the windows for Rebecca, who'd never let Janey out of the car seat in the back. Ansel and Janey had visited them alone the past few months. Rebecca had been promoted at the television station and wouldn't get home until after nine most nights, Ansel had told them. He hadn't looked for a new job after the radio station went off air. "My own wife put me out of business", he'd say.

"That's how bad she wanted me to be a stay-at-home dad." Bill and Carol never found it funny.

As the car came to a stop, Janey bent down to grab the pink Disney water bottle Bill had given her for her fifth birthday, holding it over her head like a sword. She was out before Ansel could walk around to open her door – shooting past him to her grandparents, who slowly bent down to kiss her cheek. A beep sounded from the SUV as the trunk opened.

"Hi Mom, Dad. I like the ghosts in the bushes", Ansel called out. His head was deep in the trunk. Bill walked over and clapped him on the back.

"Good to see you. You look strong. These for Mom?" Bill asked, bending down to pick up a bag of Lindt truffles next to the spare tire.

"How'd you know?"

Ansel slung Janey's polka-dot duffle over his shoulder and walked inside with Bill leading the way, waving the chocolate at Carol's face. Sometimes he'd find her sneaking candy from the goodie bags they had ready for next week when she went to get her coat from the closet. Carol beamed, then smoothed her sweater over her stomach.

"Maybe after lunch", she said as they headed to the kitchen. "Sit down while I warm up the sandwiches."

———

Janey looked through their bin of VHSs by the television and picked out *Balto*, the same one they'd watched last time. It felt new to Bill – he remembered Balto as a bear, not a husky, but he pretended it was all familiar, laughing with Ansel at her choice.

"Lunch is here", Carol said, setting a wooden tray on the coffee table. They gathered around the plates of grilled cheese and started the movie.

Soon, Janey was asleep on Ansel's lap, leaving her sandwich mostly untouched. Bill watched Ansel as he moved Janey's soft blonde hair out of her eyes, then down at Carol's hand resting on his own knee. She pulled away when he placed his on top.

"I'm going to head out, guys", Ansel whispered, wrapping a blanket around Janey. He stacked the dishes back on the tray and went to load them into the dishwasher. Bill followed.

"How are things with Becca?"

Ansel looked back at him, unmoved. He took his grey fleece from the chair, zipped it up, and flipped the hood over his sandy hair.

"We're all right, Dad. The night off will be good for us. We appreciate this a lot", he said as he started for the front door.

"Well, we're happy to get some time with Janey. I planned something special for tomorrow." Bill struggled to unlatch the bolt, looking to the floor when Ansel reached over to help him with the lock.

"What is it?"

"Something in the woods, Ans. She'll have to tell you on her own", he teased.

They walked out to the driveway and hugged before Ansel got back in the car. The trunk was still open as he pulled out, headed south towards I-95. Bill laughed when he got a glimpse of it between the bushes, flapping like an awkward wave goodbye. He waved back at it for a while before it dipped out of sight, imagining Ansel getting halfway to the highway before someone alerted him to it at a stoplight, how he'd blush and pretend it was on purpose.

The honeysuckle bushes were full of dying buds that Bill pulled off easily, one by one with their browning leaves, dropping them to the ground. The frost had dried whatever sweet juice was inside. It had come too early. This was happening more and more in Maine, confusing the crops and the people. A dandelion peeked out from where the buds had landed. Bill plucked the small flower. When he came back inside, Balto was being thrown against the snow by another dog. Janey was asleep. Carol too, and he tucked the flower behind her ear.

———

The phone rang a few times that evening before Bill decided to put down the paper he was reading on the couch. There was an article about a campground owner who'd created a haven for deer on his property: no hunting within a half mile either direction of the lot, plus ten new trees added each year to the camp woods. Under his photo, the man was quoted as saying the only friendly faces he ever came across in the woods were of the deer. Bill's glasses fell from his face as he struggled to find the green button on the receiver.

"Hello."

"Hey, Dad."

"Ansel! How's it going? Just reading the paper here."

"All right. I wanted to call to say goodnight to Janey."

"Oh, Mom's giving her a bath right now. Rebecca there with you?"

"No. It's just me. She went out with a friend tonight, Diane from …" he paused, "yoga, I think, maybe work—"

"You know, we can keep Janey an extra day if you need", Bill offered, flicking the corner of the paper with his thumb. It was getting harder to keep it steady.

"We're all right. Becca just wanted some time out with a friend. It's good to have alone time for me, too. I miss that sometimes. People aren't really meant to live every moment one on one with another person their whole lives. Can't be healthy."

"Maybe not. But it's important. What's that beeping?"

"The microwave's going off. I've got a pizza in there. Tell Janey I called."

"All right. Have a good night. We'll see you soon." Bill placed the phone back in the receiver. The upstairs bathroom was above his head. He could hear Janey get out of the tub and giggle as Carol rushed her into bed.

"Hurry, Janey. Your hair is going to freeze like an icicle if you don't run", she called out. Bill used to tease Carol this same way when they'd take evening swims at the beach. Right before the sunset, Carol would circle around the house and find him, usually harvesting some vegetables. The backyard was his domain, home to pea and tomato crops that climbed up planks he'd found in the free and exchange shed at the dump.

She'd take his hand and lead him down the woods to the shoreline. Her hair was long then, made of icy blonde strands that covered her back. She'd braid her hair, then coil them up into a bun to stay cool while she weeded the front yard. When they reached the ocean, Carol would let her hair down as she stripped to her underwear and jumped into the water. Bill would watch her in amazement, like a sailor discovering a new creature. They worked this way for the first three summers they owned the house, before Ansel was born and the money from the farm stand wasn't enough.

When Ansel was two, the farm started to fail. Carol's dream of packing up the pickup bed only once a week with flowers and vegetables for the Portland market slowly turned to three. Then, five. Soon, they went most days and the truck came back nearly full. Bill would come up with a new excuse for the lack of interest, telling her that a grocery store had gone up too close to the farmer's market lot or it was too chilly for people to walk around.

Carol decided to drive down and find out for herself. As she set up their stand, Carol noticed how their blue banner, "Grown by the Sea", looked dated among the laminated white signs with big, black fonts. Most tables had scales and cash registers that moved the lines along quicker. They had refrigeration systems in the back of their vans to sell prepared food: smoked gouda sandwiches, tomato salads with basil and vinegar, fresh-squeezed juices. The food was packaged in plastic and labeled with a promise of "handmade" and "organic," each brand claiming to be a family farm that was deeply a part of Maine's history.

She drove past one of the farms on the way home and parked the truck a couple yards up the road. Walking down, Carol pulled her hood up to hide her face and snuck into the backyard, following the smell of the smokehouse to the farm. There were hired hands scattered across the yard, some taking eggs from chickens, one pushing at the back of a cow to move him out of the water pit, and all around them danced glistening metal tools and machines. As she backed away, back to the woods that led to the road, Carol yanked out several carrot plants and left them in the cool evening air to rot.

———

That night, after Bill put Ansel to bed, they sat together at the table in the kitchen. Carol told him to stop by the food bank in the morning and drop off the produce that didn't sell. He agreed, and asked her if she had any ideas for next week's market, a new banner maybe.

"You should go back to teaching", she said. This was something he'd been offering for the last few months.

"What about you?"

"I'll have Ansel to take care of. I'll keep selling the seeds and maybe do some more landscape consulting. It's okay."

After that summer, Bill never could get Carol to come back down to the beach with him, alone. Ansel always went with them or Bill would take hikes by himself after work while she finished dinner. As he heard Carol laughing upstairs, he wondered what another day down there together would be like. He wondered if maybe they had tried harder to find time back then – to swim, to make a new banner – they could've had another baby. Maybe staying away from the ocean, from the evenings at the beach in her underwear, had done something to Carol's body, frozen it like an icicle.

Bill remembered the last time he saw Carol drifting off with the waves, a look of peace overcoming her face as she treaded down the sand. Maybe he had stolen that from her. Maybe he'd hogged the woods by taking hikes alone, pushed her away from openness of the world, left her to maintain what was left of their garden, this small piece of land that would be turned to an asphalt parking lot once they were gone like what they'd done with Jeffrey's place after he died. The bath drained loudly through the pipes in the ceiling, leaving a loud, hollow echo as the final drops were sucked down.

———

The next day at lunch, Carol, still in her light blue nightgown, asked Bill if he and Janey would be taking a walk. She had pie dough settling in the refrigerator and wanted to get started. It was already four o'clock.

"I think Grandpa has a surprise for you, Janey girl", she said, winking at Bill. "I've got some things I need to get started on here."

Bill looked up at her, almost angry, then back to his macaroni. There were hard chunks of cheese drying on his fork. She watched as he scraped them off against the rim of his bowl.

"Why don't you come with us, Carol?" Bill asked. "Don't you want to see the water?"

"It's too cold for me out there. I'm not even dressed." She pulled at her nightgown. "You've been wanting to show her, alone." Her voice cracked. Why was he asking her this now? She had to work on the pie. Chocolate pie with fresh whipped cream!

"Will there be a mermaid at the ocean?" Janey jumped up, knocking Bill's hand against her cup of juice. He ignored it and went over to Carol, to touch her.

"Maybe, sweetie. Grandpa will help you look. You guys should go before it gets dark." Carol moved quickly from him to mop up the spill with a napkin from the table. There wasn't even time for her to get changed if he really did want her to go. That's what he was doing. He was pretending he wanted her to come, knowing that she couldn't, that there wouldn't be time. Carol thought of how beautiful the wooden faces were, imagining how special they'd feel to Janey, how she'd laugh and point and wave at them. But Bill never told Carol about them, never brought her out to the shed and showed her how he planned to fit them together. She'd had to go on her own this morning, secretly. Alone.

"I want you to come with us", Bill answered. The juice was dripping to the floor. Carol went over to the drawer by the sink. She pulled out more napkins and a pumpkin-shaped lollipop for Janey. Bill got their coats and came up behind Carol, grabbing her hand. The room felt heavy and uncomfortable to Carol, almost as if she was being teased.

"I want you to see them too. The trees", he said.

"Come on, I don't want to. I've got to clean this up. I'll be here when you two get back", she said, pushing them out the door, watching as Bill draped her coat over the back of a chair. "There'll be pie!"

———

Janey bobbed as she ran up and down the beach, gathering shells from the sand and cleaning them off before stacking them on top of each other, building a wall against the cascading sea.

"We don't get wet in my world, Grandpa", she told him, focused on the arrangement of the shells. He squatted down far enough behind her so that when he squinted, it looked as though it were true.

"Wow, Janey, what a sturdy fort."

"It's not a fort", she cried out, "it's my world." Her sneakers lit up as they stomped up the beach as Janey searched for more shells. Bill watched for a while longer, keeping an eye on the sun as it dipped in the sky.

"Time to go back home, time to have dinner and wash up", Bill said as he picked her up, tickling her. His shoulder cushioned Janey's face. She whispered bye-bye as they reached the small incline that led to the main trail, then squirmed against Bill's hold. He turned to see a wave sweep away the shells.

"I want to walk on my own", Janey said. Bill let her down, and she burst ahead, her small legs pumping faster than his unsteady walk could manage. The lingering smell of salt water on his skin made him feel sick. Had he gone in the water? Bill heard something rumble: maybe thunder, maybe one of the monstrous waves bringing in the tide.

"Slow down", Bill warned. The sun seemed to be moving from the sky faster than ever before. Backwards, away from the Earth altogether. Janey stopped running and grabbed Bill's hand, trying to laugh with him again. Her laugh felt like a heckle. A twig cracked under his sneaker, then the woods were silent for a while as they moved through. The tall brick chimney that Bill had built 30 years before rose above the treeline. That's always how he knew they were close. He reminded himself to just follow that, to keep his eyes glued up there. And he did, until Janey started to giggle and poke at his side. He wanted to yell at her to stop, to leave him alone. Didn't she understand how hard it was to look ahead? Didn't she know that all he had were pieces of brick to guide them home?

"Grandpa, is that tree alive?" she joked, pointing up at the willow. It had two eyes, a nose, and lips made of a light cedar that stuck out awkwardly against the dark grey bark. Why did it look so angry? What had he done to it? Bill spun around, scanning the woods for a dark shadow, someone on their heels.

"That doesn't belong here, Janey. I don't think it was already here, was it? That tree never had a face before", Bill said, nervous. Her hand shook with his growing speed. She tilted her head up to him and started to laugh again. Quieter.

"We met all these trees before, Grandpa. That one is Danny. See." Her voice perked up, trying to lead them back to their games. She dropped his hand and pointed up at the trunk. "I don't know what any of this means. Someone is playing a joke on us."

He scrambled to find her hand again, held it tight, and moved fast through the rest of the trail. Her face reddened and puffed out with tears as she was pulled along. There were faces on the lindens and hemlocks, even one on the burnt stump of a lightning-struck oak. *Hurry*.

Bill went down, thrown over by the knob of a root poking up from the dirt. He landed on the side of his face, his grey beard pressed against a small patch of grass that had survived the years of feet stomping down the trail. By the time Bill turned himself over, Janey had stopped crying. Her face was back to its pale white and her breath had settled. She stood by the pine at the top of the trail, waiting for Bill to catch his own. When he did, she bent down, kissed his bald head, and sat crosslegged by his side.

"Are you dead?"

"No, Janey. Grandpa didn't mean to scare you like this. It was getting dark in the woods – I just wanted us to get back here in time for supper. It was just an accident. I shouldn't have run", he told her, remembering all the faces, that they were all his. He tried to push himself off the ground, but couldn't quite make it. "Why don't you tell Grandma I need her help to get up?" His hand was steady again as he wiped a dirt clod from his knee. He looked at this little girl, his granddaughter, and felt a terrible, confusing guilt. How had he ruined this day for her? Does she have to know that this is how life gets? Behind her, he saw a light on in the kitchen and a figure, Carol, sitting behind the screen door.

"Okay." Janey nodded and started up for the house.

———

That night, Bill took a long shower, loosening the dirt from underneath his nails with the lid of a shampoo bottle. He tried to understand the dread that had sat with him through dinner. Nothing. There was no reason for all that had happened, no reason for him to have fallen, no reason for Carol to come bounding out of the house with Janey close behind. His wife, Ansel's little girl. His two girls. He reached for a towel from the bar outside the shower door and dried himself off, breathing in the steam the water had made.

He fell softly into bed and wrapped his arm around Carol's waist. They laid this way as Bill imagined himself back at their rocky beach, the Atlantic pouring in with heavy waves. He pushed the rocks down to block the water, the cold, salty waves, from crashing into him. He stacked grey boulders atop each other, lifting them with enormous strength. Once settled, they became darker as the ocean soaked them, but a small spray snuck past the cracks and wet his face. He'd almost fallen asleep when a wave struck the wall. The rocks slipped, collapsed, and rushed toward him. Bill opened his eyes before they could strike. The dark of the room comforted him, and soon he was asleep.

———

Carol went to wake Bill up after Ansel came for Janey, carrying a large mug of coffee with vanilla cream up the stairs. It was the latest he'd slept since his first week of retirement. Rebecca had come with Ansel this time, and Carol had told her how worried she was that Bill was still asleep, that maybe it was a sign of something terrible, but the only response Carol got was that it sounded like heaven. Things were hectic at the station, and Rebecca longed to spend an entire day in bed, to be allowed such wonderful silence.

"You don't understand", Carol said and felt herself opening up. Carol wanted help, for Rebecca to offer to come inside and talk. That's what family is for, to help, to listen. Why hadn't Carol tried this before? Ansel would unpack the car and say they would stay for a while longer. It would be so simple. "Bill couldn't get himself off of the ground."

"My father fell on his last birthday. Shock is mostly what keeps them on the ground. The soreness healed up in a few days. Just make sure to use ice. Plenty of ice", Rebecca told Carol as Janey tugged at her hand, asking to go home and try on her Halloween costume. Rebecca opened the back door and strapped Janey into the car seat.

"Thanks for having her", Ansel called out from the driver's window. He had the engine running so the car would warm up. It had snowed earlier that morning.

"Yes, thank you so much. Janey must have had such a good time." Rebecca gave Carol a quick hug. Her red sweater was cut low, and the firmness of Rebecca's breasts made Carol despise her own.

"I think so, but Bill's fall. I hope it didn't spook her too much."

"Oh, I'm sure she's fine. Everything will be just fine." Rebecca made her way over to the trunk and pulled the hood down, then walked over to the passenger's seat. Her long black skirt swayed against the wind. Carol watched her body, jealous of the elegant, easy way she moved.

"I hope so", Carol said, giving up.

"He will be. Promise." Rebecca looked up at her, turned her mouth into a small frown, and said goodbye before shutting the door. Ansel was busy jumping through the radio stations.

Carol waved from the front steps, hoping for Janey to crane her neck around to get a last look before they turned out of the driveway. It never came.

———

She didn't go up to Bill right away, but sat at the kitchen table, running her hands across the glass. She felt as if she'd been pushed out of her own life. Didn't she have a sweater like Rebecca's? Maybe it was purple instead. Ansel hadn't even bothered to give her a hug, instead had tried to entertain Janey, who'd already forgotten about watching her grandfather fall the day before. The short run the girl made up to the house to get Carol, to guide her down the yard to where Bill was hunched and crying, had blended in with memories of eating chocolate pie while watching movies on the couch. The taunting wooden face that hung on the tree above Bill's spilled body, the careful touch that could be seen in its design, the threat Carol made to rip the pieces off of the tree: gone, unremembered.

Rebecca no longer tried to impress Carol, and the promise of Ansel's new family showing care for them as they aged seemed hollow. Bill's accident had pulled Carol with him into this new *thing*. They'd become a nagging obligation that could somehow be managed by not listening too carefully. Carol poured coffee beans into a grinder, held the button down, and let the noise drown out her crying. She wished Ansel had come alone, that things with Rebecca weren't going to work out, that he and Janey would need to stay with them a while longer. Or even that she could find a new wrinkle on Rebecca's face.

There was still a crease in the covers from where she'd slept next to Bill. Setting the coffee down on the headboard, Carol woke him. He edged easily to the middle of the bed, patting a space for her.

"Here." Carol climbed in, letting some of the hot coffee spill on his hand as she handed him the mug. "Morning."

Juliana Roth grew up in Nyack, New York and received her BA in English from the University of Michigan in 2015, where she was a Cowden Memorial Writing Fellow in her senior year.

HEANEY AND THE MODERNS

Manus Charleton

Nature's unknowable purpose.

For a poet who came of poetic age in the 1960s it's surprising that Heaney's poems aren't part of the modernist turn which poetry took with Eliot, Auden and others. By comparison they are traditional in content and style. Heaney was aware of this as an issue for him when he was starting out. In a number of his published lectures and essays he writes about his relation to modern poets, and it troubled him initially that he wasn't drawn to write as they did, especially since their way of writing had already become established.

In his essay "Learning from Eliot" he recalls that when he read Eliot's poems first (he got a gift of his *Collected Poems* aged 15 or 16) he was "daunted by their otherness", and that he continued to find them difficult in his late twenties when he was lecturing on them in Queen's. At school he was told the "The Hollow Men" was about disillusion, loss of faith, lukewarm spirit and the modern world. And while he was able to understand the poem in these terms, it didn't speak directly and vitally to his own experience. There's a question of the extent to which he identified with the modern sensibility evident in Eliot's poetry. For, as he says, "I was never caught up by Eliot, never taken over and shown to myself by his works, my ear was never pulled outside in by what it heard in him."

Consider loss of faith. In "A Found Poem" he writes: "There was never a scene / When I had it out with myself or with an other. / The loss of faith occurred off stage." And he made the same point in *Stepping Stones* in response to a question from Denis O'Driscoll. Yet, in the West, the effects of loss of faith flow strongly from Nietzsche's declaration of the death of God in the late nineteenth century through the twentieth as one of the strong currents of modernism. With it came liberation, but also uncertainty and a strong impulse to replace the security of belief in a benevolent God with the security and power of material success or unquestioning political allegiance. There was also the response of remaining uncommitted and haunted by feelings of absence and loss.

Disillusion with human hopes and aspirations is another strong current in modern sensibility – the disillusion which was an understandable reaction to a century that included two world wars, a cold war and a nuclear arms race. More deeply, it was disillusion with the very possibility of human rationality where the supposedly rational was exposed as a mask for a more powerful irrationality at work. And in modern novels and plays characters are shown to be disillusioned, notably Meursault in Camus's *The Stranger*, who has been emotionally numbed by his life's lack of meaning and purpose. Beckett's characters, too, are disillusioned, trapped in a swing between black humour and anguish. Disillusion is present also in the tone of Beckett's poems, as it is in poems as diverse as Allan Ginsberg's "Howl" and Thomas Kinsella's "Mirror in February." But it's not present in Heaney's poems.

There's a question also about the extent to which he identified with the youth movement and culture of the sixties with its anti-establishment protests, liberation from restrictive convention, and spirit of rebellion that found expression in Beat poetry as well as rock and blues music. This movement has been seen since as naive and self-indulgent. But it expressed idealism for a better world in which people would be free, both individually and collectively. Sartre associated himself with the movement, which in France also involved factory workers, and identified its significance in Simone de Beauvoir's interview with him before he died (published in *Adieux: A Farewell to Sartre*): "But that time [1968] was important and beautiful, unreal and true."

While the absence of these modernist traits marks a limit to the range of Heaney's poetry, it is not a criticism of its merit. His engagement with the modern poetic sensibility helped him clarify his relation to his own more traditional sensibility, and to validate it as right for him. It helped him to come into possession of his own voice and deepen it. We can see this in the way he ceased trying to puzzle out the meaning of Eliot's poems and used what Eliot had called "the auditory imagination" to attend closely to their music. He was aware that Eliot insisted on "the poetriness of poetry being anterior to its status as philosophy or ideas or any other things." And by attending to the rhythmic flow of the poems he gained access to what he termed their "underworkings." He broke through to an experience of their oracular nature, with which he was familiar from his own experience of how a poem came into being.

He also came upon C.K. Stead's *The New Poetic*, which revealed to him that Eliot "trusted the 'dark embryo' of unconscious energy." And Heaney was familiar with the necessity to trust the "dark embryo", as poets have traditionally done. In *The Government of the Tongue* he writes of "the self-validating operations of what we call inspiration", and he refers to Polish poet Anna Swir's description of the inspired poet as the person who "becomes then an antenna … a medium expressing his own subconscious and the collective subconscious. For one moment he possesses wealth usually inaccessible to him, and he loses it when that moment is over." In "Feeling into Words" Heaney describes the feeling of inspiration as the "first stirring of the mind around a word or an image or a memory." It is "excitement" at the initial emergence of a possible poem. And "that first emergence involves the divining, vatic, oracular function." The water diviner is the gifted person who "resembles the poet in his function of making contact with what lies hidden, and in his ability to make palpable what was sensed or raised."

The submission of poets to the promptings of inspiration is in the Romantic tradition of understanding the poetic source in nature. Shelley wrote about nature as the source in his essay "In Defence of Poetry" where he sees the poet's sensibility as an "Aeolian lyre" moved by wind and as "a fading coal" which "an inconstant wind awakens to transitory brightness." And Heaney is attuned to the subconscious not for bare threads of modern angst and homelessness, but for inklings of nature opening up in rich veins of expression through the poet's particular experiences. It's an attempt to let nature speak for itself insofar as possible through the poet's experience. This is how Shelley and Wordsworth saw it. Where Shelley longs to emulate the soaring, singing skylark for pouring forth "profuse strains of unpremeditated art", Heaney in verse IV of "Homecomings" calls on the sandmartin to

Mould my shoulders inward to you.
Occlude me.
Be damp clay pouting.
Let me listen under your eaves.

Also, in the first Glanmore sonnet, furrowed fields are "opened ground" and "the turned up acres breathe", which leads to: "And art a paradigm of new earth from the lathe / Of ploughs." Here "paradigm" suggests not only a theory or concept of artistic expression as something which derives from nature, but also as epitomizing nature.

Yet for all his indebtedness to the Romantics (and the appeal other poets in this tradition have for him, such as Hopkins and Kavanagh), nature in Heaney's poems is not Arcadian. Still less is it inherently savage and pitiless, which comes across in many of Ted Hughes's poems, another poet he admired. Heaney's sense of nature comes from his experience of it growing up in a rural household in Ireland before mechanization, amid the sights and sounds of farm and bog. Some of the poems, such as "Clearances 3", with its image of peeling potatoes beside his mother at the kitchen basin, and "Clearances 5", with its reference to "sheets she'd sewn from ripped-out flower sacks", have a kinship with the peasant world of Millet's paintings, such as "The Potato Sowers" and "The Gleaners", both of which might well have been Heaney titles.

But Heaney's rugged word arrangements are some way from the often luminous tranquil depth in Millet's paintings. They are closer to the rough-hewn realism in Van Gogh's work, a quality characterized by Heaney's use of the word "heft." Some of Van Gogh's subjects, too, notably "The Angelus (after Millet)" and "Pair of Shoes", are subjects which Heaney might also have written about. In a "Pair of Shoes" nature is shown as a stretch of light coming out from the depth of the painting to illuminate in the foreground a pair of dishevelled black hobnailed boots, light which a man of the soil seems to have trod through before taking the boots off. It's an image which brings out the life of a human being who has walked the earth and worked it for sustenance. Heidegger wrote about this painting in his essay "On the Origin of the Work of Art", in his attempt to bring out how a work of art embodies truth. It is also a painting which you could imagine a solitary Samuel Beckett standing in front of for a long time in the Van Gogh museum in Amsterdam.

So, for all his affiliation to the Romantic tradition, there is at the same time a rugged realism in the quality of Heaney's poetry, which brings it closer to the modern insistence to see things as they are. There's a nuanced quality to his attitude towards nature which manages, at times, to sound something of both the modern feeling of disenchantment and the Romantic sense of belonging. This is perhaps best expressed in "The Tollund Man", in the last verse in particular:

> Out here in Jutland
> In the old man-killing parishes
> I will feel lost,
> Unhappy and at home.

This ambivalence is part of his stance towards the world even though ultimately he sides with the feeling of being at home rather than lost. As he puts it in "The Fully Exposed Poem", his essay on Holub, "the attempts by the will or ego ... to pervert man's indigenous genetic at-homeness in the world are sooner or later doomed to cave into his stronger, submerged sense of belonging." His tie to the Romantic tradition is umbilical, and frames his poetic outlook. He hears its "narcotic music" still infusing East European poems, such as Holub's, and coexisting with their "wire-sculpture economy" and wry irony and intelligence.

Heaney's outlook of "at-homeness" in the world is what distinguishes him from the moderns, and in "Feeling into Words" he sees a poet's basic attitude to the world as the essential element in his or her technique; technique which he sees as more important than craft. Technique includes "a poet's stance towards life, a definition of his own reality." And it "entails the watermarking of your essential patterns of perception." Technique requires the employment of the poet's attitude to life and to its worth, drawing from his or her experience of it in depth. And it comes into play in particular during what he termed "the second, the making function" after the oracular. Technique in this sense characterizes what he called in his 1997 *Paris Review* interview "the shape-making impulse, the emergence and convergence of an excitement into wholeness." And in emphasizing a poet's basic outlook as the essential element in technique we can see him indicating why he writes as he does, in faithfulness to his more traditional sensibility.

———

In his essays and lectures Heaney also engages with the view that poets should have something valuable to say about the human condition and social and political circumstances. This association has come down through the role of the poet as bard in the courts of kings and chieftains, and has formed the perception of the poet as a wisdom-speaker. In "Sounding Auden" he describes it as the aspect of poetry in which it "is a matter of making wise and true meanings, of commanding our emotional assent by the intelligent disposition and inquisition of human experience." And Heaney credits Auden with giving this voice new life as a continuing and distinguishing element in modern poetry. It is personified in the voice of Prospero in contrast to that of Ariel. Heaney's voice is more Ariel than Prospero, and we can see him in his essay on Auden clarifying for himself how best to accommodate the Prospero voice in his own poetry without smothering its lyrical birthright. He traces a path from Auden's earlier Ariel-sounding poems with their dependence for meaning on a new type of rhythm and intuitive premonitions of catastrophe to where Auden "began spelling out those intuitions in a more explicit, analytic and morally ratified rhetoric." But if this explication is what modern poetry requires, it's not a requirement Heaney wants to meet. It is a step too far away from Ariel. He shows he is reluctant to wear his social and political stances on his poetic heart lest his poems lose their compressed and latent force. We can see this in his clear preference in the later Auden for a return to his "insular experience" which can sound forth in universal terms, as in the tone and images in "The Fall of Rome", whose last two verses he quotes, the final one being especially memorable for its disturbing ripples across the subconscious:

> Altogether elsewhere, vast
> Herds of reindeer move across
> Miles and miles of golden moss,
> Silently and very fast.

Heaney regards it as a false dichotomy that poetry has to be either lyrical or political. The lyric can be implicit with recognition of historical and political conditions, and express the poet's attitude and view in nuanced ways. In "Place and Displacement" he writes: "It is a superficial response to the work of Northern Irish poets to conceive of their lyric stances as evasions of the actual conditions." It is in a poet's nature to be "often displaced from a confidence in a single position by his disposition to be affected by all positions, negatively rather than positively capable." By this he means a more detached but no less morally concerned and felt stance can be evoked. And he cites Derek Mahon's "A Disused Shed in County Wexford" as a powerful, resonant example.

There is also the dimension of the poet as a conscientious public witness to unacceptable events and conditions. Heaney engages with this dimension in "Lowell's Command", where he characterizes Lowell as wanting to feel he was "forging the conscience of his times" both through his poetry and through taking a public stand. And for Heaney there is an inherent connection between a poet being true to his conscience and writing poetry that commands attention for its truth. He gives the example of Mandelstam, who in writing against Stalin must have known he was signing his death warrant, "yet this was the only way in which his true voice and being could utter themselves, the only way his self-justification could occur." Heaney adds:

> After this moment, the hedonism and jubilation of purely lyric creation developed an intrinsically moral dimension. The poet's double responsibility to tell the truth as well as make a thing would henceforth be singly discharged in the formal achievement of the individual poem.

The poetic moral and political dimension is not to be commanded or directed at the reader; it is to be seamlessly woven into the texture of poem as poem. And Heaney writes of Lowell's middle period during which he wrote such poetry, a period of "roused poetic voice" when he was in his "prime" and regarded a poem as "an event", carried on what Heaney calls "the up-draught of energy." At the same time, poems need to have, in Mandelstam's phrase, which Heaney quotes, "the steadfastness of speech articulation." And for Heaney it is this steadfastness in Lowell's middle-period poems which directs attention to "the very source of that music, in conviction of the tongue's right to speak freely and soundingly." And again, as with Auden, so with Lowell, Heaney makes clear his preference for poems from this period, such as "Waking Early Sunday Morning", in which Lowell's conscientious moral and political view is submerged in the flow from the poem's wellspring. And Heaney cites Eliot's criticism of his poem "Little Gidding" in which "the acute personal reminiscence" (which Eliot felt the poem lacked) was "never to be explicated, of course, but to give power from well below the surface."

———

Heaney's allegiance to the intuitive feel for poetry's lyrical root in nature brought it back centre stage at a time in the modern period when it was at risk of getting lost. But arguably his strong attachment to this root left him less open to the new strains that came with modernism. His poetry can be seen as occupying a place somewhere in the tension between both pulls. For it's a moot point to what extent Heaney succeeds in being able to infuse his own poems with a tone and images that do poetic justice to social and political conditions. The tribal nature of the conflict in the North, and his ambivalence about the social and cultural influence of the Catholic Church, come into the long poem "Station Island", but they come in bound up with an almost confessional self-examination rather than by way of the stored and matured detachment he identified as needed. And in writing *The Cure at Troy* and *The Burial at Thebes*, perhaps he takes his sounding from the ancient Greek plays to have a more detached location from which to voice his present-day moral and political concerns.

At the heart of Heaney's legacy is his instinctive allegiance to poetry's lyrical root in nature. And there is a direct link between his allegiance and Kant's account of the source of artistic judgment. In his *Critique of the Power of Judgment* Kant posited the idea of nature having an inner unknowable purpose as the basis for understanding how our judgments about art can be true, judgments which are manifestly subjective while also carrying a claim that other people should agree with us; a claim that they can apply universally. For Kant "nature gives the rule to art" – rule not in the sense of any formula, but in the sense that when the artwork embodies something of nature's unknowable purpose, it provides an experience which everyone can have and admire. When we look at a painting or read or hear a poem or experience some other art form, it's precisely because it can unsettle us by its lack of knowable purpose of the kind which characterizes nature that it also astonishes and intrigues us with admiration for something greater than us which we can't explain but which is integral to our lives. And where Kant regarded nature having an inner unknowable purpose merely as an idea to solve the problem of how aesthetic judgment can be valid, the Romantics took it that nature is in fact driven by some unknowable purpose or force, with the poet as a channel for nature's power.

Moreover, the artist doesn't have it in his or her power to think of how to initiate an experience of the unknowable purpose so as to incorporate it in a work. It is a matter of nature giving it, and of the artist having a predisposition to receive it. Kant drew from the etymology of "genius" as a natural gift or a particular spirit which some people are born with to explain how "the rule" gets into art. "Genius is the inborn predisposition of the mind (*ingenium*) through which nature gives the rule to art." And there's a link between having this predisposition and trusting, as Heaney did, in a poem coming to him from nature through an oracular experience.

Kant's understanding of art influenced the Romantics. And beyond the Romantic period it's an understanding which artists, such as Heaney, have instinctively felt. When Cézanne, the progenitor of modern art, was reminded by Émile Bernard of the approach classical painters took, he replied that "they created pictures" whereas he was "attempting a piece of nature." He was trying to get under nature's skin and show the way it emerges into shapes under the eye and mind. And Cézanne added: "Everything comes to us from nature; we exist through it; nothing else is worth remembering."

Manus Charleton lectures in Ethics and Politics at the Institute of Technology, Sligo. He is the author of the textbook Ethics for Social Care in Ireland: Philosophy and Practice *(Gill and Macmillan, 2007). He has been published previously in* Irish Pages, *in the* Dublin Review of Books *and in* Studies: An Irish Quarterly Review.

DISTRACTION AS INSPIRATION: HEANEY, O'DRISCOLL AND *STEPPING STONES*

Bernard O'Donoghue

Trust in his gift – and the gift in his trust.

My title is a pretty obvious one, prompted as it is by the opening page of Dennis O'Driscoll's "Introduction" to *Stepping Stones* (Faber, 2008). O'Driscoll begins by describing his misgivings about distracting Heaney from his primary work, in a poet's life in which there were plenty of distractions already: Heaney's required "presence at a book launch, his speech at an art-gallery opening, his place at a Friday-night dinner table; his reading, his lecture, his review, his blurb, his oration, his nomination, his reaction to some public event – everyone has plans that involve snatching him away from his poems." It is a set of variations on Yeats's "Fascination of What's Difficult" which lamented the poet's distraction by "theatre-business, management of men." Other writer-biographer relationships (something of which *Stepping Stones* is a kind of variant) have dwelt on the same concerns: some, like Ian Hamilton's first tape recordings with Robert Lowell, coming to a different outcome when Hamilton abandoned the face-to-face recordings, finding that it took Lowell too far from the very subject of his poems, let alone the writing of them, as the poet dwelt on the circumstances of his life rather than the work. I'll return to this matter of "confessionalism" later on, since I think it was a major issue for poets in the mid-twentieth century.

Predictable as my title and subject is, it might of course have been couched differently because all these relationships vary depending on the personalities of the interlocutors. It might have been called "The Civil Servant from Porlock", recalling the most famous interruption in English poetry of the poet in full flow, when Coleridge says a "man from Porlock" came and knocked at his door, causing the continuation of "Kubla Khan" beyond its surviving fragmentary state, to fade from his post-visionary mind. As early as his first book, *Kist*, in 1982, O'Driscoll evokes this dilemma in his poem "Porlock":

this is a poem of distractions, interruptions, clamouring
telephones, this is a poem that reveals how incompatible with

verse my life is ...

this is the lost property office of poetry

It is a very favoured O'Driscoll image: as another example, in his rather acerbic
account of Simon Armitage's aspirations and election as poet-in-residence at
the somewhat ill-fated Millennium Dome, he says, "The stately pleasure-dome
at Greenwich needed a poet as prominent as the edifice itself; old-fashioned
sensitive souls who were likely to be distracted from their poetic reveries by
busloads of schoolchildren from Porlock were never likely to be front-runners
for the job." And now here is O'Driscoll in 2008 encroaching on Heaney's
"dream-time" more than the distractors he has itemized, like the Frustrators
who kept cutting across the exchanges between George Yeats and the inspiring
communicators who are dictating the material of *A Vision*. He tells us that his
"original plan had been to visit the poet on a specific day each week to record
material which I would then transcribe": of course, such a plan could not be
incorporated into Heaney's pressed programme. Similarly, he asks Heaney if
he had worried that "the professing" might drive out the poetry when he
became a professor in Harvard and Oxford. Later in the book Heaney
reassures us: "Never once did I think of the professorship as either a distraction
from poetry or in conflict with the Harvard appointment."

Against this idea of frustrating interrupters we might pit the opening
words of O'Driscoll's "Introduction": "A wise man's wisdom needs to be
extracted", Bertold Brecht's observation about the cross-examining
customs man who seizes the knowledge which Lao Tsu is smuggling out of
China into exile. A certain amount of debriefing is salutary, and O'Driscoll
goes on to plead the case for his interruptions and distractions over the
several years in which the question-and-answer structure of the book was
being made. At the very end of *Stepping Stones* Heaney says that some of the
poems he likes best "were written in the lay-bys of a lecture" he was
preparing. He referred to the book as "a potent stirrer-up of memories",
memories out of which O'Driscoll tells us some of the poems in *District and
Circle* were written, including "Anahorish 1944", "Tate's Avenue" and "Home
Help." We will come back to that.

The reader's misgivings about how welcome this catechetical process
was to its addressee is allayed by what Heaney said in his funeral address for
O'Driscoll (and elsewhere): "He devoted years to collaborating with me on

a book I needed to write but one that, without Dennis as interviewer, might never have got written." So the first crucial matter is to decide what this necessary book was and exactly what kind of book *Stepping Stones* itself is. O'Driscoll makes it clear in the "Introduction" that Heaney was very adamant throughout about what kind of thing it was *not*: "he would not engage in detailed analytical discussion of individual poems." O'Driscoll therefore says, "this book does not pretend to be an authorized 'reader's guide' to Seamus Heaney's poems but rather a survey of his life, often using the poems as reference points." This makes it a pretty remarkable project in the annals of twentieth-century writing, considering New Criticism's insistence that the poem is the thing and the exploration of any exterior material is the action of what W.K. Wimsatt called an intentional fallacy: the mantra was that we can know what the poem is about without bringing in any context. It is a matter that arises repeatedly throughout *Stepping Stones*: the question of confessionalism and the relations between "perfection of the life or of the work", Yeats's famous "Choice." In discussing Ted Hughes – one of Heaney's great friends and literary heroes – O'Driscoll asks "*In the long run, won't* Birthday Letters *be regarded as of biographical more than literary interest?*" Heaney says that is not how he sees it, saying, "You're dealing here, after all, with a book by a poet of genius", listing the individual poems from *Birthday Letters* that he most admires. The appearance of the book is then discussed in relation to Hughes's cancer of which he was to die not long after, and Heaney goes on to quote Hughes citing and laughing at J.B. Priestley's advice to young writers: "'Never do anything for anybody' – meaning you should avoid piecemeal jobs and do only your proper writerly work."

Still, even without pondering the relation of *Stepping Stones* to usual critical or biographical procedures, the book came into being in a very unusual way. O'Driscoll tells us that the first set of questions, in the great traditions of Shandyism, were "confined to the themes of childhood and the early writing years, but they already consisted of sixty-two packed pages; many hundreds of additional pages – interlaced with question marks – would eventually reach the poet."

To start with, this was not a simple biography or autobiography or memoir, even if it is what O'Driscoll called "a survey of his life." The structure of *Stepping Stones* is significant for the question of priorities. It is divided into three parts: 56 pages of "Bearings", concerned with the poet's childhood; 400 pages "On the Books"; and a "Coda" of 15 pages, about the poet's life and views after his stroke in the summer of 2006. The proportion of the sections looks revealing, but it is soon evident that it is misleading. Of all writers, it is least possible with Heaney to divide the "bearings" (a decidedly Heaneyesque term: you wonder who adopted it here) from the "books", the writing life. On the face of it, *Stepping Stones* starts as a kind of memoir and increasingly opens out into what Yeats called in his great late essay in 1936 "A General Introduction for My Work." But it is not surprising that Wordsworth is the poet Heaney singles out as having had a lifelong influence on him. His soul's "seedtime" remained the primary inspiration for him, right up to *District and Circle*, the title of which of course implies that the originary district is what he always circles back to, and *Human Chain*. There is a striking passage in *Stepping Stones* where Heaney describes the process of composition, still in his seventieth year, the same as it was from the first: "Generally speaking, my poems come from things remembered, quite often from away back … I'm a great hoarder, of course", and he goes on to recall his poem "Shelf Life", about hoarded objects. But the hoarded objects are less significant than the hoarded experiences and memories, and the greatest service of *Stepping Stones* is the provision of a more fully recalled context for the events and figures in the poems. If anything could improve a masterpiece like "At the Wellhead" it is a fuller knowledge of the blind musician-neighbour Rosie Keenan, whose visionary blindness became a figure for poetic insight. Similarly, we have a better grasp of the working of major poems like "The Strand at Lough Beg" and its counterpart in *Station Island* by learning more about the extent of Heaney's acquaintance with his cousin Colum McCartney, and by being reminded of the absolute obligations of family attendance at Irish country funerals.

Heaney is well aware too that the imperative to "do only your own writerly work" (in Hughes's words), insofar as it can be taken seriously at all, has application to both workers on the *Stepping Stones* project. When *Stepping Stones* was launched with a Heaney poetry reading in London, he ended by reading a poem of O'Driscoll's and called him back on to the stage as O'Driscoll characteristically shuffled off towards the side with a self-deprecating downward wave of his hand. O'Driscoll was indeed a matchless example amongst the "hearers and hearteners of the work" for Heaney – the Yeatsian acknowledgment that Heaney often inscribed in his own books – but what he was acknowledging there was the distinction of O'Driscoll's own writing. A few years after his death now, there is no longer any need to make the case for O'Driscoll's poetry as something more than the work of a professional civil servant. But, even as late as 2008, it was a salutary reminder of his standing as poet and not just as the keeper of the Grail of Irish poetry. The claim in his Wikipedia entry that he is one of the most important European poets of his era was still somewhere in the future. Just to remind you of what kind of poet he was first thought to be: he was a very fully employed public servant who, it was said, drew on the language of his career as civil servant to write a series of books of poetry drawing on the terminology of his work. Yet the obvious grand parallels – say Wallace Stevens or William Carlos Williams or Miroslav Holub – were never invoked. The assumption remained that the scope of O'Driscoll's imagination was somehow enclosed by the ironies of his attitude to his work. It was similarly assumed that his attitude to work in general was more like Philip Larkin's – "the toad work" squatting on his life – than that of Stevens or Williams. And, most curiously, the fact that the government taxation department in which he worked included responsibility for death duties was thought to explain the highly elegiac nature of many of his earlier poems (rather than the tragically early death of his parents, which left him with another kind of responsibility too – for younger siblings).

T.S. Eliot, of course, as O'Driscoll reminds us, said to Ezra Pound, "Of course I want to leave the Bank, and of course the prospect of staying there for the rest of my life is abominable to me." But that wasn't at all how O'Driscoll saw his case, as his essay on Larkin in *The London Magazine* in 1996, "Philip Larkin and Work: *Toad Hull*", makes clear. Larkin, O'Driscoll tells us, "turned to librarianship, having failed interviews for the Civil Service and the Foreign Office", because – quoting the characteristically brutal diction that Larkin reserves for his letters – "I must obviously show that I don't give a zebra's turd for any kind of job." This is very unlike the language of O'Driscoll, but the sentiment is not as foreign to it as one might expect. What I mean is that O'Driscoll, like Larkin, is not without career ambitions, even beyond writing. To give a piece of anecdotal evidence: after O'Driscoll took early retirement, I said in a letter to him – taking the line that is often taken about retirement, especially when it is chosen – "I suppose you are glad to be relieved of the daily grind and to be free to read and write", to which he replied vehemently how lost he felt without work and without the shaping obligation to go into Dublin every day. True, O'Driscoll continues in his essay that "Larkin's letters are not exactly glowing testimonials to his job satisfaction." There are also philippics against work as a "vile thing" and as "something you do in order to have spare time." But that is not the whole story.

O'Driscoll then says, though, that Larkin's "letters are not always to be taken at face-value." In fact, Larkin was devoted to his work as librarian, and he "derived evident (if not invariably acknowledged) fulfilment from being at the top of the library ladder." All this is even more true in O'Driscoll's own case as he pondered that great Yeatsian "Choice" between "perfection of the life or of the work": more true because the connection between the poetry and the day-job was extremely close. Looking back, it seems strange that the metaphorical way he used the terms of his civil-service life as titles of poems and volumes of poems should have been assumed to be foreign to the poems: their figurative resonance is witty and suggestive in all cases – "Hidden Extras", "The Bottom Line", "Quality Time", "Exemplary Damages", "Foreseeable Futures" and so on. In these titles we can see the same gift with metaphor and idiom as in Heaney's famously suggestive titles: *Wintering Out*, *The Spirit Level*, or *District and Circle*. From the first O'Driscoll's poetic language was founded in the everyday – after all, nothing could be more everyday than the current language of bureaucracy – in all its urgency. His Anvil *New and Selected Poems* in 2004 begins with the poem "Someone", which all reviewers greeted as a masterpiece of general truth ("someone today is seeing the world for the last time / as innocently as he had seen it first") when it appeared in *Kist* in 1982 – all reviewers including Heaney, who described it in *Hibernia* as O'Driscoll "hitting his stride."

But perhaps as valuable to the project of *Stepping Stones* as O'Driscoll's own poetry is his gift as a memoirist, especially in the early sections of his critical and autobiographical essays *The Outnumbered Poet*, published in 2013, just a year after his sudden death, and in the marvellous 1989 "Thurles Prospect" at the start of *Troubled Thoughts, Majestic Dreams*. If there is an Irish literary tradition that O'Driscoll most singularly belongs to, as they say, "in his own right", it might be seen as the satirical memoir represented at its most distinguished in Yeats's *Autobiographies* and *Memoir*, and in George Moore's *Hail and Farewell*. Perhaps Moore's great book (maybe the most underrated major work in Irish writing) has a harsher edge to its satire; Yeats's wit too has a graver kind of mockery to it. But some of the encounters (and O'Driscoll was a great seeker-out of literary encounters) have a fine edge to them. To give just one example, his "Readings Remembered" contain several passages like this:

> If [Sorley] Maclean overplayed his lines somewhat, William Empson
> underplayed his so absurdly that scarcely a single coherent word
> escaped; little wonder that his wife had once bawled out from the
> audience of a similar charade, "Speak up, you silly old fool!" A lip-

reader, rather than an amplification engineer, was needed as he gyrated pathetically to the lines he mumbled and mangled. What did he say? What poems did he read? Other than a vague sense that he was hitting "Let it Go" in spots, I had no idea and will never now know; he had nothing of any kind to declare when he mechanically signed my copy of his *Collected Poems* afterwards.

This is much closer to *Hail and Farewell* than it is to the seeker out of great literary acquaintance that O'Driscoll has sometimes been expected to be. And, though it is not entirely to the point here, his memories of a Thurles childhood are masterpieces of autobiography in a strong, under-acclaimed Irish tradition including such things as John Healy (Backbencher of *The Irish Times*)'s *Nineteen Acres.*

This may seem to be straying from the point, but it is relevant, I think, for two reasons (beyond, of course, the interest of determining what kind of writer O'Driscoll is: what his *mentalité* is). First, the impulse towards satire means that O'Driscoll's questions are by no means inclined towards the obsequious (as we will see in a moment). The second is more important: Heaney is one of the great critical poets, universally placed in the illustrious tradition of practitioner-poets in a line from Sidney to Coleridge to Arnold to Eliot. It is another way in which he steps beyond the constraining lines of the New Criticism. And, when he calls *Stepping Stones* a "necessary" work, he means that it will *serve* as an autobiography without quite being one. O'Driscoll's myriad questions mean that Heaney can bring anything he likes into this peculiar kind of autobiography – and of course, equally crucially, leave anything out.

It is important to stress, too, that *Stepping Stones* does not remain at the level of autobiography or memoir, even if it is a kind of autobiography by other means. In some ways they are better means than the traditional, self-selecting variety. For all his friendliness and good manners, O'Driscoll asks some uncomfortable questions, including in the area where Heaney himself has always seemed – to his credit – already to be uncomfortable: the interface of poetry and politics. Heaney has tried, like his touchstone Yeats and the majority of other poets, to assert the primacy of the artistic within poetry. In a much-quoted passage at the end of Heaney's *Station Island* referred to in *Stepping Stones*, the revenant ghost of James Joyce tells the pilgrim-poet to "Let go, let fly, forget … Now strike your note" because "You lose more of yourself than you redeem / doing the decent thing."

When in *Stepping Stones* Heaney refers to this advice, saying that Joyce in the area of poetics is "our chief consultant", O'Driscoll wittily counters (his chastely brief questions often have a dry, informed, unstated irony that is one of the book's great pleasures) with Joyce's coinage "bullockbefriending" to describe Heaney's cattle-dealing family. Joyce's world, at least in its origins, was a long way from Heaney's.

As *Stepping Stones* proceeds and the life-context can be taken as established, Heaney dwells more on poetics, on the function and use of poetry (rather as T.S. Eliot turned increasingly towards such matters as *The Use of Poetry and the Use of Criticism*). By the end the summaries in the closing pages do indeed have something of Yeats's "A General Introduction for My Work" about them: an association which became more poignant with the deaths of first O'Driscoll and then Heaney within five years of its publication. So, even if he doesn't offer guided readings to individual poems, Heaney speaks of his writing process in a generally enlightening way. Examples could be taken from anywhere in the last 50 pages; here is a striking and enlightening observation:

> One of the difficulties is to know whether a little, quick flash of lyric is sufficient. You have the invitation and the inspiration, *for want of a better word* [my italics], but the question that I can never answer is this: to what extent the will should do the work of the imagination, as Yeats said; how far you should push a thing. A lot of poems I have a fondness for came smartly through. On the other hand, the poems in North were grimly executed, and I really like them because they are odd and hard and contrary.

A few pages further on, getting near to the end of the book, comes a wonderful image for the sense of vocation in the poet. Asked whether his writing is humorous, Heaney says yes, but with this caveat: "For better or worse, when I sit opposite the desk, it's like being an altar boy in the sacristy getting ready to go out on to the main altar. There's a gravitas comes over me."

I think this is a good example of the distinctive strength of *Stepping Stones*: the mixture of self-mocking humour with a sense of significance – a significance that the writer could not claim for himself without an introductory nudge. And for that matter, *Stepping Stones* is by no means without its moments of brilliant critical insight from Heaney. Immediately after the altar-boy image, O'Driscoll asks about obscurity in poetry and

Heaney answers by reference to the modern poetry which "exults in its far-fetchedness and in which privacy of reference is not an anxiety … The Internet quality of the information that is being pulled into the poem is part of the poem's self-fashioning." He then goes on to quote an observation about Auden – from which he maybe exempts Auden himself – that "he didn't have the *rooted normality* of the major talent" (my italics).

This of course raises the whole grand question: where does inspiration come from anyway (if it can be said to *come* from anywhere at all)? This is a matter that *Stepping Stones* repeatedly returns to. In discussing the poems in *The Haw Lantern*, O'Driscoll notes that two poems that Heaney has just mentioned, "Alphabets" and "From the Republic of Conscience", were both written in response to commissions, from Harvard and Amnesty International. O'Driscoll says: "You clearly don't regard commissions as inhibiting. Would you go so far as to say they are a stimulus?" Heaney says he *would* go that far, "but in a viciously circling way, because there can be no stimulus unless you discover a way of responding to them that brings them to life." Nevertheless, he goes on to discuss poems by other poets that have helped him to get started, by Milosz and Richard Wilbur. Another source of inspiration is literary pilgrimage (though Heaney says it is nothing so calculating that makes him make those pilgrimages to "Carleton's birthplace, Tennyson's birthplace, Dylan Thomas's Fern Hill, Alphonse Daudet's mill, Hopkins's grave in Dublin, Joyce's grave in Zurich, Wilde's grave in Paris, Emily Dickinson's house in Amherst, the Keats House in Hampstead, Akhmatova's 'House on the Fontanka' in Petersburg, Brodsky's 'room and a half' in the same city, not to mention Stratford and Abbotsford, Coole Park and Spenser's castle, Lissoy and Langholm." Those visits were "a moment's memory to [a] laurelled head"; only one poem resulted from them – "The Birthplace" in *Station Island*, about the Hardy home in Upper Bockhampton.

More significantly for *Stepping Stones*, despite Heaney's declared determination to avoid providing a reader's guide to his poems, O'Driscoll's claim that the question-and-answer method of *Stepping Stones* did on some occasions trigger a poem is clearly true. A perfect example of this prompting of a poem noted by O'Driscoll is "In the Attic", one of the most magical of the wonderful series of late family poems in *Human Chain*. When O'Driscoll asks Heaney if he had "a grandchild's special relationship" with his maternal McCann grandfather (he never knew his Heaney grandparents), he says, "I have a distinct memory of only one thing he said and I remember it only because he made a mistake." Heaney aged nine or ten watches the film of *Treasure Island*. "Well, my grandfather says to me when I come back in from the picture, 'Well, son, did you see Isaac Hands?' Somehow in that little slip [Isaac for Israel] I was vouchsafed a glimpse of the mysterious gulf between childhood and old age – I mean I had an *intuition that I can only now put into words* [my italics]. What that shift from Israel to Isaac told me was that he had read *Treasure Island* decades before, and that it had stayed with him and was a part of everything that had happened to him in between and the fleetness of all that was somehow processed into his slip of memory." Ever since the essays in *Preoccupations* ("The Fire i'th' Flint" on Hopkins, for example) Heaney has been an outstanding commentator on the mental and sensory perceptions out of which poetry is constructed. And he has never put it better than this.

"I can only now put it into words", he says to O'Driscoll, presumably some time early in the first decade of the new century, leading to a point when he was able to put it into even better words in "In the Attic."

"And Isaac Hands," he asks, "Was Isaac in it?"

His memory of the name a-waver too,
His mistake perpetual, once and for all,
Like the single splash when Israel's body fell.

What other kind of book – biography, memoir, autobiography or interview – could establish so perfectly how the jogged memory creates a narrative which is then reworked into a poem? What is so striking here is the grand theoretical claims that Heaney founds on these slight pieces of memory: "his mistake perpetual" and "a part of everything that had happened in between." This is perhaps the essence of the sense in which *Stepping Stones* was a necessary book: its questions that make the poet scroll back and find the germ of what makes poems permanent – the "monuments" of Shakespeare's sonnets.

Stepping Stones is mostly organized under the headings of the individual poetry volumes. The section of the book concerned with the writing of this poem is chapter 13, "'So Deeper into It': *Electric Light* and *District and Circle*", though the resulting poem is in *Human Chain*. Another example that prompts interesting principles about inspiration and its sources, also mentioned by O'Driscoll, is the intriguing poem "Anahorish 1944" in *District and Circle* (2006):

ANAHORISH 1944

We were killing pigs when the Americans arrived.
A Tuesday morning, sunlight and gutter-blood
Outside the slaughterhouse. From the main road
They would have heard the squealing,
Then heard it stop and had a view of us
In our gloves and aprons coming down the hill.
Two lines of them, guns on their shoulders, marching.
Armoured cars and tanks and open jeeps.
Sunburnt hands and arms. Unknown, unnamed,
Hosting for Normandy.
                    Not that we knew then
Where they were headed, standing there like youngsters
As they tossed us gum and tubes of coloured sweets.

One way and another, we know a good deal about this poem, partly because of a moving reading and discussion of the poem by Heaney with John Kelly of RTÉ. O'Driscoll says it was written for the volume during the period when *Stepping Stones* was being assembled. Heaney revitalizes the memory of this event as one of the "secret sources of poetry", he says; O'Driscoll claims – entirely convincingly – that it is one of the examples of the cross-questioning involved in preparing *Stepping Stones* acting as a salutary and productive prompt towards writing a poem. When Heaney is recalling the childhood memory from 1944, he finds the whole event finds shape in this short and eloquent poem; it may have prompted too another poem, "The Aerodrome" in *District and Circle* (O'Driscoll is still anxious, like all dedicated interviewers, to be innocent of the charge of distracting Heaney from his rightful work, writing poetry.) Heaney says in the interview with Kelly that the events in the poem – a rare encounter with World War II from a rural location which, despite the Belfast Blitz, Heaney's rural world was almost cut off from – come back to life partly through witnessing the American-Afghan war after 9/11. He explains, too, the most striking thing about the poem: uniquely within his work, I think, the whole poem is set in quotation marks. It is the story as it would be told by the family, neighbours of the Heaneys, who had a slaughterhouse. It is interesting that the poet gives the narrative over entirely to those tellers, despite the fact that the voice of the poem has unmistakeable tell-tale Heaney touches. But of course the subject of the poem belongs to a much earlier period in his life, when he was five years old. As with "In the Attic", Heaney revitalizes this memory as one of the "secret sources of poetry", he says.

To return in conclusion to *Stepping Stones* and take the two writers together again, we might remind ourselves what their relations were and the suitability of O'Driscoll for this project. Of Heaney's many supporters, none has been more consistent or informed than O'Driscoll, a poet who has been the tutelary guardian of poetry in Ireland over the past generation. He has been particularly important in this role because of his deep knowledge of the poetic worlds beyond Ireland and beyond English. When Heaney pays tribute to the eastern European poets who were his inspirations – the status he claimed from the 1970s as *inner émigré* – he knows that O'Driscoll as the watchman of world poetry will know exactly what he means. Furthermore, O'Driscoll is also an ideal interviewer because, while he is a highly acclaimed poet himself, his voice has a disinterested courtesy more characteristic of the committed scholars of poetry who are not themselves competing poets – writers like Christopher Ricks, Helen Vendler, Nicholas Jenkins and Edna Longley. For all these reasons, including his own distinction as a poet, O'Driscoll has Heaney's total confidence. As a consequence, Heaney relaxes to a degree that gives greater depth to our understanding of his work and life, even in areas that are already familiar.

In addition, it will be clear from what I have said already that O'Driscoll does not pull his punches. He is the very rare case of a critic of contemporary poetry who says what he thinks and is still loved for it. In his forceful essay called "Troubled Thoughts: Poetry Politics in Contemporary Ireland" (it provides the first half of that rather ungainly title of O'Driscoll's "Selected Prose Writings" in 2001) for *The Southern Review* in 1995, the year of Heaney's Nobel Prize, he delivers a sharp reprimand to the reception of Heaney: "Seamus Heaney, a prophet who has been received somewhat carpingly in his own province." We have heard him already on Empson and Armitage. In fact he has been a consistent evaluator and advocate of Heaney from his first encounters with his work, and Heaney's long-established trust meant that he was already able to confide in him (as when he says in an interview with O'Driscoll about the medieval Sweeney story in 1983 that he had recognized in it "something here for me.")

I think the most instructive section of *Stepping Stones* is the beginning of chapter 15, the last chapter apart from the "Coda", "In Conclusion." It is called "'An Ear to the Line': Writing and Reading", and it is the place where the two friends and poets have the most productive exchanges. As well as belief in the responsibilities of the writer – "doing the decent thing" – Heaney does of course have the Arnoldian, Romantic's belief that "poetry is in the realm of the gift and in the realm of the sacred." He knows that O'Driscoll takes poetry as seriously as he does himself (indeed, more seriously than Heaney's farming forebears), and this makes it possible for him to make grand claims that in himself he would be shy of making. His fundamental beliefs about what poetry is have never been so precisely stated; in the "Coda" here, in answer to the question, "What has poetry taught you?", Heaney replies succinctly, "That there's such a thing as truth and it can be told – slant." He goes on to claim for poetry the properties that Stephen Dedalus claimed, but he adds "a quality of moral excellence." This book captures Heaney as nothing quite has before. It explains, for example, how he assigns poetry to the realm of the gifted and the sacred, but also keeps it within the realm of the intelligible.

So where would we be without this "necessary book"? We would still have Heaney's astonishing corpus – poetry, most importantly, of course, but also major critical interventions, translations for the theatre, some salutary interventions in political debate. But we wouldn't have this sustained exploration of what made and makes him write, and of the things he believes to be important in the private and public era. Often we find what we deduce from the poems corroborated by this book. And, like all encounters with Heaney's work, we find our trust in his gift and his achievement was well founded.

This essay was delivered as the annual Heaney-O'Driscoll Memorial Lecture at the John Hewitt International Summer School, Market Place Theatre, Armagh, on 27 July 2015.

Bernard O'Donoghue was born in Cullen, Co Cork in 1945. He is an Emeritus Fellow of Wadham College, Oxford, where he taught Medieval English and Modern Irish Poetry. He has published six collections of poetry, most recently Selected Poems *(2008) and* Farmers Cross *(2011), both from Faber. He has published a verse translation of* Sir Gawain and the Green Knight *(Penguin Classics, 2006), and is currently translating* Piers Plowman *for Faber.*

SEAMUS HEANEY'S GLOBE

Jahan Ramazani

A detour through Delphi.

In "Alphabets", one of Seamus Heaney's most ambitious mid-career poems, written for Harvard's 1984 Phi Beta Kappa Exercises, this arch-poet of the local, the ground, and Irishness prominently uses the world "globe" twice. "A globe in the window tilts like a coloured O", he writes at the end of the first section, and at the beginning of the last he adds, "The globe has spun. He stands in a wooden O." Temporarily deferring close consideration of these lines, I cite them at the outset because they raise several questions about Heaney's poetry – questions of a sort that haven't yet been engaged with fully. Is Heaney in any way a poet of the global? What is the relation between the evidently local qualities of his poetry and any global dimensions we might identify? And is there anything to be learned about his poetry from the global, and about the global from his poetry? The time seems ripe for such questions, in part because of the extraordinary outpouring of worldwide public and academic interest in Heaney at the time of his death, and in part because the words "globe", "global", and "globalization" seem everywhere in higher education today, with academic institutions working to "globalize" themselves and enhance the "global" aspects of their curricula. At the same time that such questions should be broached, there is a risk and possibly even violence in putting together the nuances of Heaney's poetry with such a large and bland abstraction as the word "global." Global studies emerged primarily in the social sciences, and so it often fits poorly with the qualitative reflections of the humanities. We should bring a word like "global" into contact with poems like Heaney's only if we're willing to see how the poems test, challenge, and revise assumptions about it – and only if it enhances rather than damages attention to the poetry as poetry, its language, technique, and self-reflection.

What might the student majoring in global studies notice in Heaney? Maybe that his extensive travels, as a celebrity writer in demand in much of the world, especially after the Nobel prize, result in an ever-wider range of geographic and cultural reference in his poetry. Maybe that his reading in the Classics (say, Horace and Virgil) and in poetry from England (Hughes and Larkin), the United States (Frost and Robert Lowell), Eastern Europe (Milosz and Mandelstam), and elsewhere extends his understanding of the formal possibilities and ethical significance of poetry. Obviously that his public image and his poetry were and are globally disseminated, the subject of heavy media interest before and immediately after his death, his words on the lips of pundits and politicians and poets, and translated into many languages. Maybe, too, that his academic perches at global institutions of higher education such as Queen's, Berkeley, Harvard, Oxford, and Emory brought him into contact with writers and academics from around the world. No doubt global-studies papers will be written on poems inspired by global matters including climate change, such as the poem "Höfn"; the September 11 attacks in New York in "Anything Can Happen" and the July 7 attacks in London in "District and Circle"; and human rights, such as his Amnesty International-requested poem "From the Republic of Conscience" and the Art for Amnesty book publication of "Anything Can Happen" with translations into 23 languages.

But somewhat similar things could be said of other Nobel laureates and celebrity writers of our time, such as Derek Walcott and Salman Rushdie. To delve meaningfully into these questions, we need to turn from global-studies positivism to interpretation, from extrinsic to intrinsic analysis. The complexity and specificity of Heaney's engagement with the global will remain hidden, I think, unless it is teased out of the formal and conceptual intricacies of his poems – which is where the poems live as poems. The poems I mention regarding climate change, terror attacks, and human rights would reward such close examination. But I focus on two others that might be overlooked in such discussions because less obviously "global" in their purview, starting with "Alphabets", a kind of proem to his 1987 volume, *The Haw Lantern*. Like the other of these two focal poems, "Electric Light", "Alphabets" tells a story about Heaney's emergence as a poet, in this case through the experience of learning different languages – English, Latin, Irish, and Greek. So in a poem that repeatedly points to the globe, he has, in a way, already posed the question: what is the relation between the globe and the act of writing, especially the writing of poems?

In the first of the poem's three parts, a boy learning his alphabet and numbers at primary school sees them in comparison to familiar shapes – a Y looks like a forked stick, a 2 like a "swan's neck and swan's back." Like the poet he will become, he sees signs not just as stand-ins for meanings but as sensual, material things in their own right. This early attention to the graphic dimension of language, its differential sounds ("the letter some call *ah*, some call *ay*"), and its metaphoric resemblances lays the ground for this poet's extraordinary alertness to the riches and resonances of words. But the section's last line suddenly reverses the direction of figuration – reverses, that is, tenor and vehicle: "A globe in the window tilts like a coloured O." Now instead of the written character being compared to a thing in the world, the thing in the world is compared to the letter O. Except that the globe isn't just a thing in the world, of course: it is itself a representation, a spherical map, a vehicle for the tenor of the world, and not just of any random thing in the world but of the world itself. Even at this early moment in the personal development traced by the poem, when the simple diction and rhythms ("he can see now as well as say"), when the repetitions, linking verbs, and declaratives ("There are charts, there are headlines") convey a child's perceptions, among them is the complex idea of a global totality as the construct of the mind, of language – the roundness of the letter O encountered more directly than the roundness of the world. The globe, as Wallace Stevens might have put it, had to be imagined. It is an imaginative totality different from the materiality of written characters and of the worldly things they evoke but partly projected out of its resemblances to them. Like ever-expanding smoke rings, the capital letter O in the poem evokes the "coloured O" the child drew, which evokes the O in the window, which evokes the O of the world. Highlighted at the end of the line, the letter O already hints at both the astonishment of glimpsing global totality and the connection between poetry and the globe, O as the empty cipher of poetic apostrophe. The globe, like poetic language, is simultaneously a form of representation that signifies something beyond itself and an object of representation, a made thing, a result of *poiesis* (literally "making"). Maybe it's not preposterous after all to see an intimacy between poetry and the globe, both belonging to the imagination, wonder, making.

In the poem's second section, the child learns Latin at secondary school, a language compared to military conquest ("column after stratified column", in appropriately Latinate diction with a buried pun on St Columb's College, the name of Heaney's school). Heaney remarked that, like Borges, whose "immersion in several languages in early childhood" was formative for his sense of being a writer, his "own fascination with words was keenly related to … learning Latin as a young boy. And the way words travelled and changed between languages, the Latin roots, the etymological drama." The initiation into poetry comes with the dislocations of cross-cultural and inter-lingual travel, a small-scale encounter with the global, and Heaney's mature poetry indeed moves noticeably among words of different origins, as in this Anglo-Latinate-Irish-Greek poem. But at the poem's structural center – the middle stanzas of the middle section – it is especially when the boy learns Irish script that he is visited by the muse, as evoked in the wordplay on "feet" and the self-consciously poetic diction:

> Here in her snooded garment and bare feet,
> All ringleted in assonance and woodnotes,
> The poet's dream stole over him like sunlight
> And passed into the tenebrous thickets.

Drawing on the *aisling* tradition in which Ireland appears in a dream vision to the poet, Heaney's lines become markedly assonantal, as one might expect given his association of Irish with vowels (*snooded* and *woodnotes*; *poet's, stole, over*). This system of writing is special and distinctive, a welcoming habitation (with the emphasis thus: it "felt like *home*") yet with an acknowledgment of a remove (it "felt *like* home"). This calligraphy, like the written English characters, is understood in comparison to things in the world – the letters as trees and capitals as blooming orchards – although for Irish, there is a long tradition of association of specific letters with particular trees, an almost magical way of thinking about trees that anticipates the allusion to Robert Graves's *White Goddess*.

But in the poem's third and final section, when Greek is the new language, the direction of figuration is again reversed, with the linguistic world primary and the natural world seen through a screen of signifiers, parts of a (now-vanished) cultivated field looking like lamdas and deltas. "The globe has spun. He stands in a wooden O", begins this section, in a direct echo of the previous line about the globe. The university lecture hall is the poet's stage – as is all the world, in the *theatrum mundi* topos. Now the globe has still more meanings: it is the Earth, spinning as the years pass; a model of the Earth, as earlier in the poem; Shakespeare's theater, the Globe, and the "wooden O" of the prologue to *Henry V*; the literal space of the round theater in which the lecturer speaks; and even the world of the poem in which the lyric speaker speaks. The poet's education has made language and literature primary, a literary globe that he inhabits and from which he evokes that secondary, real world. The poet is like a necromancer, who hangs from his ceiling

A figure of the world with colours in it
So that the figure of the universe
And "not just single things" would meet his sight

When he walked abroad.

Drawing on Frances Yates's account of the neoplatonist Marsilio Ficino, as Neil Corcoran has shown, Heaney joins that first schoolroom globe, the second – the globe of literary language and imagination – together with this third, the magician's globe meant to reinforce a sense of the interconnectedness of things. Heaney frequently refers to poetry's special power as lying in, to quote from several different essays, "[t]he secret between the words, the binding element", "that binding secret between words in poetry", "a religious, a binding force" – well aware that in doing so he is attributing to poetry "a religious force, especially if we think of the root of the word in *religare*, to bind fast" (*Preoccupations: Selected Prose, 1968–1979*, Farrar, Straus and Giroux, 1980). It is that binding force in poetry – phonological, semantic, etymological, mythic, psychological – that is linked to an ability to imagine and figure the totality of the globe, "not just single things" in their scattered nonrelation. Early modern neoplatonism is the avatar of a contemporary global vision – the concept of the world, as globalization theorists put it, as a "'single place," a "singular system," a "global ecumene" (Roland Robertson, "After Nostalgia? Wilful Nostalgia and the Phases of Globalization", in Bryan S. Turner (ed.), *Theories of Modernity and Postmodernity*, Sage, 1990).

The poem is both about the globe and is itself a globe. Formally exemplifying this binding force, its verbal architecture holds it together not only with the parallelism between the lines about the globe at the end of part one and the beginning of part three, and with the Irish muse's visitation at the center, but also with the parallelism between the first stanza's fall into representation under the sign of the father (as if in fulfillment of Lacan's linguistic retheorization of the Oedipal fall) and the last stanza's inscription of the father's name on the house, anticipating Heaney's signature on this poetic structure. At the sonic level, too, the poem englobes its heterogeneity through heroic quatrains of rhyme and slant rhyme and much-varied iambic pentameter, and above all an insistent echoing of the "O" at the end of lines at the close of the first and beginning of the last sections, first rhyming *hoe* / *O* (1), then *O* / *window*, and then again *window / O* (3), as well as "IN HOC SIGNO" rhymed slant with "good luck horse-shoe", let alone line endings like "Mer*o*vingian" and "*o*vum", as well as the word "gl*o*be" itself. Fatherly frame joins with motherly center, or ovum-like O, to produce the poet. The binding force of the poem's sonic and structural form represents the globe in uniquely poetic fashion – neither as an economic system of equivalence nor as an imperial domain but as an auditory and visual artifact, an imaginative structure, that binds together and sets free meanings, resonances, analogies, languages, and patterns. For the global-studies major, used to exploring the "global" through an economic-development paradigm, it might well be surprising to learn that there's something poetic about the global in its interlacings across discrepant spaces and scales, a sublime congeries of connections that exceeds measurement and calculation, even as the MFA student, likely to prefer the local in food and in action, might be surprised to hear that the binding force of the global has something poetic about it.

Another way of seeing the world whole is to leave it, a possibility the necromancer could only dream of and that the child in the poem has experienced through writerly and linguistic defamiliarization, but that modern space travel has made even more fully possible. When the letter "O" appears for the third time by itself at the end of a line, it signifies again the globe, this time literally the Earth and not only a model of it, as seen by an astronaut from afar, his vision of this "singular" whole akin to the necromancer's seeing "not just single things", in lines that sound trisyllabic substitutions: "The risen, aqueous, singular, lucent O / Like a magnified and buoyant ovum." The roundness of the globe is mirrored in an expression of wonder at seeing it, the utterance of an apostrophic O, like the child's "wide pre-reflective stare / All agog" at the sight of his family name written on his home's gable. Heaney implicitly rhymes the O of poetry with the O of the globe. He explicitly compares the wonder felt by a child perceiving his earthly and linguistic origins (his name written "letter by strange letter") to the wonder of an astronaut peering down on the world, "all that he has sprung from", just as the poet in this poem gazes down on the languages he and indeed this poem have sprung from. The global is often conceived of not only as the spatial but also as the temporal opposite of the local, in the sense of development beyond the local toward the global (say, from rural backwater to world metropolis). But Heaney holds the global and local in balance: his poetry's origin in exposure to multiple languages, with Irish at the center; the boy gazing uncomprehendingly at the patrilineal family name from which he has sprung; the astronaut looking down on mother Earth and seeing it as a location, exemplifying what a theorist calls "the localization of globality, the perception of the finite and limited nature of our world" (Mike Featherstone, *Undoing Culture: Globalization, Postmodernism and Identity*, Sage, 1995). So too, written characters, multiple languages, and literary texts have both dislocated the poet and revealed him in locality. Globalization has often been described as an intensified interconnectedness across the world's surface, and if poetry is for Heaney above all a binding force, as exemplified in this poem's multiply nested verbal, aural, and analogical design, then perhaps it shouldn't surprise us that one of his major poems about coming into being as a poet is also a globe-like poem about the globe. But where the globe is sometimes thought to be a preexisting order of reality, Heaney's emphasis is on the imaginative apprehension, the literary and linguistic construction, the binding *poiesis* of the globe. And where the globe is often opposed to locality, parish, province, region, or nation, Heaney enfolds within the global his locatedness in a name and a culture, his education in particular languages and literatures that shape how he sees the world, his wonder toward "all that he has sprung from." A vision of the global intensifies rather than diminishes a consciousness of the contingencies of local origins.

But Heaney as a global poet? Surely that's a stretch, for all his worldwide fame. There are few poets more firmly located in place than this rural County Derry-born poet, author of a book titled *Opened Ground* and a poem called "Digging", of poems filled with a rural Ulster childhood's peat and bogs, frogs and cows, plows and pumps. A crude mapping of his poetry's geography along the lines of the *New Yorker*'s *View of the World from 9th Avenue* by Saul Stenberg would give us one version of Heaney's globe, particularly if it ignored the formal complexities and just went with toponyms: County Derry would be at the center, with Ireland occupying most of the space, some of the remainder devoted to other parts of the British Isles and Northern Europe, especially Denmark or ancient Jutland, and lesser space devoted to Spain, Greece, and Italy, with distant outcroppings of peripheries like Massachusetts, Iowa, and California to the west, and China and Japan to the east. Heaney's poetry has often been distinguished, as in a standard anthology, from exilic and less obviously "Irish" Irish poetry, or what a poetry encyclopedia calls "cosmopolitan" poetry by the "European-Ir. poets" affiliated with Beckett and by Ulster Protestants such as Louis MacNeice and Derek Mahon, because it is firmly grounded in a sense of Irish "cultural identity" and "of history, place, lang., and religion" (Anthony Bradley, "Irish Poetry", in Alex Preminger and T.V.F. Brogan (eds), *The New Princeton Encyclopedia of Poetry and Poetics*, Princeton University Press, 1993). Similarly, in *Irish Poetry after Joyce* (Syracuse University Press, 1997), Dillon Johnston separates Heaney and other poets who write "about areas of Irish life" from poets who "thoroughly avoid Irish modes and write in a more European, even Eastern European mode". While this is a neutral distinction for some critics, for others it is to Heaney's detriment. In a transnationally sophisticated study, Cheryl Herr differentiates the laudably "cross-regional" or "dislocational" poetry of Paul Durcan from Heaney's verse, which she associates with "a reclaimed, centered, historicized, and wholly indigenous viewpoint" (*Critical Regionalism and Cultural Studies: From Ireland to the American Midwest*, University of Florida Press, 1996). More severely, David Lloyd castigates Heaney for his "reified … bourgeois ideology": "his work relocates an individual and racial identity through the reterritorialization of language and culture"; his metaphors and language "promise a healing of division simply by returning the subject to place, in an innocent yet possessive relation to his objects". ("'Pap for the Dispossessed': Seamus Heaney and the Poetics of Identity", *Anomalous States: Irish Writing and the Post-Colonial Moment*, Duke University Press, 1993). Nor, in Lloyd's view, is there anything plural, transnational, or heterogeneous in this forced Romantic equation of poetry with the land: Heaney's writing is said to allow the culture "to be envisaged as retaining a continuity with an homogeneous, undifferentiated ground."

But if Heaney has been condemned for his rooting of poetry in the Irish ground, he has also been applauded for it. In a recent book, *Local Attachments: The Province of Poetry* (Oxford University Press, 2010), Fiona Stafford sets up her entire argument about Romanticism with a discussion of Heaney's "celebration of local truth", as "a poet who not only celebrates local connection, but makes it central to the existence of true poetry." Heaney is credited with "elevating the idea of the 'local' as the touchstone for the best kind of art." Far from seeing Heaney's work as being in concert with the global, Stafford speculates that it is formed in reaction against it:

> His very recognition of the value of the local, the particular, and the distinct may have been heightened by a growing awareness of globalization, which has facilitated both easy international communication and the growth of a somewhat homogenized consumer culture.

She repeatedly returns to Heaney's Nobel lecture, "Crediting Poetry" (*Opened Ground: Selected Poems, 1966–1996*, Farrar, Straus and Giroux, 1998), which affirms "local setting" and "local work" in the arts.

But while Heaney considers the local and the indigenous to be crucial as "bearers of value" in art, and while scholars such as Stafford are right that, as we've seen in "Alphabets", his poetry is deeply responsive to his rural Irish origins, a localist account is insufficient to the complexities of his work. In the Nobel lecture, he is leery, as he puts it, of "being sentimental or simply fetishizing – as we have learnt to say – the local." He begins the lecture with the formative experience of growing up on a farm in County Derry, but this local site is always traversed by spaces elsewhere. There is "the voice of a BBC newsreader speaking out of the unexpected like a *deus ex machina*", a voice that mingles with the local voices and with the sounds of Morse code. By virtue of modern technologies and media that have accelerated globalization – what the anthropologist Arjun Appadurai calls technoscapes and mediascapes – the "here" is layered with the "elsewhere" (*Modernity at Large*, 1996), even in this seemingly isolated spot: along with "the names of neighbours being spoken in the local accents of our parents", there were

> in the resonant English tones of the newsreader the names of bombers and of cities bombed, of war fronts and army divisions, the numbers of planes lost and of prisoners taken, of casualties suffered and advances made.

Like the languages he learns in "Alphabets", these alien voices and names both dislocate the boy, defamiliarizing his local experience, and relocate him, contrastively illuminating the specificities of his cultural experience. As he grew older, Heaney says, "my listening became more deliberate", and

> I had to get close to the actual radio set in order to concentrate my hearing, and in that proximity to the dial I grew familiar with the names of foreign stations, with Leipzig and Oslo and Stuttgart and Warsaw and, of course, with Stockholm.

As he heard "short bursts of foreign languages", he listened to the dial sweep

> from the intonations of London to those of Dublin, and even though I did not understand what was being said in those first

encounters with the gutturals and sibilants of European speech, I had already begun a journey into the wideness of the world. This in turn became a journey into the wideness of language …

It is that interrelationship of an initiation into the wideness of the world and into the wideness of language that Heaney explores in "Alphabets", and that he associates with poetic consciousness.

It might be unfair to rely too heavily on his Nobel address, written after all to be delivered in continental Europe, to support my argument for a more expansive view of his poetry than "redemptive localism", in Ian Baucom's terms, based wholly in the "identity-endowing properties of place" (*Out of Place: Englishness, Empire, and the Locations of Identity*, Princeton University Press, 1999). But even if we return to the essay "Mossbawn", Heaney's first in his inaugural collection of essays, in which he describes in intimate detail the specifics of the childhood farm that shaped him, he similarly notes in the oft-quoted first paragraph the groaning of American bombers and the sight of American troops maneuvering in the field. The Northern Irish ground isn't sealed off from the wider world, the movements of people, aircraft, and weapons. Moreover, at the start of that inaugural essay his most emphatic affirmation of his rootedness is a ritualistic incantation of "the Greek word, *omphalos*, meaning the navel, and hence the stone that marked the centre of the world", which he compares to the sound of someone manually pumping water. In Joyce's *Ulysses*, Stephen Dedalus famously thinks of an *omphalos* as interconnecting all humans, like a telephone line going all the way back to Eve. In Heaney, the *omphalos* is emphatically Irish, emblematic of rural Derry's primordial rhythms and reminiscent of Joyce, but it is also emphatically cosmopolitan, a foreign word, after all, that ultimately connects Heaney with Homer through Joyce, and that figures a shared humanity and writerly tradition across divisions of time, culture, and language. "I would begin with the Greek word, *omphalos*", says Heaney at this other beginning, and in doing so, he begins with a split signifier of both rootedness and travel, indigeneity and the cross-cultural. It's through a detour to Delphi that he affirms his relation to the Irish ground. "I began as a poet", he wrote, "when my roots were crossed with my reading" – a crossing seen in his Greek trope for his umbilical connection to the land.

The title poem of Heaney's 2001 collection *Electric Light*, placed last in the book as a kind of summa and so occupying a special place like

"Alphabets", echoes many of these motifs. Like the Nobel lecture, it traces poetry to the crossing of the local with the foreign, Heaney's deep rural roots with cultural sites elsewhere. Like "Alphabets", this similarly ambitious three-part lyric – the first and last parts in five unrhymed tercets, the middle part in four, all alluding to *terza rima* – is again about the poet's origins and genesis, but whereas polyglossia is a primary site of the global and of poetic emergence in "Alphabets", this poem's emphasis is on travel and technology. The first house where he saw electric light is also, ironically, where the poet recalls his grandmother as an almost primeval and immobile figure. By means of the ancient transcultural technique of allusion, she is made to resemble the Cumaean Sibyl, her strange language – the word "ails" nearly rhyming with her fearsome "nail" – initiating a childhood journey into poetry, like Aeneas's into the underworld, and indeed the poet comes out of the London tube in the next section after his katabasis. Although the grandmother is unmoving, light and radio cut across the space over which she reigns:

> If I stood on the bow-backed chair, I could reach
> The light switch. They let me and they watched me.
> A touch of the little pip would work the magic.
>
> A turn of their wireless knob and light came on
> In the dial. They let me and they watched me
> As I roamed at will the stations of the world.

Both electric light and radio give the child an experience of freedom, albeit contained by (grand)parental will: "They let me and they watched me" sounds as an incantation in the same stanzaic position, casting the two magical acts in perfect parallel. In these moments, the verbs endow the child with more agency than he has elsewhere in the poem: "I could reach", "I roamed at will". The language suggests a kinship, too, between these acts and the making of poetry: "A touch", "A turn" gives the power and freedom to "work the magic" and to roam "at will the stations of the world" (perhaps contrasted with the Stations of the Cross). To create light, to fly across space – these aren't just the textbook's global flows of technocapes and mediascapes but imaginatively charged acts filled with wonder.

The poem also closely associates poetry with travel, albeit from one deeply known place to another, from literal to literary origins. Its middle section recalls, as Heaney wrote elsewhere, his "first trips to London, by ferry and train, but is also meant to suggest a journey into poetic vocation", or as he puts it in the poem,

> ferries churned and turned down Belfast Lough
> Towards the brow-to-glass transport of a morning train,
> The very "there-you-are-and-where-are-you?"

> Of poetry itself.

For a world-famous poet to plant in a poem the phrase "Of poetry itself" is to make a strong claim, and the claim is not for poetry as founded in rootedness, locality, or unchanging place, but in travel and disorientation: "The very "there-you-are-and-where-are-you?" // Of poetry itself." In Heaney's case, there are multiple dimensions to this dislocation, as he indicated years earlier to a reporter:

> Everybody's in exile to start with, everybody who writes. Especially if you're in the minority, you're in two places at once at the very beginning … I never had a feeling of comfortable consonance between myself and a place. The travel reinforces a condition that would be there anyway.

And as Richard Kearney wrote, in a philosophical rebuttal of the idea of Heaney as statically insular, "Heaney's poems are not in fact primarily about place at all; they are about *transit*, that is, about transitions from one place to another" ("Heaney and Homecoming", in *Transitions: Narratives in Modern Irish Culture*, Wolfhound Press, 1988). The resonance of this poem's word "transport" with *metaphor* – etymologically, to transfer or carry across – strengthens the idea that poetry is intimately allied with travel, and that travel is a kind of poetry. The image of a young man with his brow pressed against the glass of a train encapsulates something of the simultaneous distance and movement, stilled contemplation and mobility that the poem suggests is endemic in poetry.

It's not that this travel is placeless wandering in an empty nowhere. In another context, Heaney attributes the expression "there-you-are-and-where-are-you?" to the rural area around Bellaghy where he grew up, and so it bespeaks displacement with a peculiarly local twist. The travel in the poem is highly specific and translocal, a straddling of Ulster and London, taking the young poet not accidentally to the seat of the empire and of English-language poetry. It is the journey to the metropolitan center that so many young colonials have made, once again a recovery of localized (in this case literary) origins at the same time as a venture across space. On his way he sees

> fields of grain like the Field of the Cloth of Gold.
> To Southwark too I came, from tube-mouth into sunlight,
> Moyola-breath by Thames's "straunge stronde."

If the evocations of Shakespeare's *Henry VIII* and Eliot's *Waste Land* weren't clear enough, the young poet arrives at Southwark on the Thames, site of both the Tabard Inn, where Chaucer's pilgrims begin their travel, and of the Globe Theatre, where certain plays began their global travel. The young poet superimposes his originating Moyola River on the Thames's Strand. The breath or *spiritus* of his poetry combines metropolitan Englishness ("from tube-mouth") and rural Irishness ("Moyola-breath"), like the verbal fabric of this London poetry-soaked stanza. His poetry is born in the travel between, and the confluence of, these spaces, these histories, these discrepant Englishes. Albeit a limited, archipelagic piece of it, the global here is lived not in the transcendence of places but in the specific interconnections among them, which in turn retrace and partly reverse patterns of movement in trade, colonization, and demography – what Appadurai calls the "ethnoscape" of the global.

So, what does Heaney's poetry indicate about the nature of the global, and the global about the nature of his poetry? Surely Heaney isn't "global" in the same way as Yeats, Eliot, and Pound in their Asian excursions, let alone contemporary writers whose poetry seems to log frequent-flyer miles. Even so, his poetry articulates global flows at all five of Appadurai's different levels: the technoscape of electric light, morse code, airplanes, weapons, diesel, "combines and chemicals"; the mediascape of radio-transmitted voices from London, Europe, and the "wideness of the world"; the ethnoscape of peoples moving from country to city, rural underdevelopment to global metropolis, let alone the ancient traces in Ireland of Vikings, Romans, Phoenicians, and Anglo-Saxons; the financescape in the trade enacted by these and other peoples; and finally the ideoscape of political and cultural ideas exported abroad and imported from elsewhere, from fearsome Viking violence to modern human rights. Heaney's poetry acknowledges that modern and contemporary technology, media, and travel have sped up globalization, as theorists such as Appadurai emphasize, but in the debate over *when* was globalization, he also gives the nod, like the sociologist Roland Robertson, to a much longer, older history of the global. As he writes in "Viking Dublin: Trial Pieces", about the Viking settlement of, and remains in, Dublin, the artistry on a piece of bone leaves

> foliage, bestiaries,

> interlacings elaborate
> as the netted routes
> of ancestry and trade.

The pun on "routes" and "roots" – well before it was developed by scholars like James Clifford and Paul Gilroy – calls attention to how even the most deeply planted Irish roots are entwined with peoples and trade patterns from elsewhere, like the inwardly netted roots and outwardly networked routes of his poetry. Examining the intricate Viking design, Heaney uses a vocabulary that points both toward the literary – textlike "interlacings" – and the global, what theorists have emphasized as the ever-greater enmeshment of globalization. And here we might add a sixth "-scape" to Appadurai's – "poetryscape", the binding force of poetic language and form within a poem and among poems of different times and places. The stretch, the enmeshment, the connectiveness of the global – these aren't just objective forces; they are also imaginative experiences, embedded in and made visible by the binding texture of the parallels, allusions, figurations, architectonics, etymologies, and resonances of Heaney's poetry.

Rather than merely reacting against various globalizing forces, from the tenth to the twenty-first century, Heaney's poetry participates in and illuminates them. He shows globalization to enter individual lives even in remote rural sites, introduced by radio, electric light, mobile populations, war, travel, poems, and different languages. He reveals that the global is not only a social-scientific datum but also an imaginative projection, a difference-spanning construct, as mirrored within the intrinsic binding structures that hold together a poem's teeming patterns. Heaney's poetry's attention to itself as medium, as globe-like microcosm of complexly homologous sounds, sights, and meanings, helps remind us that the global is partly given, partly made. In these poems that are keenly attentive to their own and the poet's genesis out of locality, poetry becomes a space in which the local isn't simply opposed to or contrasted with the global – a last hold out against the brutal and indifferent and homogenizing forces of globalization – but rather reveals and revels in the interpenetrating vortices of localization and globalization. Heaney's is a poetry thickly textured with the impasto of local history and experience that also shifts among places, registers, and identities; that travels between figure and frame, the literal and the metaphoric, origins and ends; and that retraces a transnationally sedimented and fluid history in Ireland, in the north Atlantic, and in the English language – all within the binding euphonies and parallels of his richly patterned lyricism.

Finally, there is also an ethical dimension to the global in Heaney's poetry. His poems owe partly to Wilfred Owen and other poets of the first global war an emphasis on compassion toward a common humanity amid what Heaney called, with reference to Owen, "the shock of the new century's barbarism." What Isaac Rosenberg termed "cosmopolitan sympathies" in "Break of Day in the Trenches" is another thread in the "binding force" of the poetic that Heaney brings to our often positivistic understanding of the global. His poetry always registers an awareness that he comes from a place, a community; yet he tries to think with and through it to forge human connections, to rhyme his experience with that of others. Examples include his empathic poem about a Protestant neighbor, "The Other Side"; his dramatic monologue "Bog Queen", written from the vantage point of a woman long preserved in, and reborn from, a bog; and his multiperspectival poem "Punishment" that performs identifications with the executioner ("I can feel the tug / of the halter"), the adulteress (the same words, with the opposite construal of which end of the rope the speaker is on), the adulterer ("I almost love you"), the stone-throwing crowd ("would have cast, I know, / the stones of silence"), the outraged witness ("civilized outrage"), and combinations of these viewpoints.

Heaney's work also demonstrates what might be called an etymological cosmopolitanism, and it, too, has an ethical dimension. When translating *Beowulf*, Heaney discovered a cross-cultural connection in the word *thole* as straddling his local Ulster speech and a supremely canonical Anglo-Saxon text, just as he had also found it in John Crowe Ransom's Scots Irish-inflected diction of the American South:

The far-flungness of the word, the phenomenological pleasure of
finding it variously transformed by Ransom's modernity and
Beowulf's venerability made me feel vaguely something for which
again I only found the words years later. What I was experiencing
as I kept meeting up with *thole* on its multicultural odyssey was the
feeling which Osip Mandelstam once defined as a "nostalgia for
world culture." And this was a nostalgia I didn't even know I
suffered until I experienced its fulfillment in this little epiphany
("Introduction", *Beowulf*, Norton, 2000).

It is easy to dismiss the connective force of such cross-cultural, cross-
temporal sympathies as sentimental, and indeed the word "nostalgia" hints
at Heaney's wariness of going too far in that direction. Elsewhere he warns
against poetry that "rampages so permissively in the history of other
people's sorrows that it simply overdraws its rights to our sympathy" (*The
Government of the Tongue: Selected Prose, 1978–1987*, Farrar, Straus and
Giroux, 1988). But for all such ethically astute hesitations about the
excesses of nostalgia and sympathy, his etymological engagement with a
world-traveling word affirms the interconnectedness of widely scattered
cultures – the expansive ethical sensibility that "Alphabets", "Electric Light",
the bog poems, and other works are built on.

Heaney's poems exemplify a post-Enlightenment cosmopolitanism
that, as Bruce Robbins writes, isn't neutral or detached but "plural and
particular", including "(re)attachment, multiple attachment, or attachment
at a distance" ("Actually Existing Cosmopolitanism", in Robbins and Pheng
Cheah (eds), *Cosmopolitics: Thinking and Feeling beyond the Nation*, University
of Minnesota Press, 1998). His is a poetry of engagement with the
complexly apprehended, layered, and imagined space of Irish locality and of
cosmopolitan openness to wide-ranging traversals and translocations of
language, culture, and geography. No wonder, as Paul Muldoon said in
eulogizing him, that Heaney "was recognized worldwide as having moral as
well as literary authority and, as such, may be the last major poet to even
entertain such a possibility" ("Paul Muldoon on Seamus Heaney: The Mark
of a Great Poet", *The Daily Beast*, 30 August 2013). That moral authority
derives in part from his poetic affirmation and interlacing of both local
fidelities and cosmopolitan sympathies. Reprising a favorite metaphor for
poetry, Heaney said in his Nobel lecture that "poetry can make an order as
true to the impact of external reality and as sensitive to the inner laws of

the poet's being as the ripples that rippled in and rippled out across the water in [a] scullery bucket." The singular, minutely local O of his poetry ripples outward by means of large-hearted sympathies and verbal magic to the multitudinous O of the globe and back again, "letter by strange letter."

This essay first appeared in The Irish Review *(Nos 49–50). It was a keynote address at "Seamus Heaney: A Conference and Commemoration", which took place 10–13 April 2014, at Queen's University Belfast.*

One of the foremost critics in the United States, Jahan Ramazani is University Professor and Edgar F. Shannon Professor of English at the University of Virginia. He is the author of five books on modern and contemporary poetry, most recently Poetry and Its Others: News, Prayer, Song, and the Dialogue of Genres *(2013) and* A Transnational Poetics *(2009), winner of the Harry Levin Prize of the American Comparative Literature Association.*

IN OTHER WORDS:
FROM THE CLASSICAL LATIN

—

Ciaran O'Rourke

In the spirit of Heaney.

VIRGIL
(Publicus Vergilius Maro)
70 BC–19 BC

BURYING TURNUS
(Juturna speaking – his sister; Virgil's Aeneid, *Book XII, ll. 872–884)*

Could I slow the sun, retain
the heat of seconds in the air,
let shadows tremble

round the dial, by art,
or skill, or barely human need,
to hold you here, my brother,

far from the gnash
of falling wings, from Death
the monster, and his calling lair,

to hold you back, brother,
from the gap you enter,
this darkness you've become – but how?

And how could a sister,
a nymph like me, a grieving girl,
a soul to flowing mosses

and to floods, how can I,
immortal as the rain, as swept
and washed with loss of you,

how will I beat the earth
to ease your limbs,
how heal the stillness

that you've sunk into:
the blood-shut eyes, the un-
responding mouth ... what can I do?

And since you're gone
from fact and life, if not
from dreams – what god,

what murmur-loving listener,
in room or cloud, am I
forever speaking to?

Will your words repeal
the river? Your hands
scoop out

the spring-
suggesting ground?
If not to bring him back,

cleansing the hair,
the blinking skin, then
to lower me down,

down to the black, half-
empty, sleepless place,
where I might join

my brother, and
the disembodied others,
in the lonely heaven.

Translator's Note

The above is a translation of a passage from Virgil's *Aeneid*, Juturna's lament for her brother Turnus. Such a submission is made mainly in acknowledgement of Seamus Heaney's erudite and exemplary engagement with the *Aeneid* on a number of occasions throughout his career. I hope that my own translation can be taken in a similar spirit – that of turning to the work of old masters for articulate assurance or example, particularly at moments of grief, aphasia, or seeming helplessness in the face of inevitabilities.

The lines from the final book of Virgil's *Aeneid* are spoken not of the epic poem's titular hero, but of his rival, Turnus, Aeneas's match in all things but fortune's favour. As it is Aeneas's purpose and destiny throughout the poem to secure Italy as the seedbed of the Roman race, so Turnus is fated to be defeated in combat with the Trojan leader. The speech occurs before this combat ensues, and is given by Juturna, Turnus's sister, who is also a nymph, and so immortal. Aware of her brother's impending death, and conscious that she herself is unable to die, she addresses Turnus not only for the last time, but also in light of the terrible blankness, the stretching interval, which is to separate them for all time. Juturna's fierce love for her brother, the wild clarity of her sadness, is one of many internal retorts, in the poem, to the notions of manifest density and imperial glory on which the narrative initially appears to be based. In a sense, Juturna gives voice to everything that a merely imperialistic tribute or commemoration would excise – most of all, perhaps, to the loneliness, fragility, and clear-eyed love involved in having to face a reality that seems impossible to imagine, but is utterly real nonetheless.

CATULLUS
(Gaius Valerius Catullus)
84 BC—54 BC

TWO CLOCK-TICKS

II

Red-breast, her favourite,
whom she plays with
and pockets in
her palm, unfurling
a fingertip for your quick
bite and beak,

while I sit, pleased
to comfort, if needs be,
goggle-eyed just
for a taste, and, yes,
guessing that love-time
will have to wait,

I wish I could tattle
and sing with you,
as she does,
and lighten the load
of this heavy heart.

———

LXV

And will there be no more talk
of the dead?

Nothing to say
to your full-lipped shade?

Left to love what cannot
happen now, with dark songs
I shall sing the days
of losing you,

as the nightingale,
netted in shadow and leaf,
sings night by night
for the riven brood.

BASIA

V

Let us live, my Lesbia, and let us love,
counting only as coppers
the austere mutterings of old men.

Suns can sink and rise again,
but we when our brief wick sputters out
must sleep through one unending night.

Give me a thousand kisses, then a hundred,
give me another, another, another …

And when we have many thousands,
let us cast them to the wind, so that
we may not know their number

and no heartsick soul can envy us,
and our tallied kisses.

———

VII

You wonder, Lesbia, how many more
would fill and over-brim my cup.

Why, as many as the silt-heavy sands
that stretch the desert:

no-one, keen-eyed to catch them all,
could count them, then,

no forking tongue would
witch away your spell.

Or as the stars, with the dark a-hush,
that watch our secret love accrue …

To kiss you so many times
might be enough.

ELEGY FOR A SONG-THRUSH

III

Shed your tears, you Gods of love,
and all warm-hearted people
of the world.

The song-thrush my lover loved
has left, the bird who thrilled her
more than sight itself,

and who with his sweet
spatter of feet,
now here, now there,

chirred softly for her alone,
as a babe burbles
to his mother.

Now, forever gone, he sings
only on that dark road
where all things beautiful
find their end.

Song-thrush, little bird:
your small stilled heart
stings with tears
the eyes of my love.

TO A POET

LV

Speak to us of love. Holler
it out for all to hear,
trust yourself to see it clear.

Do the pale arms you desire
now cradle you at night?

Don't shutter up the light:
the fruit you pluck
will pile and rot.

Beauty loves a poet,
so sing up!

Or stitch your lips, if you like,
but let me, at least, be one
with the quiet passion
you keep.

BROTHER

CI

To fling your death
on the hundred winds,

to recite your dust
in the lapsing wave,

to loose your bones,
to lieve your lips,

to stand in a sun-dim
mist of prayer,

to be
without you, brother,

a shadow gnawing
on the vanished air,

my voice the rain
that journeys here

continually, to sing
the dirt, to lift the seas,

to bring the ancient
gifts to ground,

like the urn upheld,
and the aching throat,

the buried breath
on the risen road,

the stone in the heart,
or the golden cup,

which now
I proffer, brother,

raise to greet
your dark embrace —

to meet your sightless
silence with my own.

LAST NOTES ON LOVE

XI

Whether I trawl to deepest India,
where in the blue dawn the beaches
batter back the ocean mob,

or go to gentler deserts
in the East, shot through with arrows
of the reddened sun,

or if I fathom
the seven shades of dark
the river keeps, step through valleys
where great ghosts once slept,

if I journey with the world's
cast-outs, uncouth and shunned
to the end,

no matter, I say, just give
her this, and utter it
as truth:

tell her to go on lying
and living, as she has done,
with her three hundred men,

to spin her webs
of whispered ties to each
and let them snap,

but not to come back idly
and again pick up
my love,

which now has fallen
from her touch, as the smallest flower
in the meadow

will fall, when
grazed by the tip
of the passing plough.

TO A FRIEND

XCVI

If anything we have to give, Calvus,
is ever felt with quiet gratitude
in the graves

by which we stand, empty-eyed
and lovesick for the ghosts
that do not reappear,

then know that Quintilla feels
even more than the grief
of her early dying

the love that you
still hold for her.

POSTSCRIPT

LXVIII B

I cannot keep in quietness
the name of this one friend
of mine, Allius,

or let all time ahead
forget his kindness to me,
and to many,

or lay that kindness
in the darker plot
of unremembered hours,

so I say it plainly,
here, to you, as to a god
who lives by whispered air,

to carry the page
this name grows old within
to a thousand others,

listening in tomorrow's
brightened room,
where Allius

may still be known,
and the spider spinning there
its veils of breath

withhold her web
from the memory
of my friend.

For, more than once
he gave me ease
and helped my mind,

when I was fitful,
burning in the gorge,
my body rock-dull

in a scorch of tears,
eyes all sick with salt
and face raw red,

in a rain of want,
my lover gone.
Allius

was like a breeze
which lifts the muttered prayer
of sailors

into sky, scattering
the sea-deep storm
with light,

or like the water-
falling glint
of water in the sun,

its moss-lit clearness
flowing to wet
the fingertips

of two heat-
bitten travellers,
stooping on the track.

Allius, my friend,
was this to me,
when he unlatched

the field-gate
on a barely beaten lane
to the house he left

unlocked for us,
that room to which
all yearning strayed:

my lover's footstep,
treading the doorway
and pale in shade,

her sandal softly
creaking
on the sill …

As soft, perhaps, as one
who walked in the same
slow heat of need

another time:
Laodamia,
whose husband's half-

built house of love
remained a soldier's
early work, and last,

and who once, at daybreak,
untwined both arms
from his boyish neck,

to rise from the bed
which they had drifted
all the winter in,

and feel
a colder flame
at work on air,

the fainter
urge of war
for flesh,

and the bone-deep
vanishing it was to bring
to husbands

in the Trojan dust,
like a tremolo
of light, that day,

a sense too slight
to wake him yet,
but near enough

to alter
easiness in her,
as she pauses

by the bridal bed
at morning, far from the un-dug
graves of Troy ...

Troy, Allius,
where my brother
was also lost of light,

taking
into alien ground
his high parade of dailiness,

the brittle joys,
which Laodamia must
have known

and missed in hers,
a lack in the abundance,
usual as rain –

as her passion proved,
pulling her down
to a seep of emptiness

when he was gone,
bottomless as the earth
to which all waters reach.

And yet an ordinary pain,
and one which, in my way,
I understand.

To see always my love,
like some goddess
come close, pale

in the saffron
drape of dark,
and yet to know her

not for me alone,
me as one of many,
the hunger-haunted poet,

Catullus
of stray midnights,
and not the marriage bed!

Though the give-and-take
can be enough
to live in touch, and learn,

each day a sky-
white stone to keep,
weighted in the palm ...

Ah, Allius, you say
you knew all this before,
but know, too,

that should tomorrow
and forever
take from you your name,

or leave your lifeline
rusting in the rains
of time,

in return
for the gifts of love
you gave, my friend,

this song of mine
is given
with the wish,

new now,
and now eternal:
that your love and you go softly,

in a light
akin to what
your kindnesses allowed,

to that unshadowed way
I lived my life
a while with her,

whose living
even now makes sweet
the endless

bitterness of night.

Ciarán O'Rourke was born in 1991 and studied English and History at Trinity College, Dublin. He received a Masters in English and American Studies from Oxford in 2014. His poems have appeared in a number of publications, including Poetry Ireland Review, Poetry Review, The Irish Times, The London Magazine, New Welsh Review, The Spectator, *and* The SHOp. *His pocket-pamphlet* Some Poems *was published as a Moth Edition in 2011.*

"TOO CHRISTIAN FOR HIS OWN GOOD": REFLECTIONS ON A FAITH IN POETRY

John F. Deane

Risking a vantage point.

I was born into a strictly Roman Catholic family and environment. For decades, I was impervious to other thinking, impermeable to a struggling and evolving world outside the constricted boundaries of my Church's teachings. Much later I began to find the signposted paths inadequate; they had trailed off into marshland quakes and grasses and on across a vale of tears to nowhere. I have been wandering among infinities and found no guide save poetry; I have been working to discover a faith in poetry. This entails working towards a fullness both of life and vision and, as far as possible, not having to choose between them. It entails an integrity to that vision and saying no to the blandishments and demands of the marketplace. But it is also invidious to throw away the fruit with the peelings, the censer with the burned charcoal, and so I have tried, through poetry, to redeem the Christian elements still fruitful in Catholicism. And so, as personal introduction, I offer a recent poem:

ALL SHALL BE WELL
for Laura, on her birthday, April 2015

How comes it I have been reasoned down to thinking
that miracle is not so? Not really wine, then, save
in the minds of those blessed at the feast; no actual storm
swamping the boat where the Christ slept before rising

to rebuke the winds and the waters; the Christ whose word
or touch might release a soul from torment. I cannot doubt
the everyday wonders through which I move, for the mere
commonplace is life and life is miracle. And love.

Firefly and anaconda. Pollen, seed, and catkin. Gravity
and uplift. Poems gifted and the soft inducements
of music. How bread was broken, blessed and shared
in a hostelry at Emmaus. And so the morning candle

is plea and offering, faith's seduction, that we may keep
a wise heart and live in perfect peace amongst impossibles.

In February 2015, I published a memoir called: *Give Dust a Tongue*, a
phrase from a poem by George Herbert, suggesting how humankind is but
dust yet has the gift of language. Here's the stanza from that poem,
"Deniall," addressed to a creator and a contradictory God:

O that thou shouldst give dust a tongue
To crie to thee,
And then not heare it crying! all day long
My heart was in my knee,
But no hearing.

I gave the book a subtitle: *A Faith and Poetry Memoir*, thus limiting and
clarifying the focus of the book. A review by John Boland appeared in the
Irish Independent. His characterization of what I was doing boiled down to two
things: firstly, as he wrote, "the agnostic reader has to slog through a fair
amount of religiosity, with faith-based assertions." That's the point, I thought,
for a book that is a "faith memoir." Alongside that, Mr Boland wrote: "And
there's a lot of verse to be slogged through, too, some of it from Herbert and
Hopkins …" Imagine, having to slog through those poets. Mr Boland's
further quibble was with the narrative side of the book, stating, "it's hard not
to feel that Deane is being too Christian for his own good – or for that of the
reader, anyway, who might have wished for the occasional indiscreet aside or
confession of dislike." So, a faith and poetry memoir without sleaze, without
indiscretions. Too much Christianity and too much poetry.

Reviewing poetry has become problematic in our time, and taking
poetry of faith seriously is anathema. Our age is one of insistence on the
actual, the value-systems of the time are focused on economies, wealth,
physical well-being, pleasure. Nothing wrong with any of that; but if the
deeper side of our humanity, our spiritual side, is neglected, then are we
poor indeed.

A review of my 2009 collection, *A Little Book of Hours*, began: "Who, in the still, small hours of the 21st Century, would want to write religious poetry?" But the review goes on:

> Deane creates a highly contemporary form of religious meditation here and the Christian elements are used with a natural, unconscious grace. If you are at all interested in how religious poetry can still be written, this book will impress and stimulate you.

If you are at all interested: to be a "Christian" writer, or to mention God or Jesus in a poem, draws a tetchy antagonism. In a review of my selected poems, *Snow Falling on Chestnut Hill*, the reviewer begins:

> I am now probably as biased against religious poetry as I may once have been towards it … I would never have read this collection had I not been charged with its review. That resistance would have been foolish. Deane is a true poet.

The admission ought to be a lesson to all who approach poetry with jaundiced eyes (a kind of CCTV, closed-circuit, mentality) because of the theme or emphasis. I feel, with our secular society at odds with faith and spiritual yearnings, it is the Christian artist who stands, in our time, as nonconformist rebel and as challenge to a vapid secularism.

T.S. Eliot wrote, "Real poetry survives not only a change of popular opinion but the complete extinction of interest in the issues with which the poet was passionately concerned." And Seamus Heaney, quoting Ted Hughes, has written, in "Preoccupations:"

> Poetic imagination is determined finally by the state of negotiation – in a person or in a people – between man and his idea of the Creator. This is natural enough, and everything else is naturally enough subordinate to it. How things are between man and his idea of the Divinity determines everything in his life, the quality and connectedness of every feeling and thought, and the meaning of every action.

This speaks well to the notion of the writing of a poetry that is going somewhere. And Heaney quotes W.B. Yeats:

A poet is by the very nature of things a man who lives with entire sincerity, or rather, the better his poetry, the more sincere his life. His life is an experiment in living and those who come after him have a right to know it.

So, I find myself apologist for "choosing perfection of the life" *and* "of the work": and if a poet sees the Christian virtues as the finest way to try to live a good life, then the poetry must, of necessity, follow. These are the twin arms on which I hang my coat. I smithy towards a faith in poetry and a poetry in faith.

A life dedicated to poetry, then, is a life dedicated to a meaningful understanding of both life and poetry, rather than the haphazard production of "Sunday driving" poems. The possibility of regaining a faith poetic received impetus with the work of writers like Eliot, like R.S. Thomas, like Czeslaw Milosz. Milosz has written:

The mainstay of the Catholic Church appears to be the faithful who refrain from questioning, either because it's of no interest to them or because they have surrounded themselves beforehand with an impregnable barrier.

Thomas Merton, in *Conjectures of a Guilty Bystander*, quotes Julien Green, who says: "Religion is not understood. Those who wish themselves pious, in order to admire themselves in this state, are made stupid by religion ..." Merton agrees that the word "religion" has been made profoundly ambiguous by religious people themselves. Two things emerge here: firstly, to speak of "religious poetry" is far too vague and generally misleading, and refers almost always to work that is sentimentally pious or too closely allied with one or other institutional church. Secondly, to achieve a profound poetry, in any area of reference, is to devote a great deal of thought and effort into understanding how to live meaningfully; in other words, the work of a good poet forms a deeply meaningful trajectory, an *oeuvre* that develops with language, music, rhythms, a search for wisdom, a deepening of understanding and artistic worth that is vital, rare and rewarding.

It is too simplistic to categorize contemporary living as merely wealth-seeking and self-serving. Merton says:

It is precisely because we are convinced that our life, as such, is better if we have a better car, a better TV set, better toothpaste, etc., that we contemn and destroy our own reality and the reality of our natural resources. In losing touch with being and thus with God, we have fallen into a senseless idolatry of production and consumption for their own sakes.

This is, doubtlessly, true. But it is not the whole story. The re-emergence of the work of Teilhard de Chardin – in demonstrating how the evolution of the earth and of humankind go along together in holistic harmony – shows the closing together of all peoples, into one, as a rich and evolving growth of the human spirit. The encyclical of Pope Francis re-emphasizes this unity. True belief, true faith, works in harmony with the earth, not against it. As *basso profundo* to the trumpeting of production and consumption, poetry that projects human spiritual development alongside a love and care for the earth, is where poetry and poets are best to be prepared.

I am asking, then, for the poetry undertaking to be a sustained, probing and ever-deepening sounding of the human condition in its most positive aspects. I insist, of course, on the need for what Hopkins called "the roll, the rise, the carol, the creation": let me remain clear on the technical side of things, the value of an awareness of, and a skill in, craft and assignment. Poetry workshops abound in our age and produce a finely wrought barrelling of verse which is technically correct, sometimes pleasing, and overall unsatisfying. For what is the use of learning how to say something when there is nothing of value to say? Versification going nowhere.

I will touch on some true poetry paths. A short roll-call, from about our own time: Czeslaw Milosz, T.S. Eliot, R.S. Thomas, Rowan Williams, Geoffrey Hill, David Jones; and among Americans, Wendell Berry, Denise Levertov, Mark Jarman, and Andrew Hudgins. These, and so many others down the centuries, have proved themselves "too Christian for their own good." Edging on that list are four poets I want to touch upon. In terms of the integrity of poetry and life, a kind of secular Christianity informs the work of the late Seamus Heaney. I am not speaking of a theology or even a faith; these do not enter, as such, his work as poet. I think of the ground and grounding of the poems, their foundation in the givens of a Christian heritage and their growth in a flowering of those givens.

The first poem of Heaney's to make a strong impact was "Digging"; it announced a new voice committed to a view of poetry as a way of seeing life and what life was to be: "Between my finger and my thumb / The squat pen rests, snug as a gun." Poetry as subject, and poetry as method. That poem also initiated a series of viewpoints, literally, that Heaney took as a perspective from which to understand the world. In "Digging" he is watching from a vantage-point, above ground level:

> Under my window, a clean rasping sound
> When the spade sinks into gravelly ground:
> My father, digging. I look down …

The poem announces an exciting entrance into a faith in poetry. During his career the kind of physical perspective taken in "Digging" appears occasionally, a vantage-point, a viewing platform. One of the sonnets in the sequence "Glanmore Revisited" has the poet recently moved into a cottage and choosing a writing-place, at first opposing his wife's suggestion of opening a skylight into his "nest-up-in-the-roof":

> But when the slates came off, extravagant
> Sky entered and held surprise wide open.
> For days I felt like an inhabitant
> Of that house where the man sick of the palsy
> Was lowered through the roof, had his sins forgiven,
> Was healed, took up his bed and walked away.

Heaney's early Catholicism offered him a richness of metaphor from which to find his bearings. From up in this newly enlightened space, he could write more fluently, as he could from his home in Sandymount with its window offering a view across the Irish Sea to the world. In a late poem, "In the Attic", he writes:

> A birch tree planted twenty years ago
> Comes between the Irish Sea and me
> At the attic skylight.

He recalls the story of Jim Hawkins aloft in the cross-trees of *Hispaniola*; the viewpoint leads him to an awareness of age and illness:

It's not that I can't imagine still
That slight untoward rupture and world-tilt
As a wind freshened and the anchor weighed.

The poem tells of the setting sail of the poem itself, and the high viewpoint from which the start is made. In his 1987 collection, *The Haw Lantern*, there is a poem about sticking to the plan, a poem called "Holding Course", and the lines, "The outlook is high and airy where you stand / By our attic window"; a sense of the potency in perspective, the urgency of the imaginative life up there. But it is that memory of the man who was lowered through the roof to be healed by the Christ, that moment used in the Glanmore sonnet just mentioned, that recurs at vital moments in the last years. In the collection *Human Chain*, he reflects on the stroke he suffered and how he was helped by others; it is a poem where he uses that same metaphor of the palsied man lowered through the roof; but in this poem it is the people who helped towards the healing, those who lowered the palsied man, who are in focus. The poem is called "Miracle" and is a cry of gratitude at a moment of intense relevance for the poet. There is continuum of perspective, and a placing of the work on the ground of his early Christian beginnings.

When I asked Seamus Heaney if he might write a poem for the issue of *Poetry Ireland Review* I was planning, seeking new work that might offer a personal answer to the question of what the personal Christ meant to contributors, he answered enthusiastically: "I will definitely keep the project in mind. It's quite a commission, a test of truth and art, but one worth risking." Eventually he sent me "The Latecomers." It reads, to me, as a poem in which Heaney sees himself, not as the palsied man, nor as the helpers, but as Christ himself, surrounded by the needy who press around seeking help and healing. Seamus was then constantly being badgered for signatures, for readings, for statements. The poem is written from Christ's perspective and I will quote it in full:

THE LATECOMERS

He saw them come, then halt behind the crowd
That wailed and plucked and ringed him, and was glad
They kept their distance. Hedged on every side,

Harried and responsive to their need,
Each hand that stretched, each brief hysteric squeal –
However he assisted and paid heed,

A sudden blank letdown was what he'd feel
Unmanning him when he met the pain of loss
In the eyes of those his reach had failed to bless.

And so he was relieved the newcomers
Had now discovered they'd arrived too late
And gone away. Until he hears them, climbers

On the roof, a sound of tiles being shifted,
The treble scrape of terra cotta lifted
And a paralytic on his pallet

Lowered like a corpse into a grave.
Exhaustion and the imperatives of love
Vied in him. To judge, instruct, reprove,

And ease them body and soul.
Not to abandon but to lay on hands.
Make time. Make whole. Forgive.

Heaney's, I hold, is an *oeuvre* that moves with purpose through the demands of good poetry and the demands of thinking things through. A work going somewhere. The fact that he also moves from a Catholic perspective to what is an agnostic stance without denying the relevance for his life and work of his early trust to faith, exemplifies something immensely rich and rewarding; a poetry of excellence and a response to his life's experience and thinking. Ask a person what they believe and there's no easy answer; but it is clear that Heaney was not a person floating uncertainly around. He did not, nor should we, tie down the idea of belief to that of having a ready answer or a set of rituals. As Rowan Williams put it: the question ought to be "how do you inhabit the world you're in, the speech you speak, and the vision you see?" Seamus Heaney remains "too Christian for his own good."

I am not attempting here, in any way, a religious colonizing of poets. What I emphasize is a life devoted to poetry, and an awareness of a ground on which that commitment rests. Let me offer another exemplar: Thomas Kinsella. Here is a hugely masterful *oeuvre*, culminating as it does in the incomparable "Peppercanister" series of poems, a legacy of work emerging from the wholehearted dedication to the craft and to an integrity of vision that is deep and reinvigorating, moving through darkness, illness, and doubt. A very early work, "Night Songs", introduces, with traditional lyric grace and musical sonority, a set of questions that Kinsella will worry over and worry into for several decades:

> Turns again in my room.
> The crippled leopard.
> Paw-pad, configured
> Yellow light of his eyes,
> Pass, repass, repass.
>
> Quiet, my hand; he is tame.
>
> Soon, while I dream, will step
> And stir the sunken dawn.

There is an animal immediacy to the poem, a symbolism and an awareness of hurt and danger. There is dreaming, there is the passing of time, and there is a sense of foreboding. Personal circumstances and difficulties held Kinsella to this view of life for a long time. But the distancing that such antique formality in the versification and language brings about was gradually worked out of the poetry; the internal turmoil and dramatic movement of human suffering were gradually extracted into immediacy of reference and language, through a long trajectory of subtle scrutiny. Through the "Peppercanister" series, which began with the shock of "Butcher's Dozen", Kinsella developed the themes already outlined, but with distinctness and accuracy in the language, always at the service of the meaning; the emotion strong where needed, but always under control, "passing, repassing" and going somewhere. "The Good Fight", for instance, focused on the assassination of John F. Kennedy; the work and death of Seán Ó Riada were treated in others. In "The Familiar", family and personal suffering were again treated, but what a development there is from "Night Songs":

I rose with need in the small hours
and felt my way along the landing
to empty my system beside the sink.

The moon bright
on the three graces above the tank.
The youngest, chosen; stripped and ready.
Her older sister nude behind her,
settling her hair. Their matron mother
to one side, holding the mirror.

I felt my way back afterwards
along the landing, into my place.
Our legs locked in friendship.

It is this continual probing of the human condition, the ongoing attrition that is our living, that has given Kinsella's work a seeming darkness. But the reader's emphasis on bleakness is misplaced. It is an integral and necessary part of the movement forward in the work; as Kinsella once wrote to me, the "Peppercanister" books "assume that the act of reading is a dynamic one, the completion of an act of communication, not an inert listening to something sweet or interesting or even informative. They are not meant to increase the supply of significant information but to embody a construct of significant elements." (Mr Boland, take note!) The life clarifies the poetry, the poetry clarifies the life, and the whole is a communication with the self towards understanding and is completed as communication with the engaged other. It is a vital process; it is not Sunday driving. It is faith in poetry, and the word "integrity" applies.

"Peppercanister 27", published in 2007, is called "Belief and Unbelief." Here Kinsella, too, is flushed with the imagery and experience of a Christian upbringing. If he has lived agnostically, he has yet explored the possibilities of faith.

I am kneeling before the altar
under the bowl of blood
with the seed of living light,

I have yielded to an impulse,
    growing in the cold mornings
    as I passed the great blank door,

and walked through the high darkness,
    in among the pious presences
    praying among their candles,

to kneel at the marble rail,
    with my palms placed together
    before the hidden Host.

Like Heaney, Kinsella places himself amongst those "who are to be found to one side, unwilling to take part." This is from a poem called "Prayer 1":

Dear God, let the minds and hearts
of the main body heal and fulfil
and we will watch for the first sign
of redemption:
                a turning away
from regard beyond proper merit,
or reward beyond real need,
toward the essence and the source.

And this "Peppercanister" has an interesting "Addendum":

And remember that My ways
that can seem in the short term
mysterious and unfair
and punishing to the innocent

will justify in the end
the seeker after justice
and not the power seeker
crumpled in his corner.

That word "My" has a capital letter; Kinsella taking on the persona of God, or the Essence and Source. Here is a poet whose searching, through the medium of poetry, has been lifelong and intense and the conclusions – because there are conclusions, though not definitive – are the highest human ones, the values of justice, integrity, love and caring. One will be aware of that underground Christian seam of imagery throughout the work. Kinsella's poetry, through a lifetime, has been a search for the essence and the source. When I asked him for a piece for the issue of *Poetry Ireland Review* on Christ, he sent me the following:

> The records differ in detail, but all are agreed
> on His nature as a man: compassionate and precise
> in His judgment of men's conduct;
> arrogant and gentle in fatal combination.
> Torn from the flesh in carnal pantomime
> – too direct for this world.

Or, as Mr Boland might adduce: "too Christian for his own good."

A younger poet is the Augustinian priest Pádraig J. Daly. His latest collection is *God in Winter*, published in early 2015, and is his fifteenth. There is, in this work, too, an ongoing development and integrity, of form, voice and content, presenting a life's work through the medium of poetry. The priest-poet begins:

> We have some urgent tale to tell
> About life; but our mouths open
> And no sound gathers shape.
> We belong out by the side of things.

Over the course of the developing work, sound does gather shape. The excitement in the individual poems increases rapidly as the whole body of work moves across a definite and deeply lived axis towards an interior resolution. His poetry registers the experience, the feeling, the passion; but the best poetry goes beyond what is pleasurable and touches what the pleasurable is an ingress to. A life given to poetry opens the world piece by piece, and it is the flowing onward that takes our attention. A poem published in 1997, "Complaint", is from *The Voice of the Hare*: here, the God of this priest/pastor is no longer addressed with love, but in anger and with a sardonic "Sir."

COMPLAINT

I will tell you, Sir, about a woman of yours,
Who suddenly had all her trust removed
And turned to the wall and died.

I remember how she would sing of your love,
Rejoice in your tiniest favour;
The scented jonquils,

The flowering currant bush,
The wet clay
Spoke to her unerringly of benevolence.

I remind you, Sir, of how, brought low,
She cowered like a tinker's dog,
Her hope gone, her skin loose around her bones.

Where were you, Sir, when she called out to you?
And where was the love that height nor depth
Nor any mortal thing can overcome?

Does it please you, Sir, that your people's voice
Is the voice of the hare torn between the hounds?

For an active priest, and the prior of a monastery, as Pádraig Daly was then and is still, this position was truly a difficult and a trying one. But his faith in poetry was both sustenance and source to him, channelling his problems, his language skills, his very voice, into the truth and radiance that is good poetry. Following his Christian path, he was able to reach a position where he could write a stanza like this one, from *God in Winter*:

A herring gull twists its head to eye me from the water,
A seal pants heavily.
A plane is labouring through the sky.
A boat going, a boat coming:
Feel how God, with warmth envelops the world.

This is Augustinian in its thrust for praise from the creation to the creator. For Daly, then, poetry is not a sideline indulged in when he gets a free moment from his Christian ministry; it is the source of his understanding, the essence and development of his soul's worth presented in the phraseology and harmony of the work. The last poem in this collection places him at a point of near stillness, that *point vierge* of Thomas Merton, the "still point" of Eliot's turning world, the compassionate Still Point of Zen Buddhism:

PLACE

Sitting before a great cathedral,
Letting my eye move up along the stone
In the last of the sunlight,

Watching pigeons find their niches,
Small birds drop for crumbs,
A dog twist, lazy-bellied, on the steps,

I am certain still
That every drifting mote has place;
And we are gathered all

In the upswell of Benevolence.

In a phrase of William Blake's, used by W.B. Yeats, we "make our souls" in works of the imagination, more surely than by listening to sermons or studying theological treatises. But the poets we select to be our companions would suit us better if they are not writers merely caught up in the glare of the coloured bulbs of superficial values, but in the steady light that is focused on the search for meaning, for truth, for order. Yeats wrote of Blake that he believed "that the imaginative arts were the greatest of Divine revelations, and that the sympathy with all living things, sinful and righteous alike, which the imaginative arts awaken, is that forgiveness of sins commanded by Christ." The views of Christ held by both Yeats and Blake were very individual indeed, and I am not pleading for a particularly Christian vision for poetry in general. Yet I have found that the greatest writers do touch, when they touch on imaginative living, on what are fundamentally Christian truths. That touch is also explicit in the work of James Harpur.

Angels and Harvesters is Harpur's fifth collection (Anvil Press, 2012). There are questions asked in Harpur's poems to which there are no answers; what is important is that the questions continue to be asked. The opening of "Finbarr and the Serpent of Gougane Barra" reads:

> Did it exist?
> For hours I'd scan the surface
> Hope for a splash, a shadow in the water,
> Anything
> To puncture the mysterious.

The language of God is silence, and Harpur makes his raids with caution. Poetry, for him, begins in those moments that are interstices between periods of indifferent living. To catch these moments, Harpur opens himself to the unexpected, the offered, the way Blake did, or Julian of Norwich. The raids are an attempt to extract reasons of the mind and heart that may reconcile spirit and soul, heaven and earth, angels and harvesters. In the title poem there's an ordinary field, "the field a world / of cutting, gathering, / cutting, gathering;" yet amidst the figures of men and women cutting and gathering are other presences, angels, who are "like ancestors / almost remembering / the world they'd left;" then they simply disappear again, "without ceremony", and all we are left with is the ongoing human sound, "the swish of scythes, the swish of scythes."

Harpur's endeavour is the ongoing search for purpose and meaning in life. There is a commitment to poetry as a major and central thrust into creation, not just a means of self-exploration or public involvement, but a commitment to poetry as the deepest expression of a human being's response to life. There is an integrity in the commitment to a faith in poetry. In Harpur's work, the history of Christian thought and experience, its saints and sinners, touches on the radical presence of the Christ. When I asked him to contribute to the Jesus issue of *Poetry Ireland Review*, he gave me what I consider the best poem in the issue, a long piece touching on his moments of intuiting the presence of Jesus. The poem outlines various moments of near contact, and how closeness to the ultimate mystery slipped always just out of reach. The poem, "The White Silhouette" is a journey of the soul, with its stops and hesitations along the way:

Or somewhere like Holycross in Tipperary,
The abbey at the meeting of road and river,
You might have stopped to break a journey
As I often do, and seen me there in the nave
Ambling down the sloping floor
Towards the relic-splinter of the Cross
Or sitting outside on the banks of the Suir
On a bench on a swathe of tended grass
Perhaps that day, when, heading north,
I paused by the car park to watch
A bride, fragile, and frozen by the door
Her bridesmaids huddled in the cold of March
Waiting and waiting to make her entrance
Into the sudden shine of turning faces
Like a swan gliding in its snowdress
From an arch of the bridge in a state of grace.
I was too mesmerised by her destiny
To see you start your car, drive off,
And raise your hand as you passed me by
On the way to Cashel, Fermoy and the South.

This deeply Christian poet seeks to know the everywhere of God in this life, in the world about him, and in himself; he sees his task as Christian to live to the full with the awareness that the Christ is the ground of our living and of the world's being. The poems reach for and hold moments of richness and grace, and the work is grounded beautifully, as this poem illustrates, in the actual world. The poem ends wonderfully:

I still write to you, poem after poem,
Trying to shape the perfect pattern
Of words and the mystery of their rhythm,
An earthly music audible in heaven –
Each poem is a coloured flare
A distress signal, an outflowing
Of myself, a camouflaged prayer
Dispatched towards the Cloud of Unknowing
And all I have to do is stay
Where I am, ready to be rescued

Not move, speak or think but wait
For the brightening of the Cloud
For your white silhouette to break
Free from it and come nearer, nearer,
Till I see your essence and I can ask
Where in the world you were
Throughout my days – and only then
Will I grasp why I never found you
Because you were too close to home
Because I thought I'd have to die
To see you there, right there, removing
The lineaments of your disguise –
My careworn wrinkled skin
My jaded incarnation of your eyes –
My face becoming your face
My eyes your eyes
I you us I you us
Iesus

The work of these four poets has a momentum and direction to it that adds to the power of each individual poem. There is a base of Christian reference that adds focus to the direction. Michael Conway, in a recent issue of *The Furrow*, outlines the changes in religious perception that have occurred over the last decades, a shift away from the definitions and prescriptions of church that worked downwards from a hierarchy to a mute and accepting laity, to what he calls an ascending mode; prescriptions and dogma are no longer simply taken for granted. Conway quotes from *Alice in Wonderland*:

Alice asks the Cheshire Cat:
"Would you tell me, please, which way I ought to go from here?"
"That depends a good deal on where you want to get to," said the Cat.
"I don't much care where …" said Alice.
"Then it doesn't matter which way you go," said the Cat.
"… so long as I get *somewhere*," Alice added as an explanation.

Good poetry is non-aligned; it is based on language, rhythms, imagery, imagination, and touches, at its best, the values by which we live. If these values are most clearly defined and expressed in the person of Christ, the

Christ who did not come amongst us to establish a church, but to offer knowledge of who or what God is, then a vital poetry that goes somewhere, touches, for us in the West, upon Christian values.

To end, more or less as I began, with a poem of my own: this tries to express a sense of universal oneness amongst all humans, that fellowship in the ongoing evolution of our world – and how we all share in life as a form of Eucharist, how the long search for understanding is a constant. For me, the base of that constancy is the person of Christ. But then, of course, I am too Christian for my own good …

EUCHARIST

I leave the pew, slowly, following
men and women old as I, and older;
no rush, we are cautious now, we –
communion of the living – holding on.

I take on my palm the white, the cosmic bread
and place it on my tongue, take a sip
of the earth-sweet and bitter wine; amen, I say,
amen. Now I am guest at the crude table

of the Upper Room, am Jewish-Christian, Hellenist,
I am Greco-Roman, Byzantine, medieval
mendicant, contemporary doubter; hold
a moment on my tongue two millennia

of a difficult history, memorial, sacrifice,
the proving – down a long bleak tunnel
scarce candle-lit – of the original
mandate of the Alpha, the Omega Christ.

This essay was delivered as The Sixth Annual Irish Pages Lecture at the John Hewitt International Summer School, Armagh, on 30 July 2015.

John F. Deane was born in 1943 in Achill Island, Co Mayo. He is the author of two novels and ten collections of poems, most recently Semibreve *(Carcanet, 2015). He is also the author of a memoir,* Give Dust a Tongue *(Columba, 2015).*

HEANEY'S LEGACY

Alan Gillis

It mattered.

"They stood. And stood for something. Just by standing." So reads the first line of Seamus Heaney's poem "Lupins." Now the man is no longer with us, it is melancholy yet inevitable to ponder what his legacy might be. To circumspectly wonder what, in years to come, might still be standing. At the moment, of course, one remains deeply affected by his loss and remembers, first and foremost, his personal and civic generosity and openness, his unstinting good nature and dedication. Long may this be his legacy. But what kind of things will be said of his verse in the future?

For most poets, the anxiety is going to be whether they will have a legacy, of any kind. By contrast, it's hard to think of any other artist who might have felt more assured than Heaney in this respect. Indeed, one would expect Heaney's legacy to take care of itself. Yet it might be best to think of the spread of a posthumous influence as an active thing. A poetic legacy, surely, must be the result, not just of people being affected by a poet, but of people then going forth and making something happen in relation to that encounter. In certain respects, Heaney's legacy will be a way of happening, in which his work will inform what we do, while we, in turn, inform and extend the reach of that work, through all the vicissitudes and changes that the future may bring.

Of course, Heaney's legacy has burgeoned since he was barely mid-career; as a personable and professorial celebrity he was taught in schools and studied by scholars, spurring intense critical scrutiny while enjoying immense popularity with readers, for some 40 years of his working life. This will necessarily shape his posthumous legacy, yet it certainly won't encompass it. At the same time, there's simply no point in thinking too far into the future. In 50 or 60 years' time, will the earth be smothered in ashes or ice? Will we have been invaded by Martians? And will they be reading Heaney? These are questions of a different kind (although the fragility and vulnerability of our sense of a future, at this present time, is something that might usefully be informed by Heaney's legacy – if poetry serves a purpose, what else might it be, other than this?).

More practically, we might focus on the mid-term future of the next 30 years or so. While there clearly will be a Heaney legacy, the interesting point is that these next few decades might seriously affect the kind of legacy this will be: what form, shape, tone, and bearing it might accrue. You might say that Heaney will stand the test of time on his own, on the strength of his own words, but literary history insists that something else will happen also. I personally don't like the phrase from Auden's elegy for Yeats: that he will be "modified in the guts of the living." But if Auden hit upon a truism – and if a writer's bearing and meaning within literary history will inevitably change, because the poetic taste and epistemological make-up of society will unavoidably change through time – then we might benefit from thinking about the kind of modifications we might have a say in, in our own time. In terms of Heaney's legacy, what would we like to happen, and what would we not like to happen? What would be good legacy, and what would be bad legacy?

Given this is Heaney we're talking about (so the least we might expect is a big legacy), what we talk about when we talk about Heaney is more than likely to affect the way many people talk about, and think about, poetry generally. Think of how the swings and roundabouts of the legacies of Yeats, Eliot, Pound, and so on, affect the ecosystem of poetry more generally. The active contours of Heaney's legacy are likely to have quite an impression on many intersecting circles and fronts, affecting contemporary Irish poetry on the one hand, and *potentially* lyric poetry on the broadest possible vistas, on the other hand.

The matter of Heaney's legacy, over the next 30 years, is therefore a matter likely to affect, among other things: how poetic language is thought of; how poetry as a rhythmic event of orchestrated sound is to be discussed; how the scope of the "well-made poem" is to be understood; how the speaking "I" of a poem is construed to be operating and affecting our understanding of human subjectivity in our time; how we apprehend the morphing and mixing of the realms of the literal and the figurative, and how we articulate what is at stake in our apprehension of their interchange; how the capabilities and potentials of the vernacular are to be grasped; and, of course, how on earth we're meant to properly pronounce that last *gh* in "Broagh."

I personally started reading lyric poetry seriously about 25 years ago, and then writing it some years after that. On both counts, what lyric poetry *was*, and what might be at *stake* in the activity of reading and writing it, was massively coloured by the influence of Seamus. I wouldn't say the Heaneyesque was hegemonic, but it was certainly a pervasive and active presence. This was in Ireland, mostly in the North. But my understanding through conversation with others is that the same might likely have applied, more or less, if I had been in Britain instead. And during the intervening years, of course, like Roald Dahl's magical giant peach, Heaney's legacy just kept growing and growing, until its circumference was not graspable by any single individual, and many of the subjects and forces at work within it had taken on creaturely characters and voices of their own. All of which is simply to reaffirm the obvious: that while we are all still coming to terms with his passing, Heaney's legacy is nonetheless something we've been engaging with for a long time.

And in my own time, in my ongoing engagement with this legacy, I think it would be accurate to say that I fought with Heaney's work for a long time. At the time, fighting with Heaney was a version of fighting the establishment. It was like fighting with the fact of being from the North of Ireland. It was like fighting against *the countryside* from the vantage of the town's estate. It was like fighting against the enormously powerful, subterranean pull of the lyric on my ear, since I seemed to be wary of my susceptibility to its calling. And it was like fighting against my family origins and against myself. All of which I did with impunity, when I was younger, for whatever reason. But in turn, eventually coming fully round to Heaney was, for me, a release and an immersion which, I think, was all the more formative for having been resisted.

It's often said that Seamus was both over-praised and over-criticized. But I run the risk of boring you with autobiography to convey the manner in which the reaction to Heaney, in Ireland at least, has often been deeply personal and highly charged. It has something to do with his work, but it also had something to do with the times. And from the slightly more level vantage point of the present, it seems to me that while the praise or criticism was sometimes excessive, whether in print or in private conversation, what matters is that both the love and rancour were expressions of how the poetry, and how it was being perceived and understood, were taken as matters of immediate importance. *It mattered.* And, I think, it matters now.

So I'd argue that Heaney's legacy should be shaped by two guiding principles. Firstly, it shouldn't be a betrayal to criticize, nor should it be a prerequisite to sign up to every single facet of his poetics. Rather, his legacy needs tough, informed, straight-talking debate and *criticism*, as well as praise and fond recitation. Secondly, while it would be grand if we could grow towards more objective wisdom as we age, it would nonetheless be wonderful if we could maintain the urgency and personal sense of consequence, regarding Heaney's work, going into the future, that so many have demonstrated and lived through in the past. Let him not be a textual effect. Let him be worth fighting over. If only in our quarrel with ourselves. This, I believe, would serve his memory, his work, and his legacy, most powerfully. It would also be at the service of the broader good of poetry, which is what he would have wanted anyhow.

Regarding Heaney's legacy, let him not be cordoned off into some ahistorical realm of great writers, petrified in the fridge freezer of a reified canon. A real, active poetic legacy cannot be a state imposition. His decisive influence will be felt in the minds of the youth of the future, with some simultaneity of enchantment and resistance. If it is a healthy legacy, it should shoot off in ways we cannot now predict. But for this to happen with substance, his legacy should also instil in future readers and writers a sense that a poetic tradition exists which is a living, multiplex, changing entity, and that this is the true ground of literary enrichment. In his formative essay "Feeling into Words", Heaney wrote: "Finding a voice means that you can get your own feeling into your own words and that your words have the feel of you about them." But he then asked: "How, then, do you find it?" And he answered: "In practice, you hear it coming from somebody else, you hear something in another writer's sounds that flows in through your ear and enters the echo-chamber of your head and delights your whole nervous system."

Crucially, it seems to me, this initiation to the heart of poetry must be an experience for the budding critic as much as for the budding poet. It describes an engrossed kind of reading, an immersion in the auditory imagination, that seems to be ever more under threat, but without which poetry means little. Towards the end of *Stepping Stones*, Heaney claimed: "The main disadvantage of being a poet anywhere at the minute is that there is no strong sense of a critical response which has lived and loved that which it is responding to." In fairness, he was himself the recipient of much first-class criticism. But the broader point was of course to note the unfortunate cleavage of creative writing and criticism. More and more critics look out above the poetic text without "close reading." More and more poets live with a vacant simulacrum of engaged consideration or evaluation. That many poets and critics seem separately content with such a scenario is part of the problem. We don't necessarily need poet-critics, but we absolutely need poets and critics to feel the pressure of one another. So let Heaney's excellence as a critic, and the consanguinity of this to his excellence as a poet, be a core element of his legacy. What both verse and criticism need is generous exactitude, borne of susceptible and alert reading. In Heaney we find this in abundance. Let it spread.

Teachers and advocates of Heaney must ultimately trust to the poems themselves. This may sound tautological, but the presentation of poetry in pre-assembled packaging and readymade contexts – this poem means *x*, this responds to *y*, and so on – is of course increasingly rife and is something that Heaney's work will be vulnerable to. But future readers must be allowed to make what they will of Heaney's work. There can be no "end product" of Heaney's legacy, just an ongoing personal relationship where readers will take his work as it comes, keeping it with them as they take life as it comes. If people new to his verse are simply encouraged to read the poems, and read them again, encouraged to know it's okay to spend time with them, encouraged to ask *themselves* "what is this?" while not grappling for an immediate interpretative fix for them, letting the savour and pith of the words and phrasings sink in, they will find the freshness and richness that courses through the lines, rhythms, and syntax pulsing through their own sensoriums, attuned to the work's abundance, the sureness and strangeness of its reverberations, and thus his work will enter their inner lives, where his legacy belongs.

This is not to suggest that we mightn't be both careful and ambitious regarding the contexts and perspectives through which we approach his work. For example, the sense of Heaney's significance as being bound up with a narrative of the Northern Irish Troubles, and of the peace process, is inescapable. But, touching wood that *that* narrative might be gasping to its finish line, then let us start to understand his work more fully in terms of other historical horizons. Let him not become a heritage figure, safely reified as a token of the Troubles. He has asserted the validity of individual sensation and immediate experience in an age of disembodied corporate utilitarian anonymity – from Althusser to Amazon and Apple. He has vividly energized the pastoral in an age of ecological disgrace. Let us explore his work in these contexts more closely. He has been the most extraordinarily self-reflexive and meta-poetical of poets, his language almost always his subject matter, and yet he has offered unwavering and sure solidity of selfhood throughout his work, in a manner that has been anathema to many critics informed by the "linguistic turn" of continental literary theory. This paradox seems fascinating. He has been one of our great poets of upward mobility, moving from the hay barn to Harvard, juxtaposing the coarse with the refined, self-critical that his "tongue went whoring // among the civil tongues." A middle-class audience accepts the perspective of the farmyard scullion as somehow representative of a shared bond underneath and beyond the vanity and pretension, materialism and mechanization, of middle-class life. But this would not happen if the farmhand's vernacular and perspective was replaced with the perspective and vernacular of the hoodied teenager in the shadow of an inner-city tower block. Why? How is class to be figured in Heaney's legacy? He has insisted on the lyric primacy of the individual, but this unique sensibility is simultaneously to be the site of something universal. Let's look, once again, at how exactly that works. But, then again, let us not worry about his work as a total system or coherent philosophy. Let us appreciate his insistence on the present tense of rhythmic utterance. And let us fully appreciate his popularity and audience. Let us applaud him for attaining this reach without compromising the authenticity or ambition of his work. And let us figure if the public thirst for poetry that he stimulated might be somehow built upon, without playing to the crowd, as a lasting aspect of his legacy.

On that note, if Heaney's legacy is something that is to happen, here and now and in the years ahead, then let us salute and support those who facilitate such endeavour. Without a doubt, Seamus's death produced a feeling of profound desolation. But the ongoing good work and will of many will help his legacy become something more joyful: a constant flowering. Seamus will be remembered for the way in which he could combine the devil-may-care individuality of creative flair with the exactitude of committed criticism; he will be remembered for the way in which he strove to meet the times head on, but was fuelled by an abiding and questing sense of tradition; and, last but not least, we'll remember him as a touchstone for social warmth, care, good faith, and good spirits. Long may other individuals and institutions – readers, writers, facilitators, publishers – continue to themselves reflect and promote such qualities and virtues. If we continue to support and encourage one another in the ongoing endeavour of honouring poetry, while having a bit of craic while we're about it, then we will continue to honour Seamus Heaney.

A poet and critic, Alan Gillis was born in 1973 in Belfast. He is a graduate of Trinity College, Dublin and Queen's University Belfast. He is the author of four books of poetry, most recently Scapegoat *(The Gallery Press, 2014). He is currently Lecturer in English at Edinburgh University.*

GRADUAL AS FLOWERS,
GRADUAL AS RUST
—

Michael Longley
& Nathaniel McAuley

A Note on the Interview

The interview that follows comprises some 50 email exchanges between the poets Michael Longley (b. 1939) and Nathaniel McAuley (b. 1990) between May and August 2015. Longley's background makes him distinct among his Irish poetic contemporaries: the son of English parents, he was brought up in Belfast and educated at Trinity College, Dublin, and has lived his adult life amidst the Northern Irish Troubles and subsequent peace process. The consistency of Longley's output, when read as a whole, presents to the reader a life of intense personal reflection and preoccupation with identity and death, made only more poignant when intertwined with his many joyous celebrations of day-to-day domestic life and the natural world. The title of this interview is taken from Longley's poem "Emily Dickinson."

Longley attended school at the Royal Belfast Academical Institution and read Classics at Trinity, where he met his wife, the poetry critic Edna Longley. He held the prestigious position of Ireland Professor of Poetry between 2007 and 2010. His many accolades include The Whitbread Prize for Gorse Fires *(1991), The T.S. Eliot Award for* The Weather in Japan *(2000) and, most recently, the 2015 Griffin Poetry Prize for his latest collection,* The Stairwell *(2014).*

No Continuing City *(1969, aged 30)*

Your first book was published 46 years ago. Do you still feel attached to it? Aside from the Classics, what were you reading at the time of writing?

Yes, I still like this collection. Its publication seems only a blink ago. It took a while for it to find a publisher. Each time it came back with a polite note of rejection I excised a few weaker poems and added some new work. So it ended up pretty hale and hearty. I am proud of the elaborate stanzaic patterns of such lyrics as "Epithalamion", "A Personal Statement", and "The Hebrides", of the prolific rhyming throughout and of the emotional depth of poems like "In Memoriam" and "Leaving Inishmore." I am pleased by the ambition and invention and liveliness of my younger self. At the time I was reading George Herbert, Robert Graves, Yeats, MacNeice, Wallace Stevens, Richard Wilbur, and the Great War poets.

You had about a decade's worth of poems written by this point: can you recall what you had in mind with the selection of the poems? The structure?

I simply assembled the poems as they presented themselves, higgledy-piggledy, no grand plan, no self-important schemes. Look after the pennies and the pounds look after themselves, as the saying goes. As things have turned out, the book is already touching on a lifetime's preoccupations. I was aware of the Horatian principle of *variatio* and put the collection together with that simple notion in mind.

Tell me a little about the many dedications. Was this purely the Classicist in you or was publication a chance for poetry to become a social medium?

Poems aren't usually born in isolation. They relate to other poems and to their authors. What was happening in poetry here in the sixties was not unlike the phenomenon of French Impressionism – the coincidence of talents, a sodality of the imagination – affection, regard, competition – artistic intoxication.

On that note, tell me a little about the finality of many of the relationships with women you included in this collection. Is this a young man fully renouncing his past and ready to cleave to his wife? "This new dimension, my last girl …"

My love poems (and love poetry in general) should not be taken literally. They are not strictly speaking autobiographical. They are, of course, coloured by my experience, but I wear masks in all my poems, especially in the love poems.

Much of this writing, I surmise, would have been under the watchful eye of Mahon. You've written about how intrinsic he was to your development as a writer. Was he simply the perfect reader or did you feel you lulled into writing for an audience?

My friendship with Mahon has been of central importance in my life, especially in the early days. We wrote poems partly to delight and intimidate each other. We are not intertwined in that way now – you can't go on for long conversing at that intensity. It now seems important for us to sing from our separate bushes. The same applies to my friendship with Heaney. From the beginning the first person I would show a new poem to is my wife, Edna, who is both encouraging and unsparing. If she likes a new poem, I am not overly anxious what anyone else thinks.

An Exploded View *(1973, aged 34)*

It's 1973. The Troubles are in full swing and you've written the collection completely in a time of immense social stress and conflict. How did this affect your writing? Did self-expression in wartime never feel a little frivolous or counterintuitive, especially when you come from a military family?

Reviewing *No Continuing City* in *The Irish Press*, the Welsh poet Dannie Abse was fairly enthusiastic about the book's artistry, but warned against escapism: I had not yet mentioned what we were soon to call the Troubles. He had a journalistic point, of course, but I didn't think this was any of his business. Towards the end of the 1960s I had run into formal difficulties. It didn't matter that I was surrounded by what Abse rather vulgarly considered rich raw material, if I couldn't write adequately about it or about anything else. My poems were becoming shorter and shorter and increasingly condensed. I feared that there was little or no rhythmic renewal. I slowly untangled the tight knots and wrote some relaxed love poems ("Caravan", "Swans Mating", "Galapagos"). The newfound emotional expansiveness made room for "Wounds", one of my best-known political poems. Over the years, I have read it on the BBC and RTÉ, and it has appeared on the Leaving Certificate syllabus in the Republic. In "Wounds" I ask my father's ghost what he as an old soldier makes of the tragic mess.

Divisions are amplified in a polarized community, yet you seem more fluid and exploratory in your own identity than ever — soda farls and poteen, the West of Ireland, and (common to many of your collections) a very Catholic lexicon. From this to multiple reflections on your father in the trenches. Was this an attempt to set an example for seeking to understand both communities or an attempt to possess or embody both communities?

"A very Catholic lexicon"? I hope not. I am incurably anticlerical! At this time I was discovering (and promoting in my Arts Council job) Irish traditional music, and reading the great geographer Estyn Evans, whom I was lucky enough to meet. A profound and lasting influence. His *Irish Folk Ways* and *Mourne Country* educated me belatedly in the pre-Christian Ireland of holy wells and magic trees, Brigid rather than Mary. Soda farls and poteen are the cultural possessions of both communities. In those days I used to get deliveries of poteen from a member of the RUC! The discovery of the townland of Carrigskeewaun in County Mayo was the ultimate revelation: my soul-landscape. The moody Atlantic light, which has been suffusing my poems for 50 years, first gleamed in *An Exploded View*.

"The West","Ghost Town", etc., portray the need for escape and headspace to write. In this collection we are first introduced to the solitude of your beloved Carrigskeewaun. As with any time of great social stress, people cry out for artistic response and engagement. Was there any part of you inclined to shy away, to stay away, even? To write what you wanted in solitude? Tell me what your responsibility to stay looked and felt like.

I don't visit remote places in order to escape. The reverse, perhaps. I want the light of Carrigskeewaun to illuminate the northern confusion. Ireland for me is defined by Belfast and the Western seaboard. That's what my poem "The West" is saying (along with many other poems). I could never entirely give up one for the other. I "hover" like an otter between Belfast and Mayo. "Ghost Town", by the way, conflates two deserted villages on the island of Hoy in the Orkneys.

You talk about "borrowing roots" from your contemporaries, seen clearly in poems like "Letters" and "To the Poets." Was there ever a personal desire for their more straightforward backgrounds, so to speak? Was poetry a way of possessing a piece of them? Did you ever feel guilty of a privileged cultural voyeurism?

When the Troubles erupted I was taken aback by the violence. I did for a while feel apologetic for being a middle-class Protestant. Mahon and Heaney seemed to enjoy more vivid hinterlands (the Belfast shipyards, the farm in County Derry) and perhaps that blinded me to the richness of my own. Partly inspired by my poet friends, I learned to be proud of my absolutely non-sectarian English parents and the nobility of my soldier father: he served in both world wars and was an old-fashioned patriot. And few backgrounds in Northern Ireland are entirely "straightforward" or absolutely bounded by "borders."

Brearton notes how Mahon refused to see the North as any different from the South — Heaney saw poetry as "restoration of the culture to itself." You had more of a "redefining" notion of the arts. The six counties and your own identity seem like metaphors for each other. Tell me a little about that.

I think the above answers cover this but I would add that in "Letters", my verse epistles to Simmons, Mahon and Heaney, I am proposing some kind of sodality of the imagination in violent times. I think my friends were right to be cautious. I myself heartily dislike the notion that discord might be fruitful for art and that in return art might provide solace for those who have suffered. To quote Auden: "Art is not life, and cannot be / A midwife to society." The arts cannot be relied on to be curative or redemptive, certainly not in the short term. But they are, I believe, a way of keeping alive ideas and perceptions that are in danger of being engulfed by conflict. Although poets may not necessarily be writing directly "political" poems, they are obviously absorbing and being sensitized by what is happening around them. It was crucial here, at that time, to avoid the poem of the latest atrocity; and to deal with our community's suffering much deeper down where something just might have "changed utterly." I like Ciaran Carson's suggestion that the true poems were "of" the Troubles rather than "about" them.

Man Lying on a Wall *(1976, aged 37)*

You dedicate this collection to your children. In general this feels more domestic than your previous collections. Was your mind becoming more content and rooted in the home? Were notions of true identity undermined by the immediate realities of family life?

In some ways *Man Lying on a Wall* is a more domestic collection, as you suggest, but it seems to me quite unsettled, full of uncertainty, even menace – the Great Indoors! I find little contentment in its pages. The wee dedicatory poem to my children is quite complicated and ambiguous.

You seem to be poking fun at the rules and expectations imposed on artists in your opening few poems – "Careful not to curtail our lives / / Or change the names he has given us" (from "The Lodger"). Were public demands becoming less of a concern? Did this clear the way for the more meditative and self-reflective tone of this collection?

If I am indeed poking fun in those poems, they are not very funny! In this book public concerns filter through in underground ways: "Company" and "Ars Poetica" (which is meant to be comic) consider the imagination under pressure from outside forces. There are two Great War poems: "Edward Thomas's War Diary" initiates my long spiritual involvement with him. I am still pleased by the political subtlety of "Fleance." So, I wasn't clearing the way, as you put it, although there is an inadvertent tilt towards the more meditative.

Tell me a little about the love poems in this book; the excitement of an adventurous sex life plays heavily from the beginning of the book in poems like "The Swim" and "The Bat."

At the start of the book there's a set of three love poems consisting of six quatrains each, twenty-four lines, a shape I adore. They are fictions and should not really be read as autobiographical. Love poetry often allows me to say quite complicated things about life in general. "In Mayo", for instance, is fuelled partly by my love of the western seaboard. Its erotic charge carries over into three straightforward nature poems ("Landscape", "Weather", "Flora") and three sequences of brief lyrics ("Points of the Compass", "Fleadh", "True Stories"). In this work I am trying to get closer to the soul of Carrigskeewaun. "Standing Stone", the fourth lyric in "Points of the Compass", feels to me like a rhythmic culmination. Here and in other pieces, such as the title poem and "Halcyon", I think I strike a lively enough balance between insouciance and concentration. In *Man Lying on a Wall* love poetry and nature poetry overlap (and continue to do so throughout my career). My wife's spirit abides between the lines of all these poems.

The Echo Gate *(1979, aged 40)*

In your opening poem, "Obsequies", we see the birth of one of your more famous soundbites: "You can't call yourself a poet. That's like calling yourself a saint." What is it about that title that irks you?

A poet is what I most want to be. It's lovely when others call me a poet, but it is surely monumentally presumptuous to equate oneself with Keats and Catullus and Homer. Poetry is a calling. There aren't that many poets in the world. A real poem is a rare event. Creative-writing programmes won't do much to alter those alarming facts.

I'm taken by the presentation of death in this collection, and with that, the seeming absurdness of life. Particularly "Wreaths" — "A bullet entered his mouth and pierced his skull // The books he had read, the music he could play" and "He kept a good shop and he died." Further, the death of poetry itself: "… Flanders // and the death of poetry there" ("Bog Cotton"). Did such grim prospects ever stunt your compulsion to write? Did the Troubles ever raise concerns about your own poetic legacy?

Death is a central preoccupation throughout my work, as in lyric poetry generally. I have never considered what people do to make a living as "absurd" in any way. Indeed, I revere the greengrocer and the linen worker (though not, perhaps, the banker!). Jim Gibson the greengrocer was part of my life and I shall never forget him. His widow approved of my elegy. Had she not, I would not have published it. People's feelings are more important than art. Total war is surely "the death of poetry." That is why Isaac Rosenberg's poems in the Great War or Keith Douglas's in the Second World War are such astonishing miracles. Their poems are for me sacred texts. I faced into the blackness of the Troubles with these inadvertent giants at my side. I would add that *The Echo Gate* contains some of my best love poems – "The Linen Industry", "On Mweelrea" – and some examples of "portraiture" from the everyday – "Mayo Monologues", "The Barber's Wife" – and as light relief at the end of the book, "Self-Portrait."

While there is a bluntness and finality in regards to death, there is also quite a sweet hint of comfort in the supernatural. In "Second Sight", for example – "My father's mother had the second sight // Flanders began at the kitchen window …." Should such poems fall in the same vein as "Lore" later in the collection – fascinating, but by-the-way, and anecdotal – or was there an openness to something otherworldly? Perhaps even an afterlife?

Art for me would be impoverished without some hint of the transcendental, but that doesn't mean that I believe in an afterlife (except in art!). A true work of art is "immortal." Perhaps all art is "by-the-way", to borrow your useful term. But generally I dislike what you call the "anecdotal." To chat within the confines of a poem is to waste time and space.

Poems *(1985) and period of silence (aged 40–51)*

Tell me a little about the impetus to release such a small collection as Poems *in 1985? Were these poems left overs from* The Echo Gate? *Or an attempt at keeping active?*

These poems were never collected separately as a pamphlet or book. In 1985 Salamander Press published my first four books in one volume as *Poems 1963–1983*, with these pieces as an addendum under the title "New Poems." For a decade in my forties I wrote hardly anything. These poems are all that emerged from my long spell in the wilderness. On the one hand I feared that I might be finished, on the other I hoped that this might be no more than a protracted fallow period. I believe in the essential healthiness of fallow periods, giving the top-soil time to recover.

We see a slight diversion from your Greco-Roman background and see you engage in the Irish classics of The Ulster Cycle, *in particular* The Táin *– poems like "On Slieve Gullion" and "Smoke in the Branches." Why wait so long to explore stories one would assume more accessible?*

So far I have found the Greek myths more absorbing, but I have always kept my ears open to Celtic possibilities. Perhaps in the future I'll explore the Irish stories more. Mind you, the *Odyssey* and the *Iliad* seem to me bottomless, endless.

I read a great interview you did with Peter McDonald in 1998 in which you talk about your 1991 quitting of the Arts Council. You pulled no punches, saying, "90% of the time I spent in the office was a waste of time, a waste of my life." Looking back now, do you feel the disdain for pomp and circumstance it left you with to be ultimately beneficial?

Most of bureaucratic life is a waste of time. I was quite good at it – framing agendas, writing minutes and reports, managing meetings – but my only really worthwhile work was with artists – writers and traditional musicians mainly. Where are all those mountains of paperwork now? Spiritually they weigh infinitely less than a single song or poem. Yes, the tin-pot "pomp and circumstance" of it all, the self-importance. It was crucial for me to see through it, oppose it and escape from its fumes.

Was it simply a lack of time that prevented you from writing? Or was it drive? Tell me a little about your writer's block.

A good poem will always make time for itself. So far as I can make out, there were several reasons for my writer's block – office politics, excessive drinking, mid-life anxieties and distractions. Perhaps I had nothing to say. I blame only myself. I love quoting John Hewitt: "If you write poetry, it's your own fault."

Gorse Fires *(1991, aged 52)*

I'm quite aware (having read your collected works in such quick succession) that I have experienced your life and output unnaturally quickly – but Gorse Fires *does seem to mark a period of contentment and calmness, not to mention confidence. Am I correct in saying this?*

I disagree with you. *Gorse Fires* seems to me an uneasy collection, a response to anxieties both public and private. In the spring and autumn of 1986 I went to live on my own in the Carrigskeewaun cottage for two months. I was desperate to regain my poetic touch. I was trying hard, possibly too hard. At first I felt lonely and tongue-tied, but then some good poems came along – "Sea Shanty" and "Detour" – that combine concentration and insouciance in a healthy way. There's even a touch of humour in them to help keep self-importance at bay. I was relieved to be writing again, but I didn't feel particularly "content" or "calm." Surely "Ghetto" and "The Butchers" (which I wrote in Carrigskeewaun) are among the blackest work I have produced. Homer enabled me to write belated lamentations for my parents. In *Gorse Fires* I also commemorated Joe O'Toole (my Mayo farmer friend), Philip Larkin, Charles Donnelly, the Ice-Cream Man (murdered on the Lisburn Road) – and not forgetting the Man of Two Sorrows. The book is predominantly elegiac.

We gain some insight into a lesser-considered part of your background in this collection, namely your mother's Jewish heritage – poems like "Terezín" and "Ghetto." As a writer fascinated by the feminine, as well as by his own identity, why did you wait so long to explore this side of your inheritance?

Perhaps I have neglected my mother. Her hinterland doesn't teem with history and incident like my father's. In *Poems* I include two tender elegies for her, "The Third Light" and "The White Butterfly", and in "No Man's Land" a glimpse of her Jewish mother. If I knew more about my Jewish background, I would probably write about it, but *sotto voce*. I value the hush of the "Terezin" couplet: "No room has ever been as silent as the room / Where hundreds of violins are hung in unison." I didn't postpone writing about these things. I wrote about them when I was ready to.

You've noted when writing this collection you felt like a young poet again: can you tell me about that? Did this lead to your revisiting the Classics in a big way again?

As I've said before, my forties were a bleak decade. There were years when I produced next to nothing. So, to be writing again with enjoyment and some confidence was renovating. I felt as though I was beginning all over again. Yes, I did feel like a young poet. At the same time Homer started to brighten my imagination again after many years. "Homecoming", my version of Odysseus's return to Ithaca, is for me a symbolic moment, as is the description of the bedchamber he constructed for Penelope, *The Tree-House*, a little hymn to married love. And I relish those moments of delayed recognition and reunion in the *Odyssey*, reunions with his father, wife, nurse and dog. I began to realize that Homer could open many doors into my life and memory.

The Ghost Orchid *(1995, aged 56)*

There is a wonderful playfulness at large in many poems in this collection – poems like "Hippomanes", and most strikingly, "According to Pythagoras" – "I could go on and on with these scientific facts / / If I wasn't so late I'd tell you a whole lot more." If we compare this to The Echo Gate *with its intense concern for accuracy, do we see a poet perhaps taking himself less seriously? Tell me a little about your musings around poetry at this point of your career.*

I'm always looking for accuracy of a kind. In *The Ghost Orchid* Ovid made his first emphatic appearance, and I was encouraged by his example to let my hair down. His *Metamorphoses* is a glorious ragbag of tall tales and shaggy-dog stories. I like to think there has been a playful element in my work from the beginning. With "Hippomanes" I was tickled to find among Virgil's somewhat official-sounding *oeuvre* this vivid account of randy mares in heat. That sweet little word "quim" has waited a long time for its Virgilian burnish! In ancient literature bad science can often generate good poetry, a rich surrealism, its own kind of truth. I hope I have never taken myself too seriously. Taking the poems seriously is another matter. I was pleased with *The Ghost Orchid*'s tonal range, its serious jokes.

Even more than your other collections, there are intensely violent-erotic overtones in this collection – poems like "Sheela-na-Gig" and "Spiderwoman." Was there ever a hesitation to publish these or indeed any other poems?

It's difficult to write well about sex – a question of tone. Sheela-na-gig carvings combine vulnerability and bawdiness. Frightening and funny, they put the word "pudenda" firmly in its place. I relish their gynaecological frankness. In "Spiderwoman" Latin myth meets David Attenborough. Sex in the natural world can be weirder than anything you'll find in art. There are some poems I wouldn't read to an audience of schoolchildren, but I couldn't explore human nature and my own psyche without some X-certificate stuff. Much of my work involves being private in public, so I do tread carefully. And I am anxious to avoid invading the privacy of others.

This collection contains "Ceasefire," one of your best-known poems. With the heartbreaking lines — "I get down on my knees and do what must be done / And kiss Achilles' hand, the killer of my son"— an obvious request for peace and reconciliation. How had your attitude towards the Troubles evolved?

Although they may be diminishing, the terrible tensions that caused the Troubles still run under the surface of life here. The so-called Peace Walls are still standing. The damaged and the bereaved remain our responsibility. From the beginning I have tried to write straightforwardly about our society's convulsions. I don't think my attitude has "evolved." I feel just as inadequate now as I did then. I am relieved that "Ceasefire" has been of some use. The old king, Priam, visits the tent of Achilles to beg for Hector's body: that episode is the soul of the *Iliad*. In my imagination I gave Priam the face of the Enniskillen draper Gordon Wilson. The "shared future" is some way off. It will take a generation or two for us to get there. The Troubles have produced some good art and that will help the slow process.

The Weather in Japan *(2000, aged 61)*

With the Good Friday Agreement signed in 1998, did you feel more at liberty to engage with wider subject matter?

Poetry is about all of the things that happen to people. In Northern Ireland one of those things has been civic violence. When I was writing poems about the Troubles, I continued to produce love poems and nature poems without any sense of self-indulgence or guilt. Love poetry is essential. Our society was seriously wounded by the Troubles. I shall be facing up to that fact for the rest of my life.

I'm interested in your often-noted use of the female speaker in your poetry. Can you tell me a little about that?

My poetry celebrates the feminine principle and is liberated by it. My soul has been shaped by all the females in my life – my mother, my sister, my wife, my daughters and granddaughters, lovers and girlfriends. Even as a small boy I preferred the company of girls. When I was six or seven I played magical games with a neighbour called Pauline Goodbody. I find close friendship with testosterone-fuelled males impossible – all elbows and knees. In my poetry I strive to be true to my nipples.

Brearton quotes a lovely passage from one of your journals when you write, "decided to send the thing (poem) to Edna before it drives me mad." Obviously as a reader, it would be hard to best Edna Longley; but more specifically, can you equate any of the success of such poems in the female voice to this close poetic relationship shared with your wife?

I don't really think in binary male/female terms. The Muse is hermaphrodite. Edna is the first and last judge of my work. I live in hope of her approval. She has looked after my sanity during the dark times when I was writing badly or not at all. She has stood between me and disappointment. When he was alive, I showed my new work to Michael Allen, another great critic. I listen carefully to everything Fran Brearton has to say. There are some other readers whose opinion I value. I am very lucky.

Snow Water *(2004, aged 65)*

In 2006 this book marked the end of your Collected Works. *Nearly 40 years since you sat with the legendary "Group," the participants get (albeit under the guise of Classical personas) close to the final thought in this collection, with your poem "The Group." Tell me a little of your feelings towards this collective, then and now?*

The Group has been grotesquely over-mythologized. Derek Mahon attended only once. James Simmons and Stewart Parker were abroad during my involvement. Hobsbaum disliked my poetry and was discouraging. The great critic Michael Allen and Harry Chambers (who was later to found Peterloo Press) were purged Stalinist-style, partly because they stood up for what I was trying to do. Hobsbaum's own verse was embarrassingly clunky. The main excitement for me was meeting Seamus Heaney and his wife-to-be Marie Devlin. Seamus and I hit it off from the word go, and he and Marie and Edna and I became a foursome totally independent of the Group. Perhaps Hobsbaum resented this. His aesthetic was narrow, but he chaired meetings powerfully and with charisma. I looked forward to them, and retrospectively I am glad I was there. But I didn't change one syllable as a result of Group criticism. The friendship of other scribblers was the main thing: as well as the Heaneys, Bernard MacLaverty, Arthur Terry (the distinguished Hispanist and translator), Jack Pakenham (a painter who wrote rangy surreal verse) and John Harvey (an inspirational professor of English at Queen's who died tragically young). Harvey unsettled Hobsbaum for a while by championing my work.

What about the generation before that? I'm struck by the passage about yourself and Montague visiting Baudelaire's grave in "The Pear." Did and do you ever feel comfortably on a par with your predecessors?

As undergraduates Mahon and I eagerly bought the early collections of Thomas Kinsella, John Montague, and Richard Murphy. They were important exemplars and remain so. They are serious makers and have kept going. I have only met Kinsella briefly once or twice, but I have enjoyed the sometimes hilarious company of the other two. I don't think of poetry as a race or competition. The relationship between poets is never "comfortable."

What about the generation after? (I'm thinking of "Owl Cases" for Medbh McGuckian, and previously "The Rabbit" for Ciaran Carson and "Stilts" for Paul Muldoon). What sort of relationship did you share with them?

Just at the point when my contemporaries and I might reasonably have felt that we had solved a few problems, along came this brilliant younger generation hell-bent on deconstructing our best efforts: Muldoon, Carson, McGuckian, Paulin, Ormsby – that's quite a line-up. They keep me on my toes. They are a blessing in my life. I read their books. I count them among my friends. Once a month or so, I meet Frank Ormsby in the Crown for bangers and mash and the exchange of poems. And there's an even younger group of sparklers that includes Sinead Morrissey, Leontia Flynn and Alan Gillis. Is there no rest for this 76-year-old?

A Hundred Doors *(2011, aged 72)*

Given your fascination with death, there is a beautiful flare of life in your poetry concerning your grandchildren. Tell me about how becoming a grandfather affected your outlook.

Becoming a grandfather is like being promoted for doing nothing. You acquire a new title and a new role – in my case, "Papa." Edna's life and mine have been lit up by our seven grandchildren. Fatherhood did not quite prepare me for the depth of tenderness I feel for these new lives. I rediscover the world through their eyes. Children are poets.

Concerning poems like "The Wren" and "The Levert", how significant was it for you to introduce this new generation to Carrigskeewaun?

Edna and I carried our children on our backs through the river and the channel to the cottage. It is a miracle that they now do the same for their children, our grandchildren. I remember showing Ben (the eldest) sneezewort beside the lake when he was a toddler, and talking about the name. This summer I named for my son's three children some of the little flowers that shiver on the duach – bog pimpernel, sandwort, eyebright. I do this in a casual conversational way. It might put them off to know what a profound experience this is for me. In the poems for my grandchildren, I suppose I do see their lives as ecologically bound up with the natural world, as epitomized by Carrigskeewaun.

In the title poem, "A Hundred Doors", you seem to lay out your religious agenda as that of "The sentimental atheist." Tell me a little about what that means. Was there a want for a deeper spiritual formation, or was it the lexicon and customs that fascinated you? Was atheism the only logical conclusion after a lifetime of religious-political bombardment? How did Anglicanism manifest itself in your childhood home?

I am a non-believer, but I have a religious temperament. Life would be lacklustre without a spiritual dimension. Although some close friends wear dog collars, I am passionately anti-clerical. Poetry is my religion. It is how I make sense of the world. Horace calls the poet *musarum sacerdos,* priest of the muses. I like that. My parents were easy-going Anglican agnostics who never went to church. On our own initiative, my twin Peter and I were confirmed at 16. Most weeks I listen to Choral Evensong on BBC Radio 3, especially for the Psalms. Two or three times a decade I take Holy Communion. I don't really know why. Perhaps my attraction to George Herbert, whose forms I imitate in some of my early poems, has something to do with his Anglicanism. In her interesting book *Northern Irish Poetry and Theology*, Gail McConnell discusses my poetry's Anglican connections. But for me, these are usually unconscious.

The Stairwell *(2014, aged 75)*

Tell me about including "Marigolds, 1960" in this work? Having your first ever published piece in the body of a poem in a work so late in your career is quite a significant statement.

At the time I was hurt and confused by my father's dismissal, but that pain passed soon enough. "Marigolds, 1960" is primarily a lamentation for my father. Weighed against his death, the five lines count for very little. It pleases me that my first published verse should resurface, transformed, more than 50 years later in *The Stairwell*. I'm not sure how "significant" this is.

This collection cannot be read but in the light of the passing of your twin brother. The second section of the book is dedicated exclusively to him. Touching on what we spoke about earlier concerning the limitations of poetry, did writing poetry while grieving not feel like a too-laborious pursuit? Or does poetry become instinctual?

Being a twin is a huge blessing. Losing a twin is a catastrophe. Catherine, my sister-in-law, and I sat with Peter when he was dying. In my sorrow I hoped that one day I might write an elegy for him. I ended up writing 23. My poems were welcomed by Catherine and my sister Wendy, who lives in Canada (she is 85). It all seemed perfectly natural. There was nothing laborious about it. Poetry for me has always been, among other things, "instinctual."

What do your own plans look like now? Was The Stairwell *your final collection or can we look forward to more work from you?*

The Stairwell will not be my final collection, since I go on writing poems.

Michael Longley was the holder of the Ireland Chair of Poetry between 2007 and 2010. He is the author of 14 collections of poetry, most recently The Stairwell *(Cape, 2014). He continues to live in Belfast.*

Nathaniel Joseph McAuley is a Belfast-based poet and graduate of the Seamus Heaney Centre for Creative Writing at Queen's University Belfast. He was awarded the Arts Council of Northern Ireland's ACES Award in 2014.

from THE WILLOW FOREST
(poem-sequence)

Frank Ormsby

A wind from Old Europe.

THE ACCUSED (I)

At the War Tribunal he sits behind bullet-proof glass.
They have confiscated his uniform.
A cardie and open-necked shirt do not constitute
the image he would like to project.
The steel-grey mortuary hair, a gift to cartoonists,
has a straggly look, as though his enemies
had tousled him for the cameras. So, when he refuses
to recognize the court and hammers a shoe
on the desk between him and his judges,
he is done-for already, takes on the purulent look
of a small, fat man in a temper –
the kind who would sign orders and feel no need
to think of the victims or picture their faces.
The evidence approaches like a wrecking-ball
that will sweep him away, though somewhere behind
that bullish face, those bullet eyes, he has not yet lost
the will to out-rant his accusers, the conviction that he will win.

THE INTERPRETER (I)

In a packed train from the suburbs I revise
irregular verbs and reacquaint myself
with the extensive vocabulary of atrocity.
I am fluent enough to know that nobody is fluent,
even in his own language. Always suspect a nuance.

What is being said in the underground tunnels
of the unsaid? How does an arrangement of the face
or a change of timbre affect what is stated?

———

From photographs used in evidence and sudden
bright doors opening in the testimony,
I begin to picture a village in remotest Europe,
unlucky in where it lies, a dozen miles
from the disputed border and at the mercy of both sides.
There are modest statues in the village square
to the dead of two world wars, and, now, the memorial
for which the place is known – the victims' names
chipped on a marble wall next to the space
I translate as "Playground of the Fatherless."
I learn of the region's rich woodland,
the lakes of bluebells and the part they have played
for centuries in the villagers' lives. A band from the neighbouring town
turned out to play when the main street to the woods
was re-christened "10 April Street." You would scarcely believe
how much I know about the village dogs,
both those that fled the soldiers' arrival
and those that died, baring their teeth at the guns.

WITNESS D

They called her the Lazarine. She wore
the necklace of death and set her face to the world
in ways beyond tears and laughter.
The others kept their distance, wary of one
who had lived twice and now, for the second time,
told how the soldiers' final act
was to step into the pit and cut the throats
of those who were still moving.
How she rolled, face-down, into a pocket of still air

between two corpses and lost consciousness.
She had no memory of the earth covering her
but carried with her the face of the Accused
as the officer-in-charge. Now chanting
her ordeal, she stopped, opened her blouse
and, to gasps from the courtroom, bared the scar on her throat.
She dreams of a country of grief, she says, under
a forest of willows, but the judges,
embarrassed, decline to hear it described.
No matter. It was as if the dead
themselves had returned to bear witness
and had the last word and were not to be doubted.

———

Later, in the park, she stood under the trees,
her upturned face dizzy with birdsong –
the same sound that had pierced her as she slipped towards death,
then sweetened her crawl back from oblivion,
trailing blood and earth.

THE ACCUSED (II)

There are few males in the courtroom,
but when the judges enter the women stand in unison, raise
the framed photographs of their husbands and sons
and cry for justice. And again when the Accused
is led in – the cry now for justice and revenge.
The Accused exudes indifference and shades of contempt.
Once, with an amused look,
he aims his finger at the gallery and feigns pulling a trigger.
The courtroom has to be cleared.
He is rumoured to be "on twenty-four-hour watch",
to have "got religion", or at least, acquired a crucifix.
Now, as the evidence against grows like a mountain,
he is given to maniacal, high-pitched laughter,

either mocking the widows, or having a break-down,
or embarking on the behaviour patterns
that will have him declared "unfit for trial."

WITNESS G

The undertaker's son has spent three years
in solitary for his own protection.
After threats to his wife and children – or so he claimed –
it was he who buried guns and explosives in the woods,
the Accused's justification for attacking the village.
A star witness now for the Prosecution
and quick to denounce the Accused, he has not,
however, been, and never will be, forgiven.
On the day before the massacre he drove his wife and children
to visit relatives in another village.
No one with family dead can ignore
such ruthless self-interest, or accept his failure to warn.
So he runs the gauntlet of kindly women's curses.
His family has moved away, his house is aerosoled
with threats and condemnations.
He will change his name and grow anonymous
among the terraces of a distant city.
He will be tracked down before the year is out
by his third cousins and left dead in the snow.

WITNESS J

The teenager, alive because he played truant
on the fatal day and has ground to make up,
breaks a leg kicking the prison van
in which the Accused arrives at the courthouse.
He delivers what evidence he has from a wheelchair.
His father and his teacher are not around
to administer the sharp rebuke.

THE INTERPRETER (IV)

God forbid I grow old as a connoisseur
of Man's depravity. After days like these –
stained with hatred and the cut-throat past –
in search of the benign, I choose to walk
home through the park.
I would, if I could, compose an interpreter's prayer –
names in a clean recital, pitched to move
whatever good may bask at the heart of things.
"Squirrel" I think, "a small arborean rodent";
"Bluebell: an Old World plant of the lily family,
with blue, bell-shaped flowers."
I think "leaf" and "light" and "water."
I think "street" and "sky."
Not much there, you might say, to counter the thrust
of a pitiless, cut-throat future –
yet it counts that the urge is alive,
that somehow the field has not been abandoned.
I think "grass" and "rabbits" and "hostels" and "hot dogs."
I think "houses" and "stone."
Let the final word be "darkness" as darkness comes down.

THE UNDERTAKER'S WIFE

My husband knew more about death than anyone else
in the village, dressed to encounter it daily
in the living quarters above the "shop" –
a word he hated, preferring instead to speak
of the "business", those two rooms on the ground floor
that were never without coffins, empty or full.
Nobody else in the village had handled the dead
as he had, laid out the elders for the grave
in their final nakedness. These family intimacies
coloured his rapport with the villagers headstone grey,
made his smile a sliver of frost, his eyes

the dark archive of a man who could write
a history of death. I married him as my last chance
and was not offended when my friends
joked about "cold hands", or were curious about the skills
he brought to our bedroom. I countered
with the traditional claims for a "warm heart."

———

The boy we adopted was from a village
beyond the mountains. It was the old time
when unidentified groups came out of the woods
and took prisoners, nobody knew where or why.
When he was six, they chose his parents
while he hid in the woodshed. He never saw them again
and came into our lives so fraught and anxious
we thought he would run away. But year by year
he took his place among the villagers
as the undertaker's son, a man of consequence,
accepted by them, taught to smile
by the village girl he married, and unpicked
from the black fabric of his past
by his own children. But for him
the past did not recede or slacken its grip.
Something or someone had him by the throat.
The less we knew the better, or so it seemed.
The day before the massacre he packed us off
to visit relatives. Our lives changed overnight.
The survivors were implacable. If he knew
enough to save his family, he knew enough
to warn the entire village. His failure to warn
meant a hand in every death.

THE ACCUSED (III)

The existing photographs, in retrospect,
seem to record an unsmiling intent,
that angel-of-death stoniness against a blurred background
suggesting a shadowy past. The Defence argues that he too is a victim.
The evidence they cite is not widely known:
the slum poverty of his boyhood,
his father's brutish presence, bequeathing hatred
and more hatred, the death of his mother
when he was five. They try to disperse the fog
of rumour – that he led a murder squad
during the War of Liberation,
that he became, for a time, a police informer,
that he smuggled guns from Africa,
was on first-name terms with half the world's tyrants.
All myth, all speculation, unprovable, the Defence avers.
The Accused stares in silence into his hands
for several days becomes a fugitive half-hidden behind
what may be a false name, among dates and events
that are plainly inaccurate.
Is the wrong man on trial? From the widows' faltering need
for reassurance, reassurance grows.
Day in, day out, their fixed, implacable eyes
begin to fathom his fear.

THE WILLOW FOREST

What with the pogroms, the genocide,
the ethnic cleansing, the secret massacres,
the mass graves, the death camps, the public executions,
at last there was nobody left,
the country was empty.
Survivors who reached the borders
became refugees.

Rebuked by that silence beyond the mountains,
the victors planted willows and in due course
the country grew into a willow forest.
The trees hung their heads
over a history that, now memorialized,
could be forgotten.

Except that the few who visited
spoke of a weight
that was more than gravity,
a wind in the trees
that stilled to a kind of weeping.

Frank Ormsby was born in 1947 in Co Fermanagh and has lived much of his life in Belfast. He is the author of four books of poems, most recently Fireflies *(Carcanet, 2009), as well as the editor of nine poetry anthologies. He was Editor of* The Honest Ulsterman *between 1969 and 1989. He retired in 2010 as Head of English at the Belfast Royal Academical Institution, where he taught for 34 years, and continues to live in Belfast.*

MICRO-PROSE

Nicholas Ruddock

Instructives.

THE GLASS FLOWERS

Should you ever feel we are a wanton race, destructive and incapable of miracle, then a visit to the Botanical Museum at Harvard would be instructive, for there, in a small room filled with exhibition cases of glass and wood, accompanied by the low hum of humidifiers, are the four thousand glass-and-wire constructs known – the wire is invisible – as the Glass Flowers, each of which is of such delicacy as to seem to breathe through its protective prison of glass: here, for example, is just a common kind of grass, lying on its side as though pulled from the earth, roots tangled and clustered and as wayward as such roots are, twisted and hung with gravity, and the green of the blades of grass is as imperfect and varied as the green of nature; here are scarlet maple leaves, indistinguishable (though these leaves will never change) from those we shuffle through in autumn; here is the elegant pitcher plant from Newfoundland, which drowns insects for its sustenance; here is the saprophytic Indian pipe, dead-white and cold as ice and shrivelling black when it dies; here are the lilies and the orchids, the celebratory laurel, the gentian, the iris and the pomegranate, all of them, one by one, created between 1887 and 1936 by two artisans, Leopold and Rudolf Blaschka, father and son who lived and worked in Dresden, Germany, at that time the most beautiful city in Europe and so it remained until February, 1945, when thousands of tons of incendiary bombs fell from the night sky and the temperature at ground level approached 2,500 degrees Celsius, sucking oxygen from those who tried to breathe in their sheltered rooms, their basements and gardens, and the ash of their bone mixed with the sandy loam and blew hot with the blast-furnace heat of revenge and coarse slabs of glass, crude glass now as black as obsidian flowed over flowers.

—

THE OXFORD BOOK OF MODERN VERSE

At the Abbey Theatre, in 1934, she came to the attention of William Butler Yeats. In this photograph, dark hair frames her face, a moonstone, her creamy pallor typical for Ireland back then, before Ryanair, before the Costa del Sol burnt winter away. An actress less than half his age, her voice was pitch-perfect for singing the old songs, and for the recitation of poetry. He saw her first outside, leaning against a shadowed wall, backlit, a parenthesis. Inside, she sang and recited and he spoke to her, his incompetence with girls and women paring him away, saying, with your permission I could edit your verse. Oh the flattering. She was bare to the world, undisguised by metaphor. Leaning towards her, over a small desk, the light flickering, he said, Margot, I find rhythm wanting in your body of work. As if she didn't know it, as if she hadn't intended it, as though she hadn't reached out for the very lack of it. Married, a mother of two, a skewed gyroscope, her chameleon moods. Finally he succumbed to her, a touch on her shoulder, unbuttoning her in Donegal in November, the hotel under direct assault by a north wind that had driven even the sheep indoors. He recovered his potency, a Second Coming, and in good faith he included seven of her poems in *The Oxford Book of Modern Verse*, 1936. Then he went to Spain with his wife to translate the *Upanishads*, but Margot distracted him still, her pulse beating in his head, her white skin addictive, her body his nightmare, a trainwreck with her brakes shot uncertain on the narrow-gauge, drive-wheel spinning, the other passengers already jumped for their lives while he stayed, unbalanced, shovelling coal into her, and the heat of her body burnt holes in his hands and his face and his falling-down underwear and his gabardine trousers which were down and undone to her until dawn broke to his otherwise empty bedroom, to the soporific breezes of Palma, Majorca. The morning post, her letters on a silver tray unanswered. Then Barcelona where she cleaved and broke, alone in the Plaça de Colón, her only friends dogs and vagrants and midnight vendors of street food, and cobblestones, and her own footsteps leading up a staircase to an anonymous roof, to a skylight in a green and rusty metal frame, down through which she fell – not as you or I would fall, thinking *oh no oh no* – with no thought in her head at all, down through shards of glass to an earthen floor where three Catalans, surprised in their kitchen, used everything at hand to staunch the blood that flowed from her now-glittering veins: tablecloths, restaurant linen, napkins, aprons stained with the juice of beets and prunes and mustard and the sauce of soups and apples, daubing and pressing until they ran to the street and they waved down the Guàrdia Urbana and the Guàrdia Urbana carried her away. Next she entered a series of hospitals from which she never recovered, and in our world today, 2014, no mention is made of her, of Margot, nor is she included in *The Oxford Book of Modern Verse*, but the wild swans at Coole still turn their heads, falcons twist against their leather restraints, and the bishops of Ireland remain as mute as ever to the sounds the wounded make.

———

HENRY HUDSON AND IRENE AVAALAAQIAK

In 1611, Henry Hudson was set adrift by mutineers, cursed into a small boat, vilified, tumbled against the gunwales, put over the side with those few loyal to him and gaffed away, open and pitching to the lee side of the ship on the vast northern ocean we now know as Hudson Bay, a dreary seascape of tidal wash, saline, tundra and muskeg semi-suffused by gray static light and little sound, as though the sun were always in partial eclipse, as though there were no birds or birds had no voice, and historians tell us that these castaways were never heard from again, that they drowned, that Hudson had no sextant, but that was the opinion of Europeans who did not take into account the appearance, in Inuit legend, of a boat with oars driven by relentless winds onto the sandbars east of Baker Lake, where white men came ashore in the thinnest of shirts and lay down on the ground inhospitable for 343 years until the northern hemisphere turned their bones to chalk, until their shoulders bristled through ragged linen, until they rose again into the crystal night of winter and walked as caribou, surprising the hunter Irene Avaalaaqiak in the year of the great starvation, 1954, when Inuit themselves lay down and died and died again, and over the shoreline hummocks these caribou came and she shot them with her .303 and amidst the blood congealing there she assembled her cutting tools, shook their hooves, a greeting, cut their tendons ceremonially, took snow into her mouth and – she was seventeen – stooped and pressed her lips to the lips, still-warm, of the sailors dead from the south.

Nicholas Ruddock is a physician, poet and fiction-writer. He is the author of a novel, The Parabolist *(Doubleday, 2010) and a collection of short stories,* How Loveta Got Her Baby *(Breakwater Books, 2014). His second novel,* Night Ambulance, *is forthcoming. He lives in Guelph, Canada.*

PLANET SEAMUS

—

Daniel Tobin

His gravity and grace.

We met on a soft November evening in the lobby of the Ballsbridge Hotel, about midway between Sandymount and the Wellington Road flat where my wife and I were living for the fall term, 2000. Our teaching week was over at the American College. We had taken some 15 students from our small liberal-arts college in Wisconsin on a semester abroad. While a night at one of the local pubs would have been *de rigueur* regardless at week's end, the present outing came as a surprise when the phone rang early in the afternoon and I picked up: "It's Seamus. Is tonight a good night for you?" A good night for me? Had I been clipped crossing Baggot Street by a swerving Dublin bus I would have found some way to splint myself together and say, as I did, "Yes, of course, that's perfect. Where should we meet?"

Though I had been his student in his Harvard poetry workshop some 18 years before and had recently published *Passage to the Center*, my critical book on his work, as well as my own first book of poems, I did not expect the kind of greeting I received earlier in the month when I attended the launch of Seamus's *The Midnight Verdict* at the now defunct Waterstone's. I made a point of introducing myself to him after he'd read. The usual crowd of literati milled around, many with copies held out for him to sign, which he did, as always, warmly and gratefully. He was still sitting in his chair when I leaned in to say hello, and I began to say my name when he shot up and shook my hand vigorously – his big farmer's hands – and asked how I was and why I was in Dublin and thanked me for the work I had done on behalf of his work and said he had read my book of poems but hadn't recognized me immediately. How long had it been? Eighteen years is a long time. But he wanted to get together while Christine and I were in Dublin, and he signed my copy of *The Midnight Verdict* "To Dan, with high regard, to a hearer and hearkener of the work, Seamus." He wrote his fax number on the back inside flap and said to send him my number and he would be in touch.

And so he was, good to his word, little more than a week later after I had faxed him our phone number.

"You'll have to go yourself", Christine insisted. "You were his student. He doesn't know me. He'll want to talk with you. You wrote your dissertation on him, you wrote the book."

"I think you should come", I said. "He's not at all standoffish – just the opposite."

"You should go yourself. He won the Nobel Prize! I'll be a third wheel. I'll be a hanger on."

So we batted it back and forth through the late afternoon and into the evening, with the one caveat that I would call her, she reluctantly agreed, if I judged my meeting with Seamus to be amenable for her to join us. I left our flat with that agreement, took the lift down, and headed along Clyde Road toward Pembroke. When I entered the crowded hotel lobby Seamus was already standing off to the right, dressed for the weather – trenchcoat, moleskin hat in hand. We waved to each other. He was smiling. We shook hands, and before I could say anything he asked with his warm northern brogue, "Where's Christine?"

———

My first encounter with Seamus Heaney was, like most, in and through the work alone. One day in my mid-teens I had gotten the notion that I should become a poet. Nothing could have been more unexpected in my family. My father lied about his age at 17 to enter the navy in 1941, at the start of the Second World War. The youngest of 10, by 13 he had lost both his mother and father, dropped out of middle school, and been bounced from one older sibling's apartment to another while he worked as a short-order cook. My mother had to drop out of Fordham University when her father developed multiple sclerosis. They met at the USO after the war and married two years later. My father was a longshoreman on the Brooklyn docks until one of the docks, Luckenback Lines, blew up with him on it. He woke with a co-worker and friend dead beside him, and promptly found a way into Marine Insurance Claims and a white-collar job. My mother worked as a bank teller. Eventually they had two children – my older brother ("The Walking Encyclopedia") and me ("The Athlete"). There were few books in our four-room apartment. Poetry existed almost exclusively in an alternate universe. My mother wanted me to be a priest or a dentist, or maybe "go into computers." Poetry was not something my parents had counted on.

In fact, I had read very little poetry until the Muse, perhaps to play a practical joke on my parents, whispered in my ear that unlikely afternoon. What poetry I had I read in English classes in high school, or found in an edition of Poe's selected work (his poems dovetailed nicely with my abiding love of horror films), or in our dog-eared copy of *Immortal Poems of the English Language* edited by Oscar Williams. How Poe's work and Williams's anthology came to reside on our one bookshelf piled high with my mother's romance novels I was never able to find out. They were just there. I remember looking at the array of oval portraits on the florid cover where Keats, Shakespeare, Donne, Dickinson, Pound, Eliot, and the immortal Oscar Williams looked out from their distant galaxy where, apparently, all the great poets lived as in some coterminous Parnassus. By the time I entered my senior year of college at what my future dissertation advisor would call "that blue-collar Roman school" I had managed somehow to compile a thick notebook filled with handwritten poems, all quite ambitious, all quite derivative, and all quite bad. Still, the strange impetus somehow born in me to become a poet hadn't dissipated.

It was during my senior year that I enrolled in my first poetry-writing workshop with the poet and distinguished translator of Dante's *Inferno*, Michael Palma. At the start of the first class Mr Palma circled the room, asking what poets we read and loved. I said John Donne and Gerard Manley Hopkins and William Butler Yeats. He looked visibly stunned – nearly everyone else invoked Rod McKuen. It was the spring semester 1980, and in one class Mr Palma handed out a poem that had appeared a short time before in *The New Yorker*. The poem was called "Field Work" by someone named Seamus Heaney:

> Where the sally tree went pale in every breeze,
> where the perfect eye of the nesting blackbird watched,
> where one fern was always green …

Nothing could have been further from my own immediate experience, growing up on the streets of Brooklyn: no sally trees, no nesting blackbirds, no ferns, but peeling plane trees in rows and pigeons at the gutter cracks and maybe a slip of wispy green growing between the stoops. I heard the lines, heard them at once, and – without thinking, without any mediation whatsoever – I hearkened to them. The poem on its own had tuned the life of itself in me.

That summer I traveled to Ireland with a friend, my first trip to my ancestral island, and took a job working in the poorer areas of Dublin, off the books, courtesy of the Irish Christian Brothers, the very order that presided over the "blue-collar Roman school" from which I just graduated. When I wasn't working, or heading with my friend to a pub, or "making hay", or not, as Kavanagh's great song goes, with a girl I'd met, or visiting the farmhouse outside of Robeen, Mayo, my mother's mother had left more than 60 years before, I was buying every book of Seamus's, devouring the poems, listening intently, sometimes writing in the manner of, and trying to move slowly into my own in the art.

After I returned, and sent some of my new poems to Professor Palma, he heard the change for the better and knew the influence. That fall, my friend told me Heaney was to read at Hofstra. We went. I recall his tweed coat and his heavy walk to the podium, the hands shaped more to a ploughshaft than a pen, the brilliance of the reading, mostly from *Field Work,* which had come out the year before. I carried my Faber copy that I had bought in Ireland with its orange map of Glanmore on the cover down the aisle for the poet's signature, more than a little nervous, holding my finger at the poem on the page I wanted him to sign, unfamiliar as I was then with the custom of poets signing the title page. "My tongue moved, a swung relaxing hinge ..." By then I had applied to Trinity College, Dublin for graduate work in Irish Studies. Soon, I heard Seamus Heaney would be coming to teach at Harvard. I applied to the Divinity School – I had majored in religion – with the intention of taking a workshop with Heaney. It never occurred to me that as a graduate student I would not be allowed to register for the class, and that I would have to submit samples of poems that would determine whether I would be allowed to enroll. The acceptances from Trinity and Harvard came within days of each other. I chose Harvard, giving up my return to Ireland, with the intention to combine my interests in religion with literature, and with the incongruous conviction that I would study poetry with Seamus Heaney.

———

When Seamus asked for Christine in the lobby of the Ballsbridge Hotel, he did so never having met her and having heard her name only once, a week or so before, when I spoke with him at the crowded Waterstone's launch. I took his inquiry then, as I take it now, as an example of his almost preternatural sensitivity, a rare regard for personal as well as intellectual and artistic nuance. It was as though Seamus had some kind of invisible antenna that enabled him to read the social gist of my back-and-forth with

Christine earlier that afternoon; as if her concern with being welcomed by the laureate had somehow communicated itself to him along the airwaves. I rang her from the hotel lobby.

"You're kidding."

"We'll pick you up in a few minutes."

Seamus drove. His car was a nicely-trimmed Mercedes. He knew our building, a modern brick four-storey on the corner of Wellington and Clyde, set among well-tended Georgians not far from Herbert Park. Someone told us the actor Richard Harris lived nearby. We were lucky to have our flat rent free for the entire fall courtesy of the American College. Christine was waiting in the doorway, clear of the rain, and hopped quickly in back as Seamus greeted her warmly – "Hello, Christine," as though he'd met her sometime before, "Wonderful to meet you." He wanted to go to one of our local pubs. Slattery's, of John Berryman fame, was farther away and had long since lost its luster – we'd made our pilgrimage soon after arriving in Dublin and had been disappointed. We decided on the Fifty-One on Haddington Road near the Grand Canal, which at the time had a grand old bar with several elaborate deep mahogany dividers that doubled as snugs. Seamus knew the place, he told us, about a block from Smyth's, he informed us, where one of his sons had tended bar for a while. On the way he apologized for the Mercedes, the one thing he allowed himself, he confessed, "with the bounty of Sweden."

We moved through the loose maze of patrons and found three stools at the end of the back bar. Seamus gave the publican a sly wink – easy enough to recognize who he would be serving, and doing so without fuss and bother: two pints of Guinness and a Powers for Christine. And so the rounds ensued – a good long night of talk on poets and poetry, how Michael Donaghy was the real thing, and compliments for my own first book, "Enviable, that 'gun wrapped like an infant in white cloth'"; and interest, genuine interest, in Christine's work, her teaching, her poetry, how and where we'd met, a *tête-à-tête* about the recent disastrous American presidential election, how Christine and I had gone to bed in one universe where Al Gore had prevailed and woke up the next day in another; "Aye, aye", – no exclusionary palaver, teacher to former student. We stayed until closing, well tended and let be. Seamus whisked us back to our flat through the drizzling rain, upbeat, un-phased by the rounds, generous, and off he told us, the next morning, to visit family in the North.

Such was our close encounter with Seamus in Dublin, all very easy and understated, as though we were all on our home turf. Four years later, another

November, some months after Michael Donaghy's sad death at 50, we would spend time with Seamus again, this time for a dinner gathering with his wife, Marie, organized by a Harvard colleague. We had moved two years previously to Boston when I became chair of Emerson College's Writing, Literature and Publishing Department. I had hoped the move would be something of a homecoming, but it had turned out differently. Among other things, with some exceptions, the Boston academic world had revealed itself to be insular and standoffish, which is why I was surprised when a few days before election night a poet-professor friend who taught at a local university phoned to let me know I was being invited to have dinner with Seamus and Marie and a few others at the house of Seamus's colleague at Harvard. The one caveat, my friend informed me, was that there could be no wives except the host's and the poet's. My friend, who knew and had spent time with Seamus, was clearly accepting of the conditions. Stunned, I confessed I was not. Seamus had met and liked Christine, I told him, and I couldn't imagine that such conditions were Seamus's idea. They weren't, he assured me, but keeping the group small was important and that meant in both of our cases no wives. I told my friend that I would love to be included, would love to see Seamus again and meet Marie who, Seamus had written me once, had very much liked my book on his work, but that under the conditions I wouldn't be able to join them.

"If you want to go you should go", Christine said after I had gotten off the phone, though she was bristling, "ripping mad", as my Mayo-born grandmother used to say.

"I have no intention of going", I responded.

About a half hour later the phone rang again. It was the poet-professor. "The wives can come."

I looked across the kitchen at Christine, mouthing my friend's words. She rolled her eyes. I shrugged my shoulders and turned over the palm of my hand as though I decided to test for rain. She nodded her head. We would go.

—

The night of the dinner party with Seamus and colleagues and friends took place on the Saturday after the 2004 election, almost four years to the day since our evening at the Fifty-One. We left our duplex condo in Dorchester, made our way up Dorchester Avenue with its slowly gentrifying storefronts, its *mélange* of immigrants from all over the world: Jamaica,

Haiti, Ethiopia, Vietnam, the longstanding working class and poor African-American and Irish-American denizens of the pocket neighborhoods that made up "Dirty Dot", where we had moved after leaving our first jobs in the American Midwest.

There was, and is still, no direct route from the likes of Dorchester to Cambridge and Belmont, in every sense of a path, though we arrived on time and were wonderfully welcomed at the door by our smiling host, and Seamus and Marie. A hearty handshake for me from Seamus – those big hands that had signed my copy of *Field Work* after the Hofstra reading – and a hug for Christine, a warm "Lovely to meet you" to both of us from Marie. My friend the poet-professor and his wife had already arrived. He gave me a knowing look. The house I could see from the outside and now from the inside was large but no mansion, and attractively appointed. "Lace curtain", my mother would have ventured, and my father also, whose great-grandfather had travelled by coffin ship from Cork to St John, New Brunswick in 1850, escaping the Famine to become "a laborer of the city" before emigrating further south to Brooklyn. That evening we mingled, laughed, drank, bantered, and ate with an inner circle neither Christine's parents and families, nor mine, could never have imagined. It was as though, for all of our education, our rise above our given station, we had somehow found our way to another planet.

In fact, we had, or very nearly. Though nothing like the "sky walk" Seamus recounts in *Crediting Poetry* and his own emergence from the potato-digging fields to "master new rungs of the air", we had arrived for this evening into a proximate orbit of Planet Seamus. My friend's news that the wives would have to be excluded from the group for it to remain small suggested just how complex entry into that close orbit could be. It was a protected orbit, and we were lucky to have briefly entered into even its lower atmosphere, I suspect (though I will never know), at Seamus's insistence – he who was himself always gracious and "the heartiest of welcomers."

It was right, of course, to protect and, if needed, to deflect the too-close orbit, for the Heaney Attractor was (and still is even after his death) nothing if not powerfully alluring, both for the genius of the man and his work, and almost the more so for the graciousness and generosity that accompanied the gravitas. After he suffered his stroke, his drawing inward became a matter, after all, of self-protection. Even so, it appeared very little to lessen the demands on him, to diminish the attractive reach of Seamus. At a reading I attended at Boston University some two years after, he was almost miraculously recuperated, and I watched what looked vaguely like a papal procession emerge from backstage, wending toward the reserved seats – academic minions, like postulants, advancing first, and behind them various members of the professoriate like bishops, then Cardinal Pinsky and Cardinal Epstein and, finally, Seamus looking to my eyes rather wryly bemused, simultaneously enjoying and nonplussed by the high formalities, more perhaps like the Buddha than Il Papa. Afterwards, I greeted him on stage, thanked him for another extraordinary reading – that same big handshake – and walked off happily to give him his space.

———

The buzz had been growing since I had taken Derek Walcott's workshop during my first semester at Harvard Divinity School, the year after I graduated from my blue-collar college, amazed that I could roam almost at will inside the offerings, both graduate and undergraduate alike. One had to apply to the workshops with samples of one's work, which I submitted. No guarantee. Though I had been accepted into Derek Walcott's there was no assurance I would be accepted into Seamus's workshop, which, if it had not been the entire reason for applying to HDS, had been its perhaps most subversive attraction. When I walked up the steps to the English Department I felt the pit of my stomach opening – would my name be on the list? I walked through the door and headed for the board where the winnowed list had been tacked – only 12 names from however many submissions. I looked and didn't see mine. I walked out, down the steps, started down the street, and stopped. Then I walked back, unaccountably, up the stairs again and over to the board and to the list. My name was there. I had somehow missed my own name.

That first meeting, I took my seat in the seminar room, in Sever Hall in Harvard Yard, grateful beyond gratitude I had made the cut. All of us who had found their names on the sheet tacked up in the English Department sat around the big table. Seamus had just taken his seat at the head near the door to the hallway. Classes were just letting in and letting out and we were about to settle in, looking to Seamus, when a second door leading to the classroom opened and in filed one student after another, making their way along the edge of the room and out the front door, I had the impression, to catch a glimpse of the famous poet.

Following the student parade into the hall that first class was a harbinger for the rest of the term. Seamus had an ease with the class and each member

of it, and a generous, responsive treatment of our work, most of it well
meaning and smart but hampered in some way and, at least in my case,
overwrought. He pushed us with exercises and individually tailored reading –
for me, Thomas Kinsella's "Nightwalker" – and took us seriously and met each
of us for tutorials. "Leave off the sky hook", was one piece of advice he gave
for one of my poems, belabored with an epigraph. In other words, trust your
own nubbed treasures. By the end of the semester he left me with a sense of
confirmation far beyond my accomplishment, and wrote a recommendation
that I still treasure and that gave me further entry into the world of poetry
well beyond my beginnings. He helped to give me a way of mastering my own
"rungs of the air" despite the gravities and necessities of doctoral programs
and the politics of academia and the vagaries of sheer happenstance.

———

The last time I saw Seamus he was in the center of a crowd of well-wishers,
orbits, epicycles of regard and self-regard approaching then departing from
the attractor, and Seamus with his interested look and welcoming smile. It
was the reception at the Associated Writing Programs Convention in
Boston, 2013 after the Big Event of his onstage conversation with Derek
Walcott, moderated by Rosanna Warren. He looked himself, older of
course since I last saw him, and a little worn, tired. I walked up briefly and
congratulated him. Christine lingered a little longer, laughing with him. He
would be dead in six months, a sonic boom of stunned silence echoing
around the world, the net humming beyond the often "sulphurous news of
poets and poetry." At the funeral – hundreds of orbiters, famous and not so
famous, and the close true friends and family members, huddling. Homilies.
A country stopped as for the loss of a head of state. And homage after
homage from heads of state.

Now he has become, as Auden said of Yeats, his admirers. When I think
of the extent of the influence of his gravity on my life, outer orbiter that I
am, I think past myself to an afternoon in Belfast some five or six years
before he died. I'm sitting across from a young Pakistani woman in a café
near the Linen Hall Library. It is the first time we've met, a rendezvous
arranged via e-mail and over time across half the globe from Pakistan to the
American Midwest. Her eyes are bright and dark and look quietly intense
with her face warmly framed by the hijab she wears. Her name is Saima
Kahn. A young scholar of Seamus's work, she has traveled from the

University of Ulster at Coleraine to meet on my brief trip to Belfast. Several years before, I received an e-mail from her when she was still living in Pakistan. She loved Seamus Heaney's poems, she said, and had read my book, *Passage to the Center: Imagination and the Sacred in the Poetry of Seamus Heaney*. She was taking a chance, an outside chance that I might respond to her questions about his work and my work. She had some insights, she said, about Seamus Heaney's poetry and its relation to Sufism. Her mother had told her not to expect a reply.

So began an e-mail exchange between a young Sufi woman in Pakistan with aspirations to pursue a degree in the West focusing on Seamus Heaney's poetry and her own faith and an American college professor, then living in Kenosha, Wisconsin. Though occasional, our transglobal correspondence lasted a few years before our meeting in the Belfast café. Planet Seamus had indeed enough gravitational pull to bring together two individuals from far-flung zones through the attractive power of his work – a centrifugal as well as centripetal force reaching out to gather apparent disparities together around the attracting center of his work and his life, at once verifying of its roots and venturesome in its routes. At the end of his great poem "Alphabets", an astronaut "sees all he has sprung from / the risen, aqueous singular, lucent O – like a magnified and bouyant ovum", and the reader cannot but be held by a figure of exquisite brilliance in which the global and the local, the many and the one, the beginning and the end, align in perfect relation. We encounter a gravity akin to grace – the same gravity and grace in the poetry and as in life that was Seamus Heaney's great gift.

Daniel Tobin was born in Brooklyn in 1958 and has degrees from Iona College, Harvard University and the University of Virginia. He is the author of six books of poems, most recently Second Things, Belated Heavens *(2011) and* The Net *(2014), both from Four Way Books. He has also published two critical studies,* Passage to the Center: Imagination and the Sacred in the Poetry of Seamus Heaney *(University of Kentucky Press, 1999) and* Awake in America: On Irish-American Poetry *(University of Notre Dame Press, 2011). He teaches in the Department of Writing, Literature and Publishing at Emerson College, Boston.*

TWO REFLECTIONS

Seán Lysaght

More truly and more strange.

WINTERING OUT

I first heard Seamus Heaney's name mentioned by my father, who had *Death of a Naturalist* and *Door into the Dark* on his shelves at home. They were housed among other paperbacks of poetry and short stories on a small bookcase near the fire in what we called the front room. It was the start of the seventies, and I sensed a growing stir around this new poet of the countryside, the natural world, and rural life. My father would repeat a phrase from the Ardboe Point poem in *Door into the Dark*:

> Right along the lough shore
> A smoke of flies
> Drifts thick in the sunset.

That "smoke of flies" brought us both back to evenings on the Camogue River in County Limerick, where we fished the evening rise for brown trout.

One summer in the early seventies, we went to the inaugural North Cork Writers' Festival in Doneraile. In those days the calendar of literary festivals in Ireland was scant: Doneraile was vying with only Listowel Writers' Week and the Yeats Summer School, as I remember it. The accent at Doneraile was on the work of Elizabeth Bowen from nearby Bowenscourt, on Edmund Spenser, who had lived at Kilcolman, and on the novelist Canon Sheehan. In those pre-internet days, several booksellers turned out to offer books for sale in the convent hall, and among the volumes on display was the distinct, fresh cover of Seamus Heaney's new book *Wintering Out*, in its first appearance in 1972.

As is the way with a teenager trying to find his own path, to establish his territory, *Wintering Out* was a book I could make my own. Its technique was less familiar than the earlier volumes. It had steered away from the longer, richer lines of its predecessors to test a sparer world, one that was troubled by the deteriorating situation in Ireland and by the writer's distance from those events. It remains for me also a new object. The blue, grey, and white cover, with its bold Albertus font, belongs to the great stable of covers designed by Berthold Wolpe for Faber. These colours were austere compared with the earlier rich greens, pink, and red. I felt that that austerity was matched by the placing of printed characters on the page; although, if I had looked carefully, I would have seen the same thrift in the three brief poems that open *Door into the Dark*.

The title page of *Wintering Out* shares a common format with the first two collections, and with *North* (after which time Berthold Wolpe retired, in 1975). The collection's title is in a font called Monotype Old Style, lettered in capitals, in a format known as outline, where the strokes of the letters are hollowed out, as it were: this has the effect of giving the letters the appearance of characters sculpted in stone; and it confers a kind of permanence, of memorial.

Underneath this, in a different italic font rather like Courier, we read "by Seamus Heaney." The preposition in front of the name was dropped in later conventions for title pages and was not always used on the title pages of contemporary volumes by Faber. When set underneath the memorial capitals of the title, this sign of authorship appears humble, tentative, almost submissive in its setting.

The poems themselves were set in a font very like Courier (Courier is currently fashionable among designers because of associations with what's called "postwar retro" and the days of the typewriter). But the initial capital of each poem was set in the outline Monotype, the font used for the title on the title page: by doing this, each poem in its authenticating Courier font was tagged at the start by memorial permanence.

Another striking feature of the layout of the first four books was each poem's title, set very high on the page, with a large space separating it from the poem itself, about seven lines' worth. This had the effect of highlighting the blank paper surface, a territory of silence around the words themselves that the poems had to work their way out of. As a result, the feeling of origination was pronounced in the placename poems and in others, such as "Bog Oak", "The Last Mummer" and "Oracle."

These were particular features of *Wintering Out* — not all unique to that collection — that I especially relished at the time, because for me they were part of an original discovery.

I still have my father's paperback copy of that early edition, in a 1973 reprint, where the layout is identical with the true first edition. Faber unusually published the 1972 paperback before the hardback, in a run of 2,500 copies; the hardback came the following year, dated 1973. So the first paperback has the status of first edition. I was browsing in a second-hand shop in Belfast a number of years ago when I came across a first paperback edition, and asked for the price: "two-fifty", I was told. I thought I had found a bookdealer's bargain, but as I walked to the till it dawned on me that the lady was asking for £250 sterling for this copy, so I retreated, and put it back on the shelf. Nowadays, I content myself with the 1973 paperback reprint; of all Heaney's books, it is the one I return to most often.

—

FINDING A VOICE

A challenge every aspiring poet faces is how to find and establish a voice at the busy crossroads of poetry. This challenge is deceptive, because language seems to offer an immediate, intimate expression, and yet as soon as we put pen to paper, or fingers to keyboard, the raw material resists, and we are haunted by the voices of others who have gone before us. Language echoes with the voices of great talents; the colours we had chosen to paint a distinctive world of our own carry the trademarks and copyright notices of others.

An aspect of this problem is that one of the voices that get us started in many instances is the voice of ambition. This voice is not one we hear, but is part of our inner dialogue with ourselves, setting a target, framing a set of aspirations. Ambition in itself is not very interesting to anyone else; in fact, it is rather unseemly. However a poet might be driven, however deep the compulsion, there is a vanity in the desire to emulate, to compete, that interferes with the poem's chance of unfolding in its own energies, on the page or in front of an audience.

In my limited experience of writers' groups and creative-writing classes, I find another impulse, which pulls in the opposite direction. That is, to lack ambition, to think of poems and jottings as private, as part of the dialogue with oneself. The very fact of coming to a writers' group or class says how lonely and unsatisfying the dialogue with oneself must be. At the end of the day, the craft of poetry usually happens somewhere between too much and too little ambition, and holds its own line between them.

If language were only at the service of our privacy, it would not stand much chance of communicating anything. The fact is – and this is the miracle of language – that we engage with a medium that has its own history, its lineaments, and associations; in the case of English, both that history and its range across the continents are awesome in their potential.

Nowadays, we are probably poorly schooled in the sense of language as an instrument. The prejudices of language teaching insist on communication; we are supposed to "pick up" foreign languages, as if they were litter on a street, and not systems of their own, with structure and codes of grammar.

Our approach to poetry as writers does not have to be formalized into a technical system, but an awareness of language as a set of tools, of our notebooks as rooms full of instruments, can be helpful. This is a strange place, you might say, for a person to find their voice, in this lumber-room of décor and device that we usually call "the tradition." Still, even the most distinctive, self-driven poets have come from somewhere; many of our strongest poets wear the badge of their debts with pride.

In this way of looking at the problem, we are thinking of a poet's language as a thing that is separate from the poet, a kind of apparatus, a weird, complicated machinery that is never fully mastered. You could use the analogy of a bicycle to picture this. The first attempts at keeping balance can be unnerving, but as you get the hang of it, you discover a new, thrilling sensation. The machine is not you, but as you get control of it, it becomes an extension of yourself: you are moving more smoothly, with more speed than before, and yet the power at your command is your own force pushing down on the pedals, translated into a new dynamic by the bicycle.

For some writers, the favourite bit of machinery is metaphor and simile, for others it's rhyme, assonance, metre, and so on. This goes against the grain for convenors of poetry and writing classes who see communication or perhaps therapy as the heart of the craft. Be that as it may, there is a delight in working with the apparatus of language in poetry akin to the thrill of learning to ride a bicycle.

I'm not trying to enforce any standard weights and measures here, but I would make the case for rhyme as part of the stock-in-trade of the poet, at whatever stage in the craft. Finding rhymes is a basic pleasure in poetry at every level of the Muse-chain, from doggerel to Parnassus, and it is part of a common expectation. Rhyme can also be practised with a view to going beyond it, as Ted Hughes did, to find what Wallace Stevens called "ghostlier demarcations, keener sounds." Even in the voice of the freest of poets, poetry has been burnished by its passage through different forms, structures and conventions.

And what of the voice? In poetry, there's no direct line from the confused knot of desires and inhibitions we start out with, to the settled appearance of a book in print. But part of that journey is the discovery of other writers and our own tentative steps in the genre. As we write, recite, revise and publish, we commit ourselves to something bigger, to that network of implication represented by language. We approach new spaces and relations that we had not come across before. Stevens expressed this memorably in the final line of an early poem, "Tea at the Palaz of Hoon":

And there I found myself more truly and more strange.

Seán Lysaght was born in 1957 and grew up in Limerick. He was educated at University College, Dublin, where he studied French and English. He has published six collections of poetry and a biography of the naturalist Robert Lloyd Praeger (1865–1953), The Life of a Naturalist *(Four Courts Press, 1998). His recent collections include* The Mouth of a River *(2007), a celebration of the landscape of north Mayo, and a volume of translations from Goethe,* Venetian Epigrams *(2008), both from Gallery Press. He teaches at Galway Mayo Institute of Technology, Castlebar and lives in Westport, Co Mayo.*

ON IRISH MUSIC

Kevin Anderson

A tuba for the wife.

When I was very young, I hardly noticed a gap between Irish music and classical music. Irish music was just music; it was taken for granted and it included a lot of music that just wandered in from all over the place and stayed put. More or less everyody I knew would consider going to see an opera, because it was there and because we couldn't see why not. I suppose Anew McMaster's audiences for Shakespeare had that attitude. Nobody had told them it wasn't for the likes of them.

Eventually I understood that classical meant a kind of emancipation, belonged with reading Dostoyevsky and with some kind of personal development that would rescue you from the undignified aspects of your own family. I don't think it implied social mobility in the usual sense; it had to do with the contents of your own head. I didn't want to be like my own family but I assumed they didn't either and that they could be set free by going to a few classical concerts, and by Culture in general. I once gave my mother a birthday present of the complete poems of Shelley. I was accused of giving her a book I wanted to read myself but I really thought she would want to read it as much as I did. And she would be allowed to read it first.

Concerts could include a bit of everything. I remember one that had horses from the Theatre Royal, some banjo playing and a tenor singing something from *Maritana* ("Let me like a soldier fall ... This breast expanding for the ball.") Operas were aimed at everybody, Waterford was quite excited about Vincent Wallace and Gounod's *Faust* would come up naturally in conversation. My grandmother held a grudge against Pinkerton in *Madame Butterfly,* seemed well informed about the anti-American feeling the opera stirred up and was willing to go and see the opera if transport was offered and brandy provided.

When my grandmother put on a hooley she'd ring up somewhere, an accordion player would turn up and play all night for dancing. What he played was what my grandmother considered music, jigs and reels and ballroom tunes as well – I remember the women of the family as waltzers and very reluctant foot-stampers. But there was no change of gear – as I think there would be now – between the jigs and the slinkier stuff.

Leo Rowsome's son Liam went to our school. The Rowsomes were a family of authority in traditional music, Leo a piper, Liam a fiddler. Liam would play at school concerts but it was usually Gounod's "Ave Maria." The Christian Brothers hardly noticed and the only thing I remember the school choir singing was Purcell's *Nymphs and Shepherds*, as schools all over the Brtish Empire used to do. The irony of the Christian Brothers dealing with the words or even the word "nymph" didn't occur to any of us till later.

My piano teacher, the 80-something-year-old George Harrison, was a pupil of Sir Robert Stewart and Michele Esposito, taught piano at the Church of Ireland Training College in Kildare Street and was organist at St George's Church in Hardwicke Place, whose bells Leopold Bloom hears at the beginning of *Ulysses*. He drove from Clontarf to my uncle's butcher shop on the Malahide Road; he had obviously learned the route before traffic lights, paid them little attention and never had an accident, although those who had to share the road with him may not have been so lucky.

Mr Harrison's Irish music was the sort of thing you could sing in parlours. He often accompainied singers at the Ancient Concert Rooms in programmes like the ones Molly Bloom sang in. The music he took seriously included the organ sonatas of Mendelssohn and Reinecke, with a soft spot for Guilmant. He used to play me Edwin Lemare's *Andantino* – the *Moonlight and Roses* tune – because he suspected me of snootiness and a willingness to play discordant modern music.

It was very comfortable and colonial. No great effort had been made towards an Irish national music, to try what Dvořák, Smetana, Bartók and Kodály had done, and nobody seemed to know about the way eighteenth-century Scottish music entered the drawing room without being entirely castrated. Musicians played whatever was around and was wanted and I think this must have been how things usually were in Ireland.

Years and years later, having been educated, I was looking at the Goodman Collection in Trinity College – 2,500 pipe tunes collected by Canon Goodman in County Kerry around the Famine years – and the repertoire looked like my grandmother could have phoned one of Goodman's piper sources and that they too would have played something of everything for her hooley. Neither Goodman nor his pipers partitioned their music. His collection had tunes from Scotland, the US and from nowhere in particular. I would love to hear *Dixie* on the pipes – it's in the collection – and to know where a tune called *Ireland Welcomes the Union* came from.

After independence the new state seems to have had a very general idea that Ireland should have music the way other countries had music and that a bit of gentrification would be good for us. But gentrification is a vague ambition and the Free State never seemed to have very definite ideas about what kind of state it wanted to be. It had plenty of hazy ideas about how its citizens would live lives of puritanical freedom but it never occurred to politicians to think of ways and means to organize this. Many hearts seemed to be in the right place but Irish heads were doing very little work of any kind at all.

I think we could have grown normally. We could have gone on enjoying *Maritana* and *The Lily of Killarney* and gone on from there to maybe deciding we didn't really need Wagner but saw the point of Bartók. Instead we decided classical music was, in a way, beyond us because of who we were; but that we'd import it ready made and eventually learn to live up to it.

A relation of ours, P.J. Stephenson, was head of Dublin City Libraries and was very proud of the music section in Pearse Street. An effort had been made. When it was pointed out that the library had bound together the violin and the piano parts of a set of Beethoven sonatas, making them impossibe to play from, P.J. didn't really see what the fuss was about. He had bought the music; it was on the shelves. It was up to the rest of us to do our bit and stop whingeing. We couldn't use the books but we owned them, didn't we?

So we blundered on and some of the blundering was excellent. We would have an army and the army would have music. Prussians were good at this so we had Prussian bandmasters and they brought their music with them. I remember playing wind music in a little group in the Academy on Westland Row conducted by a young Irish army bandmaster who I think must have been Fred O'Callaghan. He brought along the Prussian part-books from his barracks and for many evenings we played our way through some of the most irresistible military music in the world. I suspect that only in Ireland could the young have been allowed to be immersed in this intoxicating musical militarism. If Germany was the devil, it sure as hell had the best tunes.

The Raidió Éireann Symphony Orchestra existed, I think, for the same reason. Other states had a national orchestra so we should have one too. We had very few classical players so they went around post-World War II

Europe gathering players. The result was made up of various Austro-Hungarians from regions we were mostly unaware of; Italians who wanted to go home and eventually did; French Algerians; Polish Jews; some French and Germans with a Past. Their Past was hypothetical: we assumed every German had one. This group had no trouble establishing a unified missionary sense that they were better than Irish players and that, even if they didn't play better, they belonged to a superior tradition which we could never ever understand. It was music partitioning. The informal language of the orchestra was mostly German.

I remember, after a rehearsal, a Viennese lady shaking her head and telling me that of course, unfortunately, Irish people could never hope to play this music properly. I thought she meant the Delius piece we had just played with some of the right notes but very little of the right intonation. Not at all. She meant the Strauss waltz we had played quite well. Of course, we had never been to the Musikverein, were hopelessly non-Viennese and could not ever hope to be, or to approach, that condition. I said nothing. Now I realize how she herself belonged to that tradition and had fled for her life from it.

Anyway, you will understand that the orchestra knew nothing about Irish music and had no wish to learn. They did know Irish music existed, because every year they had to play a St Patrick's Day concert. This was a long slog through a series of arrangements of Irish tunes for full orchestra by the small army of licensed Irish composers. They were few and most of them seemed to be in trouble of the usual kind – Frederick May, whose piece "Sunshine and Shadow" was known in the orchestra as "Whiskey and Soda"; A. J. Potter, who taught at the Royal Academy with a bit of a gleam in his eye but sometimes, having failed to find his way home, would wander around Dublin bars explaining that he needed to buy a tuba for his wife. You can perhaps imagine the arrangements. You will probably have to; I can't imagine anyone wanting to play them now.

The concert was in the Phoenix Hall, the studio where the orchestra rehearsed and for most of the year gave Tuesday and Friday concerts to smatterings of an "invited" audience. There is something deadening about studios and this something was exemplified in every aspect of the Phoenix Hall. The sound was dead; the audience, when there was one, was distant. For the orchestra, it was their nine-to-five workplace. They didn't dress up and they behaved there like guys in their garden sheds. There were a fair number of women in the orchestra. They dressed better but it would have taken many more well-dressed women to make a real event of a studio concert. Studio audiences are not real audiences. They are allowed in, nothing encourages them to get excited or involved and there was hardly even any sense of excitement or occasion. This had a very disheartening effect on the St Patrick's Day concert.

The music, even though padded up orchestrally, would keep on trying to get lift-off but mostly it sounded like a jig or a reel being battered to death by stiff-wristed bows and by a brass section that, quite sensibly, couldn't find a good reason to play the notes they had to play.

I remember playing in one of these as an apprentice horn player. That night there was Mary O'Hara with her harp, a man playing the mandocello, a small group and the orchestra. There was only a limited amount of horn-playing needed so I was sometimes hovering offstage. The mandocellist was hovering more actively. He hated the whole thing, mostly, I think, because he thought the place was full of musical snobs. Amongst other grievances, Raidió Éireann had started auditioning traditional players before they would employ them. They had also forbidden piano accompaniments for traditional music – a very good idea considering the kind of accompaniments being played and later ridiculed into oblivion by Seán Ó Riada. None of this was popular with the traditional players, who usually had no bees in their bonnets about musical purity but had many many bees about how much easier it was to play with accompaniment than without. "No piano, no Maguire" was the position of Sean Maguire the fiddler, according to the Mandocello man, who was hanging around the entry door to the platform shuddering at every typical orchestral gesture. He particularly hated tympani – Kurt Goedicke, a very German-looking German, was doing timpani glissandos with extra enthusiasm.

Mary O'Hara did no loitering. She was fetched from her dressing room in good time for her entry and stood ready to pounce, with Michael Garvey, the producer of the show, holding one of the most neutral areas of her cardigan between index finger and thumb, ready to retain it when she marched on stage. He had married Mercedes Bolger the harpist and the pair of them discused marriage in a code incomprehensible to me. She went on and did her usual dynamic and self-contained performance. The orchestra were quite impressed but mostly they were getting ready for their next piece. They played this – me too, but I can't remember what it was.

It finished and people started clearing a space at the front for the small group. They walked on, slow and slightly stooped as if they were leaving a house on a windy night. They were dressed in what I remember as black, ancestral double-breasted suits. They looked dark, cagy, confident but with no sense of assertion. There was something about them that caught the orchestra's attention even before they played a note – their non-classical demeanour, their self-contained air. They started to play and you could feel a musical charge go through the orchestra. We now know what a slow air and a bit of magical piping can do. The orchestra had no idea what had hit them. Despite their snobbery, they were musicians and there was no denying the force or quality of what they were listening to. Or the discipline. The group was Ceoltóirí Chualann and Seán Ó Riada.

Ó Riada was known to the orchestra in ways similar to the way interesting delinquents are known to the police. He had conducted one of his Nomos pieces at a Prom wearing trousers that had given up all hope of ever reaching his ankles, waving in a very angular way and, I think, trying not to take the whole thing too seriously. It was one way to deal with an orchestra who had very little interest in new music and some disdain for anything non-continental.

There has been some critical disappointment with what Ó Riada achieved in classical music, but I think the classical world in Ireland as he found it would never have allowed him to develop. RTÉ were to appoint Tibor Paul chief conductor and music director of the whole station, a bargain basement von Karajan, a bully with an elliptical attitude to the English language. "The Representation of Chaos" became "The Representation of Cows." There was no sense that an Irish conductor would be given a fair chance. Eventually Prionnsías Ó Duinn was given a chance when, after serving his time in the salt mines of the cello section, he was given a concert, stopped the orchestra after a few bars of the Shostakovitch first symphony at his first rehearsal, had something coherent to say and went on being succinctly coherent for years and years.

Ó Riada would have been unable, I think, to fit in to all this, to take part in the ritual dances that music people wove around each other as they stumbled towards musical normality. It took Brian Boydell a horribly long time to be taken on by Trinity and you can see from Charles Acton's descriptions of his friend that what stood in Boydell's way was nothing to do with his musical abilities. Colonel J.M. Doyle was given what seemed like ritual engagements with the orchestra, to which the orchestra reacted with very little attention or respect; Éimear Ó Broin was mocked. Neither Ó Riada nor anybody like him would have stood a chance.

I think the Ceoltóirí Chualann setup was a choreographed response to all this – the deliberation, the austerely disciplined arrangements in that St Patrick's Day concert, the highly organized mischief of it all. I believe Ó Riada's guerrilla war had a far greater effect than any number of classical masterpieces would have done. And the classical masterpieces were not achieveable then. They would have needed a more developed infrastructure based on wider audiences and greater opportunities to try, fail and try again.

I remember playing in the first concerts the orchestra gave in Cork. The Cork ladies came in ballgowns and we played sensationally large pieces – Mahler's first symphony; *Ein Heldenleben*. At a children's concert the trombone was demonstrated by Novemo Salvadori playing *When Irish Eyes Are Smiling*. He stood up, grinned, warbled his way through more of the tune than anybody needed, mopped his forehead and bowed.

The Irish musical problem, like all Irish problems, was specifically Irish. But it was also similar to the way classical music locked itself away in a subsidized attic and refused to make sense during the sixties and seventies. I have no idea where we, or anybody else, stand now in relation to the most developed, complex and humanly significant music we know of. I hope we can all listen to it with innocent ears but I doubt it.

My Goodman excursion was on behalf of Brendan Mulkere's London Irish Festival. Nuala Ní Dhomhnaill had told us she had had a dream about the missing words for Goodman's tunes and we were getting the tunes so she could write her own words for them and she did a few before the festival was undermined by London Irish civil wars.

Brendan ran, by the skin of its teeth, an Irish centre in Kilburn and for a while you could hear unique things there. Groups of Connemara men would gather and sing to each other in a tight, intimate circle. When they did, silence radiated out among the surrounding crowd, who knew they had to listen by not seeming to listen. Brendan, although guilty of doing things to banjos and accordions that the Vatican would have banned if it understood them, played the fiddle the way Vivaldi or Mozart would have understood.

There was a London pub called the Fiddler's Elbow. I was a bit snooty about the name until I started to pay attention to Brendan's right elbow – an energetic and subtle musical instrument in its own right. The Raidió Éireann orchestra was dedicated, I realized, to the abolition of the elbow. The many arms of its string section aimed at elimintating the tiny rhythmic inflections and nudges that string players used to articulate phrases until the factory orchestras of the twentieth century reduced them to a chorus of unanimous automatons.

As Brendan's festival developed we heard many successful groups plugging themsleves into world music, Celtic music or any available record-shop category. Most of them had non-existent elbows and little or no relation to the most fundamental source of Irish music – the Irish language. We watched *Riverdance* do its wonderful work for dancing while its music ironed out the subtle rhythmic intelligence the dance was developed to match. While *Riverdance* was starting to bestride the world, we had Tommy Peoples, a magnificent fiddler with one of the most exact and refined ears I have ever come across. His Donegal style is maybe the most exposed and precise in Ireland and we heard him every night land precisely on the middle of every note, playing with such rhythmic subtlety that you could sense a perfect, implied rhythm section following his every move.

Something was being lost. Styles of playing we had owned but had taken for granted will now perhaps have to be re-learned in the way the early music movement has had to rethink bowing, phrasing and tempo to make any sense of older music. Maybe the two cultures – traditional and classical – should not have been so afraid of each other. The extraordinary Budapest Festival Orchestra play encores by putting their orchestral instruments aside and ranting their way through traditional tunes.

As far as I can see from over here in Scotland, the RTÉ orchestras are no longer the strange, punitive, inhibited groups I knew and Irish composers seem much more normal than the hesitant, problematic characters I came across in the fifties and sixties. I hope it's all better than it was and I really hope that England is no longer the only place where Irish traditions survive undamaged, normal, and growing. The Mulkere elbow is still operating, as are other excellent older elbows, so it might not be too late after all.

Kevin Anderson was born in Dublin in 1942. He studied at the Dublin College of Music, the Royal Academy and the Brussels Conservatoire; played the horn in various orchestras; founded the Edinburgh Early Music Centre; and was for many years on the music staff of the Edinburgh Academy. He worked on Brendan Mulkere's London Irish Festival, Síol Phádraig, during the 1990s, an experience that produced his unpublished novel London, Ireland. *He wrote* The Wolf and Peter *for narrator and the Moving Goalposts Jazz Orchestra, with Francis Cowan;* Mothers and Fathers *for school choirs and big band; a series of songs for the singer Melanie O'Reilly; and* Men: An Irish Musical. *He was one of Louis de Paor's translators for* The Brindled Cat and the Nightingale's Tongue *(Bloodaxe, 2004), as well as a for his* Ag Greadadh Bas sa Reilig *and* Agus Rud Eile de *(both from Cló Iar-Chonnachta). He organized the touring programme of* An Leabhar Mór / The Great Book of Gaelic *and wrote the script for Murray Grigor's film of the project,* Is Mise an Teanga.

EMOTION AND SONG *AS GAEILGE*

Lillis Ó Laoire

Last night.

A Phaidí a ghrá má d'imigh tú go dtige tú slán
Char imigh tú nó gur lagaigh tú an croí a bhí in mo chliabh
Dá mbíodh coite agam a d'iomróchadh do dhiaidhse long nó bád
Is go bhfuil an fharraige ina tonna gorma agus ní féidir domh snámh

A Phaidí cad chuige ar thréig tú mé mar gheall le mnaoi ná le stór
A Phaidí cad chuige ar thréig tú mé mar gheall le cíos ná le hór
A Phaidí do chúl buí daite is do bhéilín binn
Go dté mé i dtalamh beidh cuimhne agam ar do chomhrá liom.

Paddy, my love, since you've left, may you return again whole
When you left you weakened my heart and my soul
If I had a canoe that could swim after you a ship or a boat
But the ocean's blue waves oppose me and I have no power to float

Paddy why did you abandon me for a woman and wealth
Paddy why did you abandon me for rents and for gold
Paddy, with your bright yellow hair and your sweet little mouth
Till I go to my grave I will remember your encounter with me.

I first came across this song in archive recordings of Tory Island singers made by Ned Nugent and Proinsias Ó Conluain and subsequently heard live singers from Tory, some of whom have provided the RTÉ archives with this very song sung live. I went on to record the song myself with two of them in 1992 and released the recording that same year on a cassette with Cló Iar-Chonnacht. First impressions of the song for me centred on the melody, a hexatonic tune – that is, with only six notes as opposed to the standard seven, an effect that can create a soaring, spacious effect that transfers to the lyrics. The tune contains wide intervals that reinforce the modal structure and that augment the powerful lyrics, deepening and intensifying the plangent feelings of longing and loss they express.

The song belongs to an intertwining network of lyrics that encompass many other similar songs, those that Hyde made famous in *The Love Songs of Connacht*, later appropriated by Synge to such marvellous effect in his plays. Joyce himself was not immune to their power and they also feature both overtly and clandestinely in his work. These very lyrics can be found as part of a much more widely known song. "An Droighneán Donn", "The Blackthorn Bush", a Gaelic love song that existed in Irish, crossed languages, and became known in macaronic- and English-only versions throughout Ireland.

Seán Ó Tuama characterized such songs as belonging to the genre of *chansons de jeune fille* – Irish expressions of troubadour types – and found parallels in French and other European languages, connecting the lyrics to a wider European framework of emotional expression that flourished throughout the middle ages. Indeed, the concepts are still found in modern popular song. The striking apostrophe that typifies many of these lyrics testifies to their direct appeal to the emotions and links them implicitly with the genre of lament (*caoineadh*) in which apostrophe is a central trope. This song, ostensibly about a young girl deserted by her unfaithful male lover for another, more materially appealing, spouse, can be read as a text saturated with the gendered ideology of patriarchy, where double standards of behaviour allowed men the luxury of ending relationships with impunity without the censorious ostracism suffered by the women they jilted. This exclusion reached its extreme point if women became pregnant and bore children out of wedlock, so that, as another lyric from a related song puts it:

Nach trua mé inniu agus nach trua mé amárach
Mo theach fuar folamh is gan agam preáta
Níl aon deoir bhainne agam is gile ná an t-uisce
Tá leanbh óg agam is tá m'fhortún briste

Pity me today and pity me tomorrow
My house cold and empty with not even a potato
I have no drop of milk but colourless water
I have a young baby and my fortune is broken.

The reference to fortune encompasses the dowry system where women were expected to bring wealth into the families they intermarried with. Such a dowry was forfeit if any stain were known to tarnish a girl's spotless reputation. Of course, this ideology also condoned and helped perpetuate systematized, instutionalized segregration of women in the Magdalene Laundries and in mother-and-baby homes, such as have been recently portrayed in films such as *Philomena*. However, this reading of the song is a general interpretation that can be applied across the whole genre without reference to any particular circumstances. But these circumstances did exist – and Douglas Hyde learned this when he met Bríd Nic Mhuiris Rua in County Roscommon, who sang such a song for him and whose fate, he later learned, had been the same as that of the female speaker in the song she sang.

"A Phaidí a Ghrá" also accrued localized particular stories wherever it was found. On Aranmore Island Róise Uí Ghrianna sang a version and had a long narrative to precede it, naming characters and places involved. Her story centred on emigration to America and she told of how the party accompanying the man who was leaving stopped in Crolly for a rest. The man's sweetheart sang this song, which she had composed specially for the event. He was so moved by her performance that he decided to stay at home. Róise said that the need to emigrate recurred and that he did leave the second time, eventually dying of thirst while crossing the desert.

In Tory, strikingly, themes of love, emigration, and death also emerge in the narratives that anchor the performance of the song in that particular place. The song is linked to the Dixon family on Tory, and especially to one brother, fittingly called Pádraig, who emigrated to the US in August 1909. He died less than three months later of typhoid fever, in Bristol County, Pennsylvania, an Irish enclave to which his sister had preceded him in 1906 and where she subsequently lived out a long life. However, the story in Tory was different, with some believing firmly that the young man had died of a broken heart because he had emigrated and missed his home so much. The term *cumha* is always mentioned in relation to such feelings of separation and alienation, frequently being associated with homesickness. Such feelings were first identified among Swiss soldiers in the late seventeenth century by Johannes Hofer, who named the condition as *nostalgia* – a compound of two Greek words, *nostos* (return to the native land) and *algon* (sorrow or grief). Our present understanding of this term is one of trivialized sentimentality; but the harrowing scenes witnessed over the years at airports as Irish youth departed for foreign parts, and the headlines concerning the tragic and premature deaths of young Irish people abroad recently, especially in Australia, reveal that such narratives can still engage and move us deeply.

When news of Pádraig Dixon's death arrived in Tory, people would have flocked to the house to sympathize with his parents and siblings, a normal part of mourning rituals in such a close-knit community. Oral narrative suggests that his mother Méabha (1850–1942) requested that the song "A Phaidí a Ghrá" be sung in his memory and that a woman present, known to be a good singer, obliged. Ever afterwards the song remained a particular favourite of the Dixons and they requested it frequently at dances and other entertainments. This continued into the 1940s and 1950s, a whole generation after the young man had died tragically away from home. And the narrative was again told to me in the 1990s as I became familiar with the song and its background in Tory. Themes of love, emigration, alienation, independence, and connectedness cluster around the song – themes that are central to Irish emotional life. These themes and issues come to the fore when the song is performed, renewing, through art, the ways in which we are able to mediate the challenges of existence. This expression is a manifestation of *cumha*, a feeling of longing or pining set off by a sense of dislocation, indicating an emotional dissonance and a wish to end those feelings of loss and separation.

Studying the life of Seosamh Ó hÉanaí (Joe Heaney) and the relationship between emotion and song provides another way to observe similar cultural patterns and ideals. For Heaney, whose songs and singing represented perhaps his foremost emotional outlook, every song he sang was sung with conviction and passion, despite less than ideal performance conditions at times. A man known for his volatile temper, he was nevertheless a supreme interpreter of songs in Irish and in English, his wish always to inhabit the emotional core. He sang many humorous, light-hearted songs, but a sense of turbulence and emotional turmoil characterized much of his life and that came across in his singing. One religious song that became a signature item was "Caoineadh na dTrí Muire", "The Lament of the Three Marys" – or "Caoineadh na Páise", "The Lament for the Passion", as it was known in his native Carna. Heaney connected very powerfully to this piece and taught it to many of his students – explaining the story of Good Friday and how his grandmother of Carna sang this hymn in his youth on that day. The song links the keening tradition with the religious tradition, allowing for the inclusion of a strong emotional element into the story of the Passion, reducing the distance in time and space between its performers in rural Ireland and the original events. Likewise, it legitimized the practice of keening as something that Mary had performed for Christ, making it a duty for corpses to be keened, despite official attempts to proscribe it. Heaney's performance of "Caoineadh na dTrí Muire" represents the excluded voice in Irish religious practice. Cullen's reforms in the nineteenth century attempted to replace such practices that had flourished because of the organizational challenges of the church in the seventeenth and eighteenth centuries, but were now to be condemned as benighted superstition. Heaney's strong emotional connection to the traditional practices of his youth led him to include this item. Indeed, he often spoke of his attempts to gain recognition for such hymns in the modern liturgy.

Heaney's song "Bean an Leanna" represents another side of his character. The song intimates a broken love affair where the male speaker has been brought low by too great a fondness for alcohol. He remains devoted to his beloved, while acknowledging that the two of them cannot be together.

Éirigh in do shuí a bhean a' leanna
Is ná fan le do chaipín a ghléas
Nó go dtuga tú dúinn braon uisce beatha
Nó cart de do chuid leanna féin
Ó beidh muid ag ól go dtí maidin
Seo sláinte na bhfear uilig go léir
'S nuair a fhágfas an mháistreás an baile
Beidh an cailín is deise agam féin.

Bhí mise oíche is mé súgach
Is mé ag trial ar thigh Mhicil sa ngleann
Bhí stíoncán ag píobaire coach ann
Agus jug poitín líonta aige ar clár
Ó thit muide lag marbh síos ann
Níor fhan brí inár gcois ná inár láimh
Ach seo beannacht shíol Éabh is shíol
Ádhaimh díbh
Agus íocfaidh mé féin an reicneáil.

Ó is a Dhia céard a dhéanfas mé amárach
Nuair a fheicfeas mé mo ghrá ag goil aniar
Ní fhéadfaidh mé a thíocht ina láthair

Ar mhéad is bhí eadrainn riamh
Nuair a smaoiním ar a súgradh is ar a gáire
Ar fhinneacht a dhá láimhín a bhí fial
Ó titim i lionndubh is i ndólás
Agus goilim péin mórán na diaidh.

Rise up landlady
Don't wait to fix your cap
Til you give us a drop of whiskey
Or a quart of your own beer
O we will be drinking til morning
Here's a health to the men over all
And when the mistress leaves home
The prettiest girl will be mine.

I was one night and me merry
Going towards Micil's in the glen
A blind piper struck up music there
with a full jug of *poitín* on the table
We all fell down dead there
No life remained in our feet or hands
But a blessing from Adam and Eve's
Seed be upon you
And I'll pay the reckoning myself.

God, what will I do tomorrow
When I see my love coming east
I cannot approach her
Even after all that happened with us
When I think of her play and her laugh
On her two fair generous hands
I fall into depression and sorrow
And I cry profusely after her.

The writer Nuala O'Faolain, in her memoir *Are You Somebody?* (1996) records that she once spent some afternoons at the pictures with the lonely Connemara man, who had never mentioned singing. Nuala was a woman who wrote and spoke compellingly about the politics of emotion. As is well known, she died prematurely and performed her death in a very public way. Songs and singing were important elements in her life, a joy she associated especially with her participation in Cumann Merriman's activities, both at the Winter and Summer Schools. Nuala's two memoirs (the other is *Almost There*, 2003) detail her struggle with the challenges of being a modern Irish woman carrying a burden of emotion that seemed to have no other adequate means of expression. As she herself discovered, there was a groundswell of popular reaction to her books that showed deeply and intensely felt emotional lives in Ireland; but regrettably, and all too frequently, borne in silence, untold, unshared, and unresolved. Sharon O'Brien, in her memoir, *The Family Silver* (2004), bravely discusses her personal depression and its connection to her Irish-American heritage, pointing out how silence often became a weapon used by siblings to exclude and to punish each other for real or imagined transgressions. Part of Nuala O'Faolain's achievement was to help break the silence that many ordinary people felt and could not find an alternative to. Despite her experiences, a sense of wonder and joy pervades her memoirs. There is no shying away from life and its vicissitudes. O'Faolain's writing was therapeutic and brought her celebrity and financial security, about which she wrote eloquently and compellingly. In 2008, cancer took Nuala at 68, and she lived only a short time after her illness was diagnosed earlier that year. Nuala mentioned a particular song that seemed to encapsulate and bring some sense of order to the many conflicting emotions she experienced when faced with the shock of imminent death. In her highly emotionally charged interview with Marion Finucane on Radio 1, she mentioned that this song, "Tráthnóna Beag Aréir" by Séamus Ó Grianna, had music and words that managed to express how she was feeling. She mentioned in particular the line "Is a Rí na Glóire gile, tabhair ar ais an oíche aréir", glossing it by adding that it was a call to God in heaven (even though she didn't believe in him) to let her continue to taste the joys of the life that, despite all the setbacks, she still wished to embrace.

"Tráthnóna Beag Aréir" is a song by the writer Séamus Ó Grianna, "Máire", of Rann na Feirste and Dublin. One of the most prolific writers of the Gaelic Revival from 1882 to the present, his work is hardly read today. However, this song, one of at least five that he made, has become an anthem in his native Donegal, across Ulster, and more widely throughout Gaelic-speaking Ireland. Based on an English language song, "The Heather Glen", written by George Sigerson, a prolific writer and translator himself, it surpasses its English language antecedent in all respects. Published in 1926, it quickly became popular in Coláiste Bhríde, Rann na Feirste and spread quickly from there. It is a song in the mode of traditional Gaelic love songs, albeit with an added subtlety and delicacy of expression clearly recalling seventeenth-century "Dánta Grádha", suspended in a reverie about a tryst that happened the previous evening. This one-off meeting between the lovers leaves the speaker wishing for another, while at the same time he acknowledges that it cannot be. The tension between erotic feeling and decorum is one of the most deftly communicated elements in the song. Words such as "ealaín" and "súgradh" are replete with sensual undertone, and the parts of the body mentioned – "folt", "mala", "déad", "com", "béal", "súil", "bráid" – are likewise filled with sensual promise, although this is merely intimated, without becoming explicit.

A sense of charged mysticism pervades the song and I am tempted to see a kind of Mariolatrous echo in the way that the eye is described as being "mar réalt na maidne." "Star of the Morning" is one of the Virgin Mary's epithets, found in the Litany of the Holy Name of Mary, and also an epithet of the Roman goddess Venus. This very suggestion can link this song to other visionary, mystical love poetry and so give it universal appeal. It lies on the cusp of the erotic and the spiritual, a place reminiscent of many of Nuala O'Faolain's attempts to configure her own life-philosophy. Such a disposition links her adoption of this song as a vehicle for expressing strong, contradictory feelings to the long tradition of courtly love begun by Islamic poets and continued in Europe by the troubadours. Idealizing the beloved and the longing for union can be read as an emotional cry for peace and calm. Miguel de Unamuno, the great Spanish philosopher, poet, and novelist believed that faith without doubt was no faith at all – which sugggests that Nuala O'Faolain's cry to God, emerging from her atheism, was perhaps a more profound profession of faith than many less-conflicted pleas. De Unamuno claims that

> Out of this abyss of despair hope may arise, and how this critical position may be the well-spring of human, profoundly human, action and effort, and of solidarity and even of progress ... (Of The Tragic Sense of Life, 1912)

Another of his striking statements there is echoed in Nuala's use of "Tráthnóna Beag Aréir":

Our life is a hope which is continually converting itself into memory and memory in its turn begets hope. Give us leave to live! The eternity that is like an eternal present, without memory and without hope, is death.

By using this song, Nuala grasped at the last straws of hope, something that the portrayal of the character of Úna in *Every Single Minute* by Hugo Hamilton (his fictionalized tribute to Nuala) makes abundantly clear. She also made a lasting gift to the Irish language, by insisting – without labouring the point – on its continuing relevance as a central part of the emotional landscape of this island.

One more point deserves to be made about Nuala O'Faolain and her meditations on the life of the emotions. Her books, especially *Are You Somebody?*, provided many people with a way to express emotional traumas they had endured. Nuala, however, did not just write her story. She performed it at readings in Ireland and across the world. People came especially to hear her read, to see her and experience her re-enactment of this trauma through her readings. The description of one of these events in Aspen, Colorado, by Hugo Hamilton, is striking to me, for the reason that I believe it is the representation of a modern wake, and that Nuala peforms the role of a keening woman, a grief therapist, whose individual channelling of collective grief was eagerly sought by the attendees. I don't have space to enter into the brilliant explorations in *Every Single Minute*, but I invite you to read it yourself, with the words of Eibhlín Dhubh Ní Chonaill's first verse for Art Ó Laoire firmly in your minds:

Mo ghrá go daingean tu
Lá dá bhfaca tu
Ag ceann tí an mhargaidh
Thug mo shúil aire duit
Thug mo chroí taitneamh duit
D'éalaíos óm charaid leat
I bhfad ó bhaile leat.

Nuala's wish for more time is virtually fulfilled in in Hamilton's lightly fictionalized treatment of their trip to Berlin together. *Every Single Minute* details her story once again, connecting it to the story of Verdi's Opera *Don Carlo*, about a king who sacrifices his son for his own gain. It portrays again her insatiable appetite for life – and makes plain that, despite her increasing debility, she tried as hard as she could to bring back last night, to extend her life beyond her own inevitable, premature, and tragic physical finitude.

A scholar and singer, and native of Donegal, Lillis Ó Laoire is a Senior Lecturer in Irish at the School of Language, Literatures and Cultures, National University of Ireland, Galway. He has published extensively on Gaelic song and is currently researching the diaries of the Donegal forklorist Seán Ó hEochaidh (1912–2003), who is widely believed to have compiled the largest collection of Irish folklore made by a single individual (approximately 1,500 interviews).

AN CARRIA
(gearrscéal)

Eithne Ní Ghallchobhair

Cinniúint an charria.

Sheas an carria ar mhullach Shliabh Sneachta. Shocraigh sé a chosa go daingean ar an talamh tirim. Shín a chuid beann amach ar dhá thaobh a chinn. Bhí siad mar a bheadh coróin ann, á bhaisteadh ina rí ar na sléibhte mórthimpeall. D'ardaigh sé a bhráid agus a chloigeann agus d'amharc sé anuas ar na mínte agus na móinte, na locha, na linnte agus an corr-choill a bhí scaipthe amach thíos faoi. Thiontaigh sé a cheann an uile threo: Sliabh an tSruthán Ghairbh, Cnoc an Stualaire, Sliabh na Cloigne Theas, Sliabh na Cloigne Thuaidh. Níorbh fhada uaidh an lá nuair a smaointigh an carria go raibh sé féin chomh neamhfhaiteach le hiolar fíréan Ghleann Bheatha. Níorbh amhlaidh a bhraith sé inniu. Líon a chroí le faitíos.

Bhí tinte fadaithe amuigh ar an talamh, tinte an dochair, an donais agus an uafáis. D'éirigh an deatach agus an toit. Bhí spéir lár lae faoi dhorchadas. Ba bhuan an ghrian agus bogshéideadh na gaoithe fríd an ghleann le deich lá. Foinsí beatha; ábhar báis.

Chonaic an carria crainn loma locartha amach roimhe thíos sa ghleann. Fuinseog, beitheog, dair – crainn dhúchasacha na tíre, crainn a thug foscadh agus dídean d'ainmhithe an talaimh agus d'éanacha na spéire, crainn a thug beocht don chine daonna, crainn a mhair na céadta bliain: blianta dorcha an Ghorta Mhóir, blianta crua corracha na ndíshealbhaithe, blianta an tiarna tíoránta Adare, blianta fuilteacha na géarleanúna, blianta chogadh na cathrach. Dá mbeadh teanga na gcrann ar eolas ag an tsaol ní bheadh deireadh go deo lena gcuid seanchais. Ba bhinn leis an charria seal a chaitheamh ag éisteacht leo. Léim na bladhairí ó chrann go crann, ó thom go tom, ó sceach go sceach. Ní raibh de dhíth ach splanc amháin agus séideog gaoithe. Bhí tomacha agus sceacha ag fás leo ar achan taobh den tsliabh, iad uilig réidh le himeacht. Ba chosúil an tine le sruthán uisce ag seoladh le fána, na bladhairí ina rabharta ag ardú agus ag ísliú le séideadh na gaoithe.

Rith an carria le fána an ghleanna. Ba chrochta an cosán. Chuala sé liúireacht na mbrocanna agus tafann na madaidh rua de réir mar a cuireadh an ruaig orthu amach as a gcuid broclach. Líon crónán fiáin na bhfeitheog agus na mbeathóg an t-aer trom. Chuala sé caoineadh na n-uan óg agus na gcaorach, iad gafa ar ghualainn an tsléibhe, cuid acu i bhfostú sna sreanganna deilgneacha a bhí mar theorainn idir na tailte. Bhí deireadh leis na teorainn anois. Bhí siad uilig ar an taobh céanna sa chath i gcoinne na dtinte. B'ionann croí amháin agus croí eile, ba chuma faoin mhéid.

Bhris croí an charria ina ucht. Bhí a fhios aige go raibh ainmhithe dá dhúchas féin thíos i measc na gcrann a bhí ag lasadh na spéartha. Bhí a fhios aige go raibh a phór féin ann agus bhí a fhios aige go raibh deireadh leo. Chuala sé géimneach agus geonaíl a chomhghaol agus tháinig lagmhisneach air. Bhí sé buartha faoina heilití a bhí ag súil leis an tsaol úr a líon a mbroinn, an saol nach bhfaca solas lae ná oíche réabghealaí, nár bhlaisigh bainne a máthar ná duilliúr úr na gcrann, nár áirigh séideog gaoithe ag siorradh fríd na sléibhte idir Gleann Bheatha agus Gleann Domhain. Bhí sé buartha faoi na hoisíní nuabheirthe a d'fhág a máithreacha ina luí i bhfolach idir an fraoch agus an féar fada fhad agus a d'aimsigh siadsan bia. Ní bheadh luas na gcos ag na hoisíní sin go fóill agus ní mhairfeadh siad beo. Ní mhairfeadh siad beo nó bheadh siad sáinnithe sna bladhairí damanta a bhí ag tarraingt isteach agus ag scaipeadh amach ar an uile thaobh thíos faoi. Chonaic sé ceithre oisín ag rith le taobh a máthra. Rith siad fríd na crainn agus na sceachanna go scafánta, scafarach. Rith siad leo gan fios acu cá raibh a dtriall ach bhí a fhios aigesean cad é an deireadh a bheadh orthu. D'ísligh cloigeann an charria go cloíteach. Ghoin sé air nach raibh sé ábalta iad a shábháil in am an ghátair, in am an scriosta. Ní raibh sé ina rí ar na sléibhte a thuilleadh.

Fuair an carria boladh an bháis san aer. Shín sé a chloigeann in airde ag déanamh iarrachta aer úr a shú isteach ina scamhógaí. Chonaic sé fuiseogaí agus fáinleogaí ag eitilt thart i gciorcail os a chionn. Nach orthu a bhí an t-ádh, a smaointigh sé, gan a bheith greamaithe leis an talamh. Níor thuig sé cad é an mhoill a bhí orthu nó cad chuige nár imigh siad leofa agus an deis sin acu. Lean sé air ag stánadh suas orthu. Líon a scréachanna síoraí na spéartha. D'eitil siad isteach agus amach as na scamaill dhubha dheatacha. Ansin, tháinig sé chuige: bhí a gcearca óga istigh sna crainn. Bhí na máithreacha stróicthe idir dhá dhúil: an dúil a bhí iontu iad féin a shábháil ón uile chontúirt agus dúil bhunúsach an mháithreachais. Cé acu ba láidre, a mheas sé? Ba léir don charria go mbeadh siad gafa ag an bhás dá bhfanfadh siad. D'imeodh seisean – ach ní máthair a bhí ann.

Chuimhnigh an carria siar ar an chéad uair a thug sé rúideog ar eilit. Deireadh mhí Mheán an Fhómhair a bhí ann agus bhí cuid mhór carria i ndiaidh dul fá chónaí istigh i nGleann Domhain, áit a raibh an fraoch fite tiubh go fóill. Bhí sé ag innilt ar na sléibhte le seachtain agus corradh nuair a rug an dúchas greim air. Theannaigh achan mhatán ina chorp. D'áirigh sé an teannas ag ardú ann féin ó bhun a chos go barr a chloiginn. Bhí sé tógtha, faoi gheasa ag an fhuinneamh a bhí lasta anois ann. Sheas sé i measc a thréada ag coimhéad amach uaidh. Chonacthas dó eilit dhonnrua cóngarach dó. Ba ise a bhí staidiúil. Sheas sí go ríoga ar thaobh an tsléibhe, a bráid agus a cloigeann cumtha sínithe in airde aici, a súile donna ag amharc go grinn ar an tréad mórthimpeall uirthi. Ba chaol a com. Bhí loinnir ar fhionnadh a droma faoi sholas na gréine. Ba léir don charria a cosa láidre, caoindéanta. Bheadh siad ligthe; bheadh siad lúfar; iad réidh le héirí, réidh le himeacht dá mbeadh gá leis. Sheas an eilit amach i measc na n-eilití eile ar an tsliabh. Bhí sí uasal. Bhí sí maorga. Croí na féile.

Chaith an carria a chloigeann siar agus lig sé búireach fhada dhomhain amach as, tormán nár chuala sé ag teacht amach as féin riamh roimhe. Líon a ghlór an gleann. Glao chun cumainn, glao chun catha. Shín a bheanna amach go ríoga ar dhá thaobh a chinn, dhá throigh go géagach, gargach ar an uile thaobh. Ba mhisniúil an té a rachadh ina choinne. Thóg sé a chloigeann agus tharraing sé ar an eilit. Líon an gleann le búireach. Glao chun cumainn, glao chun catha. Thiontaigh an carria a cheann. Mhothaigh sé beithíoch inteacht ag teacht go gasta ina dhiaidh. Mhothaigh sé an bhúireach i ndeas dó agus stad sé dá chosán. Chonaic sé carria ar a chóimhéid féin ag tarraingt air ó chlé. Níor scanraigh sé. Bhí sé dírithe ar an eilit os a chomhar amach. Ise a bheadh mar dhuais aige. D'amharc an eilit go socair ar an dís. Bheadh sí mar thús agus deireadh acu, bun agus barr a scéil, cúis catha, ábhar cumainn. Sheas sí mar a bheadh breitheamh inti ag feitheamh go bhfaigheadh sí amach cé acu ba láidre, cé acu arbh fhiú í. Cé dó a dtabharfadh sí oidhreacht sléibhe? Cé leis an síol-aicme a chuirfeadh beatha ina broinn, brí ina beatha, brí lena beatha-sa?

Lean na carria orthu ag búireach leo go trodach tréanmhar. Tharraing siad cóngarach dá chéile. Chiorclaigh siad thart go mallréimeach. Thart leo arís agus arís eile á misniú féin, á ndeargadh féin chun catha. Súil níor bhain siad dá chéile le linn an ama. Bhí súile s'acu mar shaighde, á mbrú isteach in anama agus croíthe a chéile. Lig siad búirthí uathu arís, ghlaoigh siad in airde a gcinn, chrom siad na cosa cúil, d'ísligh siad a gcloigne agus go tobann thug said rúid ar a chéile i lár an ghleanna. Shnoigh a gcuid beann barr-ghéara isteach ina chéile – cnámh ar chnámh, géag ar ghéag. Bhrúigh siad agus bhatráil siad i gcoinne a chéile. Bhog siad leo ó thaobh go taobh, anonn agus anall, anuas agus suas. An lámh in uachtar ag ceann amháin, an lámh in uachtar ag ceann eile, iad fite fuaite in adharca a chéile. Bhí an dís acu ar comhchéim ó thaobh dúchais agus drúise. Chluinfeá an bhúireach fhiáin, fhíochmhar ar bharr Shliabh Sneachta agus ag bun Thrá Thobar Glasáin. Lean siad orthu gan amharc siar ná aniar, ag tarraingt agus ag brú go dtí ar deireadh bhí an dara carria cloíte, créachtach. Theith sé leis síos an gleann go buailteach briste.

Ní raibh an lá istigh go fóill. Sheas an carria go fuilteach, caithréimeach os comhar a thréada. Dhírigh sé ar an eilit. Chuaigh sé ionsuirthi. D'ardaigh sé a dhá chos tosaigh, chaith sé é féin ar mhullach a droma agus spréigh sé a shíol isteach i gcorp na heilite le fuinneamh iomlán fiánta a nádúir agus a dhúchais. Bhí an cath buaite; bhí an cumann déanta.

Rinne an fia cumann le cúig eilit an chéad bhliain dó bheith abaí. Gidh nach raibh baint aige lena mhuirín, bhí a fhios aige go raibh a phór féin ag innilt ar shléibhte Thír Chonaill agus go raibh fuil agus oidhreacht a athara agus a athar-san roimhe siúd beo ar fad. Thug sin sásamh dó.

Lá den tsaol bhí an carria ina rí ar na sléibhte dálta sliocht a shleachta leis na cianta roimhe. Ba de bhunús ísealchríocha na hAlban pór s'aige féin ach bhraith seisean chomh dúchasach céanna le fia mór na mbeann. Mhothaigh sé na scéalta dubha dorcha faoin dóigh a ghlac na plandálaithe a phór chun na tíre i dtosach báire ionas go mbeadh caitheamh aimsire ag lucht na ngunnaí. Lucht seilge agus santachta, lucht fola agus feola. Mhothaigh sé na scéalta faoin tiarna brúidiúil Adare. Chuala sé faoi na cleasanna a d'imir sé, na horduithe díshealbhaithe a shínigh sé, na croíthe a bhris sé. Cuireadh an ruaig ar sheacht dteaghlach is daichead amach as na sléibhte de dheoin Adare. Seacht dteaghlach is daichead. Trom-smacht na nGall.

Thuig an carria do mhuintir na sléibhte inniu ar dhóigh nár thuig sé riamh roimhe sin. Fágadh ar thaobh an bhealaigh iad – fir agus mná, óg agus aosta – caite amach gan trua gan trócaire, gan foscadh, gan dídean, a gcuid tithe curtha trí thine. Dream a bhí iontu a tháinig slán ar an talamh. Cheal talaimh ní mhairfeadh siad beo. Chuala an carria faoi olagón agus caoineadh na ndaoine. Mheas sé go raibh sé in inmhe caoineadh an bháis a chluinstin mórthimpeall air. Caoineadh an bháis, caoineadh an fhaitís; caoineadh don todhchaí agus don am a chuaigh thart. Caoineadh go dtiocfadh le duine daonna a leithéid de dhochar a dhéanamh do neach bheo eile. Caoineadh go gcuirfí baile trí thine d'aon turas gan comhbhá do chomhbheo. Briseadh agus buaileadh bunadh na sléibhte. Níorbh ann daofa a thuilleadh. Ní raibh

rian daofa fágtha ach seanbhallógaí uaigneacha. An raibh an deireadh céanna
i ndán dó féin agus dá bhunadh-san?

Bhí a chuid cuimhní ag an charria anois mar a bheadh bolgam na
híocshláinte. Thug siad uchtach dó in am an ghátair agus lig sé lán-srian leis
na smaointe a tháinig chuige. Ba chuimhin leis na fir gunnaí agus iad amuigh
ag seilg. Ba bhuan lucht na seilge ach sheas seisean go calma, cróga i measc
an scaifte. Ní bhfuair siad an lámh in uachtar air riamh. Níor rugadh air ná
níor goineadh é – bhí sé rólúfar agus róchliste daofa. Ba chuimhin leis an
chonairt ag tafann ina dhiaidh, an fhuil ag rith fríd a chuisle, a chroí ag
preabadaí i lár a chléibh, a chosa ag pocléimnigh ó thúrtóg go túrtóg idir
tamhain na gcrann. Bhí leagan amach na mínte agus na móinte breactha ar
intinn an charria mar a bheadh léarscáil scríofa os comhar fir léinn. Ní
thiocfaí é a shárú. D'éalaigh sé i dtólamh faoi scáth dhuilliúr na coille. Ba
chuimhin leis na mathshluaite ag tarraingt air ar a lán-díchill, ag druidim
isteach air ina mbuíon. Níor bhraith an carria riamh nach mairfeadh sé beo
nó nach dtiocfadh sé slán. Maraíodh ainmhithe eile, loiteadh ainmhithe eile,
báidheadh ainmhithe eile ach tháinig seisean slán i gcónaí. Ba léir dó féin go
raibh sé de dhíth orthu mar chruthúnas ar a gcuid fearúlachta, gur mhór leo
a chroí a réabadh amach as a chléibh agus a ardú os comhar na cuideachta.
Fuil chan feoil a bhí de dhíth orthu. Bhí a fhios aige go mbeadh seisean mar
a bheadh sméar mhullaigh na sléibhte dóibh siúd. Laoch nár leagadh, nár
leoiteadh, nár leonadh.

Go tobann thit steafóg darach i ndeas dó agus í ar dearg-lasadh. Tháinig
an carria chuige féin. D'amharc sé ar na tinte ag éirí agus ag ardú
mórthimpeall air. Bhí na tinte ag neartú, ag scaipeadh amach ar an uile
thaobh. Briseadh ar a mhisneach. Bíodh go raibh sé in rí ar na sléibhte lá den
tsaol, bhí sé gan rath, gan ríocht inniu.

Chuala an carria scréachanna agus mairgní na n-ainmhithe agus iad ag
fulaingt, á róstadh ag na bladhairí. Thug sé a chosa leis ina rith. Síos, síos,
chomh tiubh géar agus a thiocfadh leis idir fraoch agus fuganna. Ba chúng
achrannach an bealach ach an ghaoth Mhárta a bheadh ina dhiaidh ní
bheirfeadh sí air. D'fhág sé droim an tsléibhe taobh thiar de. Bhí na
bladhairí ag teannadh air ar dheis agus ar chlé. Amharc siar ní dhearna sé.
Lean sé ar an chosán díreach amach roimhe go gasta géarshúileach. Bhí cúl
gaoithe aige. Bhí an fraoch faoina chosa chomh tirim le cipíní. Dá dtiocfadh
splanc ar bith i ndeas dó ar chor ar bith bheadh sé ar shiúl. Lean sé leis. Bhí
an fhuil ag rith fríd a chuisle. Bhí an mórtas agus an misneach ann go fóill.
Ba bheag go raibh bun an tsléibhe bainte amach aige. Mhothaigh sé go raibh

an t-aer ní b'éadroime; thug sin uchtach dó. Lig sé ábhar a bhróin chun dearmaid.

Go tobann, chuala an carria rud inteacht i ndeas dó. Stad sé go gasta. Contúirt! Rinne sé boladh agus scanraigh sé. Thit a chroí ina ucht. D'amharc sé an uile threo. Ní raibh ach cosán amháin amach as an ifreann ina raibh sé sáinnithe. Bhí na bladhairí ag ardú ar an uile threo. Chuala sé an scairtigh, an gleo, an glór. Chuala sé an béicíl. Mhothaigh sé an bhagairt. Thiontaigh sé thart, timpeall agus timpeall. Bhí frithchaitheamh na dtinte a fheiceáil i ngealacáin a shúl. Bhí siad mar scátháin ar na bladhairí. Chas an carria thart agus thart arís agus arís eile, lig sé búireach fhada dhomhain amach as agus é ag iarraidh chroí an namhad a aimsiú. Chonaic sé buíon fear os a chomhar, iad clúdaithe le luaithreach agus smúit. Bhí scaifte acu ann, lucht sluaiste is spád. Chuala sé iad ag scairtigh go fiáin ar a chéile. Tharraing fear acu ar an charria, ag glaoch air, ag iarraidh é a mhealladh. Bhuail taom mire an carria. Bhí ciall ceannaithe aige i dtaca leis an duine daonna. B'ionann an duine agus an namhaid is measa riamh. Thit a chroí le neart a scanraidh. Bhí sé fuar, folamh agus faiteach. Ní raibh sé ag iarraidh bás a fháil. Ní raibh sé réidh le bás a fháil. Thug sé iarraidh chróga é féin a chosnamh ón bhás go dtí seo ach ba léir anois go raibh an cath caillte. Bhí an faitíos á phlúchadh; bhí sé cloíte. Rith fear ionsair ag glaoch air in airde a chinn. Stad sé; sheas sé. D'amharc an dís acu ar a chéile go díreach: aghaidh ar aghaidh, súile silteacha sreamacha s'acu greamaithe ar a chéile. Sheas an carria ag doras na huaighe, a bheatha idir dhá cheann na meá. Léim de dhearg-ruathar isteach sna bladhairí.

Eithne Ní Ghallchobhair was born in Galway in 1976 and grew up in Donegal. She received a degree in Celtic Studies at the National University of Ireland, Galway, where she also underook a PhD, editing a late medieval medical tract written in Early Modern Irish, De Anathomia, *subsequently published by the Irish Texts Society as a book in 2014. She has published four children's books of her own and translated numerous others into Irish. She works for the Royal Irish Academy, Dublin, as Assistant Editor of the* Foclóir na Nua-Ghaeilge.

TRÍ DÁNTA

Cathal Ó Searcaigh

I GCAIFÉ SRÁIDE I NEW DELHI
do Sheán Ó Coistealbha

Seo mo bhunadh féin, mo ghaolta
i bpéin na bochtaineachta.
Ísealaicme seo na broide
ag saothrú ar an bheagán
i dtoit thachtach na sráide.
Fear an bhruscair ag cartadh
an tsalachair; an táilliúir cráite
is poll ar a thóin; an gasúr
a chuireann snas i mbróga;
fear an phaca agus é báite
ina chuid allais; na cailíní seirbhíse
i dtigh an níocháin; an seanfhear feoite
is a theallachán préataí
á dhíol aige ar an chosán; an gréasaí
agus é deas ar sheanbhróg a dheisiú;
na páistí beaga costarnochta
agus iad ag reic a gcuid earraí,
balúin, bioráin gruaige, pionnaí.

Seo mo dhaoine féin, na glúnta
de mo bhunadh a bhí ar an bheagán,
a bagraíodh le bata na ceannsmachta,
a cáineadh is a coinníodh faoi.
Seo na bochta céanna dar díobh mé,
iad seo nach bhfuair ariamh
uain lae na sócúlachta
ach a bhfuil sé d'ualach orthu
urraim a ghéilleadh i gcónaí
dóibh siúd atá á gcoinneáil síos.

Seo mo bunadh féin go fíor;
mo mháthair agus mná mar í
as na Rosann agus as na hoileáin,
"tatie hokers" i Midlothian na hAlban.
M'athair agus a mhacasamhail, spailpíní
ó Mhín a' Leá ag déanamh fómhair
in Haddington, in Dunbar, in East Linton.
Seo iad mo ghaolta is mo chineál;
an t-aos óg a chuirtí chuig na haontaí hireála
ar an tSrath Bhán, i Leitir Ceanainn,
is gan rompu ach fostú na hainnise
ar fheirmeacha gustalacha an Lagáin.

Seo na cailíní aimsire as Cloich Chionnaola
ar déanadh leatrom orthu is éigniú
i dtithe na n-uasal i nGlaschú.
Seo na stócaigh urránta nach bhfuair
a gcearta ná taobh an tsochair dena gcuid oibre
i bpoill guail na Breataine Móire.

Seo mo bhunadh féin. Seo m'aicme i gcéin,
is cé gur agam atá sócúl na hócáide
anseo ag ól "latte" i gcaifé sráide,
is cé go bhfuil mé chomh feiceálach
le fiacail óir i mbéal bodaigh,
seo iad mo bhunadh, na glúnta céanna
atá curtha ionam, atá ag cuisliú ionam,
is atá anois ag éirí aníos ionam
is ag éamh ar fud mo chuislí.
Ar shráid na hainnise i New Delhi
tá éileamh as an nua acu ar mo chroí.

I gCUIMHNE MO SHEANUNCAIL
A THROID SA CHOGADH MHÓR (1914–1918)

Bhíodh do phioctúr, íomhá dhonnrua, ina mhaisiú ar mhatal ard,
cloch-chrua na cisteanadh agus mé i mo ghasúr,
sa chruth nach dtiocfadh liom mo shúil a choinneáil ó
d'aoibh ghnaoiúil ná ó do chulaith úr saighdiúra.

Sheas tú ar aire i *gkhaki*, snas i do bhuataisí, gunna crónbhuí
beaignéide ar do ghlúin, uabhair an fhir óig i do shúile.
Throid tú i Verdun, in Arras agus ag an Somme, mar i ndúil
is go mbeadh an Eoraip saor, a dúirt m'athair go bródúil.

Sa bhaile ba tusa saighdiúir cróga an teaghlaigh ach i gceacht
na scoile ba tú an té a thug cúl le cine is a liostáil in airm an rí.
Ó am go ham, chluinfinn fear na gcomharsan, fiúir ar a theangaidh,
ag cáineadh na gcladhairí a throid ar son Sheáin Bhuí.

Ach ba chuma caidé a dúradh ba tusa mo shaighdiúir breá
diongbháilte, mo laochmhíle, m'ardfhear misnigh;
is b'fhiú liom ag an am d'ainm a mhaíomh is d'éacht cogaidh
a laoidheadh i mo chuid véarsaí beaga leanbhaí.

Le deisiú an tí sna seachtóidí cuireadh do phioctúir i dtaiscidh
is nuair a d'aimsigh mé é bhí sé curtha ó chuma le taisleach.
B'olc liom an chinniúint a lig tusa i ndíchuimhne is ba ghránna
an mhaise domh gan tú a cheiliúradh a sheanuncail, a ghaiscígh.

Thug tú na cnámha leat as an ár ach ní tháinig tú chugat
féin ariamh ina dhiaidh. Bhí cneá mharthanach as an chogadh
ag déanamh angaidh i d'aigne ionas nach bhfuair tú lá faoisimh
le do bheo ach ag síoról na dí leis an bhrí a bhaint as urchóid na gcuimhní.

Chaith tú blianta deireanacha do shaoil ag trampáil na mbóithre
i Midlothians na hAlban, ó Haddington go East Linton – ceantar
ina mbíodh fearaibh Cloich Chionnaola fostaithe ar na feirmeacha –
go dtí gur maraíodh tú i dtimpist' cairr ar an bhealach go Dunbar.

A Sheáin chaoin Uí Ghallchóir, a ghaiscígh mhóir, a sheanuncail dhil,
thug tú an tseirbhís fhada dhílis, ceithre bliana doiligh de d'óige
i dtrinsí an uafáis i bhfách le síth agus socracht an tsaoil
is ní ortsa atá an locht má tá an domhan fós ag déanamh urchóide.

AG TAIBHSIÚ NA dTODHCHAÍ
OS CIONN LOCH AN GHAINIMH
do Phroinnsíos Ó Duigneáin

Tusa atá i do sheasamh anseo
os cionn na locha, ag breathnú uait go buíoch
ar an radharc sítheach só seo.

Na sléibhte á dtomadh féin
go díreach domhain san uisce chiúin;
na caoráin i bhfogas agus i gcéin

á gcóiriú féin i gcorcra, i gcrónbhuí;
an solas de choiscéim éadrom
ag déanamh ar bharr na Beithí.

Luí na gréine ag cur lí an óir
i spéir an tráthnóna ó Charn Traonach
go Fána Bhuí is go Caiseal na gCorr.

Smaointigh gur sheas mise anseo
tráthnónta fadó, ag breathnú uaim fosta
ar an radharc sítheach só seo.

Mé ag meabhrú ar imeacht na mblianta,
ar a dtáinig agus ar a dtiocfaidh, ar chasadh
cinniúnach an tsaoil ó chian go cian.

Ar mo dhaoine a shaothraigh anseo
i mínte an tsléibhe is atá anois sa chré
a bheathaigh iad, a choinnigh cothú leo.

Is chan mé an dán draíochta a cumadh
leis an taobh tíre seo a ghairm, chan mé
na hainmneacha ceana leis an Bhé a mhealladh,

Ón Mhalaidh Rua go Mín na hUchta,
ó Pháirc Mhéabha go Droim na Gréine,
ón Phit, ón Phollán, agus ón Chró Chrochta.

Chan mé an cholainn uasal álainn seo
i gcaint uaibhreach mo dhaoine, sa chruth
go ligfeadh sí a haithne leat, tusa a sheasann anseo …

Ach anocht ar mo mharana, i mo shuí míshocair
idir an dá sholas, taibhsíonn tusa chugam
ón am atá le theacht, is seasann tú anseo, a bhráthair,

Ag baint lán na súl as an radharc bhreá
atá ar d'amharc, cúpla líne leat ó sheanfhile
nach labhartar a theanga níos mó i Mín a' Leá.

Cathal Ó Searcaigh is the Irish Language Editor of this journal. He was born in 1956 and raised in Meenala, near Gortahork, an Irish-speaking district in Co Donegal. His poetry collections are Súile Shuibhne *(Coiscéim, 1983),* Suibhne *(Coiscéim, 1987), the bilingual* An Bealach 'na Bhaile/Homecoming *(Cló Iar-Chonnachta, 1993),* Ag Tnúth Leis an tSolas *(Cló Iar-Chonnachta, 1993),* Na Buachaillí Bána *(Cló Iar-Chonnachta, 1996), the selected* Out in the Open *(Cló Iar-Chonnachta, 2000),* Gúrú i gCluídíní *(2006),* An tAm Marfach ina Mairimid *(2011), and* Aimsir Ársa *(2013). His prose works include* Seal i Neipeal *(2004),* Light on Distant Hills: A Memoir *(2009), and* Pianó Mhín na bPreáchán *(2011). He is also the author several plays in Irish, and a selection of English translations of his poetry,* By the Hearth at Mín a' Leá *(Arc), appeared in 2005. He continues to live in Meenala, and is a member of Aosdána.*

ONE'S WIND IS UP!

—

Gabriel Rosenstock

A poisoned anthology.

A man who has a language consequently possesses the world expressed and implied by that language.

(Frantz Fanon)

The cover flap of *Windharp: Poems of Ireland Since 1916* (Penguin Ireland, 2015) refers to the editor, Niall MacMonagle, as "Ireland's most trusted commentator on poetry." Does Penguin Ireland really know Ireland well enough to make such a claim? Does Niall MacMonagle know himself that well?

Having "1916" in the title is an obvious marketing ploy, cashing in on the centenary. It would be forgivable if the editor and publisher had a positive attitude to the commemoration. What we have here is quite the opposite, adding extra quicklime to the 1916 martyrs and their vision of Ireland in coming times.

Firstly, two of the poet-martyrs of 1916 are missing from the roll call, Thomas MacDonagh and Joseph Mary Plunkett. What fault exactly did our most trusted commentator find with Plunkett's iconic "I See His Blood upon the Rose"? Is it, perhaps, too Catholic for this post-Catholic nation of our times, too mystic for our materialist ways, too visionary for our cynical era? Plunkett was influenced by John of the Cross, Catherine of Siena, Francis Thompson, among others, and "I See His Blood upon the Rose" is a spiritual classic. Steeleye Span recorded a beautiful version of it and you can find it on YouTube. Judge for yourself. It must have been excluded on the grounds that it has a vision. After all, our Irish word for poet, "*file*", means "seer" and one of our words for poetry, "*éigse*", is related to "*feiscint*", which is "seeing." But this is an anthology without a vision. It leads us with tunnel vision down a blind alley.

What the 1916 poets envisioned – a spiritual, cultural, linguistic, and economic revival, an equal cherishing of all citizens – is not a vision that this anthologist has warmed to; *au contraire*, he has hijacked 1916 for his own purposes. His choice of poems, for the most part, is a despondent litany that would suggest we live in a failed state, and (by implication) were much better off under the Redcoats. Penguin Ireland is skating on thin ice with this monstrous volume, it seems to me.

I read through the book and then read it from end to beginning and found, for example, a poem (in English) by Doireann Ní Ghríofa on the tragedy of Savita Halappanavar; the plague that is emigration emerges in "Neutral Ireland" by Gerard Smyth; there are no positive-sounding poems out there about our neutrality, it seems, or on some of the more positive aspects of emigration; Gerald Dawe chimes in with a poem about the blight of our ghost-estates, and William Wall is exercised by that theme as well; Stanhope Street Magdalene Laundry is the subject of Jessica Traynor's poem; and so on, a litany of disgrace.

We have a sinister pattern here, it seems to me; Caitríona O'Reilly has moving statues and a statue that wouldn't lift a finger to help a dying girl giving birth; "queer-bashing" features in a poem by Pearse Hutchinson, and a link to Ann Lovett is in the same poem.

I knew Pearse Hutchinson (1927–2012) quite well, and was aware of the profound respect he had for the men and women of 1916, and their dream of a de-anglicized bilingual Ireland. He was christened William Patrick Pearse and was, in fact, the last pupil enrolled in Scoil Éanna, founded by the poet-patriot whose name he was given. In *Poetry Ireland Review*, he told Liam Ó Muirthile:

> I was able to express myself more directly in Irish, because it was and is both an ancient and a virgin language. It hasn't been subjected, especially in the last century, to the awful stiff upper lip of English.

(Editor's Note: see Seamus Heaney above, on the same theme, in "Varieties of Irishness".)

No danger of finding such quotes in this anthology! I'm sure Hutchinson would strongly disapprove of the editor's intentions and his selection that is more Hieronymous Bosch, let us say, than Charles Lamb, Paul Henry, Sean Keating or Jack B. Yeats, if one can express it in such roundabout terms; unbaptized children rear their heads from their pathetic graves in Mary O'Malley's poem; and Ann Lovett again, in case we might have forgotten, in Paula Meehan's "The Statue of the Virgin at Granard Speaks."

This anthology fits in with what the media have been doing in recent years: giving ourselves a terrible bashing over the head. We deserve it, you say. Bashing ourselves over the head until we become senseless – with a windharp, of all things? I can see why one might want to do that, but hardly as a central theme for a mainstream anthology of post-1916 poetry. We have more to offer than a litany of woes, surely? Why should our poets outdo Frank McCourt? It's not that all our poets are obsessed with the failures of our state; it's what the anthologist has chosen that leaves a taste of bile in the mouth.

——

The oppressed will always believe the worst about themselves.
(Frantz Fanon)

The poems selected by Ireland's most trusted commentator do not stop there. Not only is this a failed state, and all of us failed citizens of a failed state, but even the bloody cows are dysfunctional: "On all sides of the open fields lies terror" ("BSE", David Wheatley).

The "silk of the kine" is now a mad terrorist, it seems. Theo Dorgan has said a lot of positive-sounding things, as poet and arts activist, but Niall MacMonagle doesn't want to hear any of that, so he digs up this quote for our edification:

If you drew a graph from Wolfe Tone, through O'Connell and
Parnell and Pearse and Connolly, down to the present, that graph
is a steep descent.

Given the disproportionate level of negativity that runs through this anthology, what is very strange indeed is to find it described as "glorious" by *The Examiner*. Am I missing something? "Inglorious" springs to mind? A typo perhaps?

Let's turn to Brendan Kennelly and his poem on one Eily Kilbride:

… Whose entire school day
Was a bag of crisps,
Whose parents had no work to do,

Who went, once, into the countryside,
Saw a horse with a feeding bag over its head
And thought it was sniffing glue.

It's unremitting. Is there no saving grace at all? What next? A plague of locusts? Or zombies? "The People I Grew Up with Were Afraid", says Michael Gorman:

The people I grew up with were afraid.
They were alone too long in waiting-rooms,
In dispensaries, and in offices whose functions
They did not understand …

You get the picture. It's grim, to say the least. Do you believe it? According to Fanon, you should. That's how the postcolonial, or neo-colonial, mind works. We will always believe the worst about ourselves. We are spiritually and psychologically programmed not to have a vision, or hope. Plunkett was a visionary. So was MacDonagh. Two signatories of the 1916 Proclamation, both absent. Maybe MacDonagh didn't fit MacMonagle's thesis (whatever that might be); MacDonagh, the sophisticated, civilized citizen of Europe, the lecturer and *littérateur* who taught Irish to Plunkett, as it happens. That image doesn't fit in with the anthologist's thesis which at times seems to suggest that the poet-martyrs were terrorists; or if not terrorists themselves, then proto-terrorists, their lives and writings giving succour and sustenance to the terrorists who bomb and shoot and maim in the holy name of Republicanism.

No, let's keep MacDonagh out of this anthology. We might get fond of him or, God forbid, admire him or come to respect him and the rest of the signatories.

MacMonagle wasn't around in 1916. James Stephens was and said of the leaders: "They were good men – men, that is, who willed no evil." Here's a poem by MacDonagh that I translated recently into Irish. It's quite modern for its time and is set in Paris. There are poems of far less interest and scope in this anthology.

I bPÁRAS

Sé seo m'fhásach-sa is táim anseo liom féin
Ina lár is níl aithne ag éinne orm.
I mo thost mar a bheadh seabhac i gcéin
Sa spéir ghorm.
Ní labhraím le héinne ó mhaidin go hoíche

Mo ghnó féin á chur i gcrích,
An slua callánach thart orm ina mílte
Gan sos gan scíth.
Buaileann clog mór an tSorbonne
Mar a bhuail anseo fadó
Siar in aimsir Villon
A scoir láithreach dá ghnó.
San áit seo is sneachta ag titim ón spéir
Leis féin ina sheomra cúng –
Ceithre chéad caoga bliain ó shin
Le Grand Testament do chum.

So, then, let's see. Instead of MacDonagh and Plunkett, who do we get in this *Windharp: Poems of Ireland Since 1916?* Lord Dunsany. He is introduced by this fanfare:

Edward John Moreton Drax Plunkett, Baron of Dunsany, London-born, inherited the family title and estate near Tara, in County Meath. He was an officer in the Coldstream Guards during the Boer War, and in the Royal Iniskilling Fusiliers during the First World War. While on leave in Dublin in April 1916, he was shot in the face when he drove into Dublin to support the British forces in suppressing the Easter Rising ...

How shockingly obsequious! It's like a death notice from the *Daily Telegraph* reprinted in the *Sindo*. The cat is now well and truly out of the bag. This anthology does not celebrate Ireland, certainly not as the 1916 leaders saw it; it celebrates the master-race we thought we had kindly asked to leave, those terribly annoying wasps – white Anglo-Saxon Protestants – described by John Bassett McCleary as "the most aggressive, powerful, and arrogant society in the world." And they haven't gone away, you know!

Is there an alternative to this waspishness? Of course there is. John Moriarty in *Invoking Ireland: Ailiu Iath n-hErend* (Lilliput Press, 2005) saw it as the living legacy of the Tuatha Dé Danann, a legacy that is scorned by Waspishness or dismissed as mere fancy:

The Tuatha Dé Danann were a highly enlightened people who spent their time acquiring visionary insights and foresights and hindsights, acquiring the occult knowledge and the occult art of the wizard, the druid, the witch, these, together with all the magical arts, until masters in everything concerning them, they had no equals in the world.

Yeats would have relished that quote, as would AE; they would have loved the company of the likes of Moriarty, whose mind was larger than the British Empire.

Meanwhile, we shouldn't get bogged down in such things as Lord Dunsany's biographical details. It's poetry that matters here, the poetry of Ireland since 1916. What has our trusted commentator chosen? What kind of Ireland is invoked? A poem in praise of the British Army! Am I joking? It's called "To the Fallen Irish Soldiers." Here's how Dunsany's obscene rant ends:

> Sleep on, forgot a few more years, and then
> The ages, that I prophesy, shall see
> Due honours paid to you by juster men,
> You standing foremost in our history,
> Your story filling all our land with wonder,
> Your names, and regiments' names, like distant thunder.

Shall our booksellers take it down from the shelves? No, they will put it on the window, for all to see. This is how we will celebrate 2016. Glorious, isn't it?

———

Imperialism leaves behind germs of rot which we must clinically detect and remove not only from our land but from our minds as well.
(Frantz Fanon)

On RTÉ's website, one Paddy Kehoe gives this anthology five stars:

This welcome new anthology [*says the bould Paddy*] whose subtitle is *Poems of Ireland since 1916* is perhaps doing its most useful thing when it turns up neglected gems, such as Katharine Tynan's *The Long Vacation*, which was first published in 1916. This moving poem mourns the young Irishmen who were dying in the trenches of the First World War at the time. The poet depicts the youths as the boys they recently were, coming home from school to fill houses with gaiety and exuberance. Now their mothers *stand in the doorway listening long* and ask: *Where do they tarry, the dear, the light-heart throng?*

Let me put my cards on the table. I'm an utopian anarchist. I have no interest in the nation-state, in flags, borders, or national anthems. Every anarchist is anti-imperialist and pledged to peace but after reading this book I'm sorely tempted to take over the GPO again and this time make sure that in a hundred years from now we will not have publishers, anthologists, and reviewers who bend over backwards in their praises of the British Army, or any other army for that matter. I would hope that most English people in their right minds, unfazed by poppies, would agree with me on this.

Let's not forget that there were many decent English people who were genuinely exercised by the Irish question and who even stoutly approved of the 1916 Rising, decent folk such as the composer Arnold Bax, who also wrote under the name Dermot O'Byrne. He saw with his own two eyes those English gentlemen who were sent to quell the Easter Rising. His poetry was banned by the British censor – and MacMonagle follows suit. You won't find the Dermot O'Byrnes of this world besmirching this anthology:

> They mixed lewd talk of girls with beer;
> One tattooed monster with a leer
> Began to sentimentalize
> About some Kathleen's arms and eyes …

We sometimes forget that P.H. Pearse himself was half-English. AE said of him: "Pearse himself, for all his Gaelic culture, was sired by one of the race he fought against. He might stand in that respect as a symbol of the new race which is springing up" (*The Irish Times*, 19 December 1917).

Let us remember that Plunkett, MacDonagh, Pearse, Connolly and all that delirium of the brave were not inspired by some rabid form of anti-Englishness, as Declan Kiberd explains:

> What they rejected was not England but the British imperial system, which denied expressive freedom to its colonial subjects (*Modern Irish Writers and the Wars*, Colin Smythe, 1999).

The anthology gets a two-star review on Amazon from American poet Thomas Rain Crowe, himself a distinguished anthologist of poetry from the Celtic realms. Crowe is outraged:

> This anthology is terribly lacking in one essential way: it doesn't include a respectful and representative number of Irish-language poets – which is key to any anthology of Irish poetry during any generation or era. And since this covers a century of Irish verse, it's appalling that Ireland's important Irish-language poets are missing. Poets such as L.S. Gogan, Seán Ó Ríordáin, Máire Mhac an tSaoi, Máirtín Ó Direáin, Michael Davitt, Biddy Jenkinson, Cathal Ó Searcaigh, Tomás Mac Síomóin, Greagóir Ó Dúill, Philip Cummings, Derry O'Sullivan, Seán Hutton, Seán Ó Leocháin, Caitríona Ní Chleirchín, Gabriel Rosenstock, Gearóid Mac Lochlainn, Colm Breathnach, Liam Ó Muirthile, Eoghan Ó Tuairisc, Caitlín Maude … all missing! Don't know what the editor was thinking (or *not thinking* would be a better description). A shame to waste the money and the paper on this anthology which could have been so much better, so much more …

Crowe has listed some Irish-language poets known to him (and to the educated reading public at home and abroad), but his list could be trebled quite easily. Instead of the likes of Seán Ó Ríordáin and Cathal Ó Searcaigh, our most trusted commentator gives us John Fitzgerald, Tara Bergin, Lucy Brennan, Susan Connolly, etc., who may well deserve the dubious honour of being included – but what possible excuse is there to exclude Ó Direáin, Máire Mhac an tSaoi or dozens more?

What would Pearse, Plunkett, and MacDonagh make of this anthology? Opening it at random on page 156, Pearse would read Greg Delanty's poem "The Children of Lir" and heave a sigh, saying, "Is the Murder Machine still with us? There is no such name as *Lir*. *Lir* is a genitive form of *Lear*. One can say *Clann Lir*, of course, in Irish, but in English one must say 'The Children of Lear.'"

Nuala Rua is here, of course. Who would dare exclude Nuala Ní Dhomhnaill?! In fact, we have two poems, in all, in Irish: "Ceist na Teangan" by Nuala and "Jackeen ag Caoineadh na mBlascaod" by Brendan Behan. How did Brendan get in? As an alcoholic IRA man, he fits the picture perfectly. Máire Mhac an tSaoi, poet, scholar, former diplomat, translator of Rilke and Lorca, that's not the image we want in this anthology. No sirree. Let's have two token poems showing us how precarious this other tongue, this most bothersome tongue is; like the Blaskets, it's really only a relic of the past, not some glowing beacon for the future. Two pages of Irish-language poetry out of 318 pages. That'll show them who's in charge – the indomitable Irishry, that's who. We go back as far as Swift, you know. It's like 1916 never happened. *INNTI* never happened. IMRAM never happened. Those poets listed by Crowe ... who has even heard of half of them, after all? Why do they have such unpronounceable names? How is it they are still popping up, like menacing mushrooms?

When we revolt it's not for a particular culture. We revolt simply because, for many reasons, we can no longer breathe.
(Frantz Fanon)

Just in case you are one of those people who thinks that the Irish language has some kind of a future, dip into this unlucky bag and you will find Mathew Sweeney's poem "The Eagle":

My father is writing in Irish.
The English language, with all its facts
Will not do. It is too modern.
It is good for plane-crashes, for unemployment,
But not for the unexplained return
Of the eagle to Donegal.
He describes the settled pair
In their eyrie on the not-so-high mountain.
He uses an archaic Irish
To describe what used to be, what is again,
Though hunters are reluctant
To agree on what will be ...

And so on. What's happening in this poem? What is being said? Sweeney is quite prolific. Why pick this particular poem? What's the agenda here, the mindset? Could someone explain? The "Introduction" evokes "English poet and soldier Sir Philip Sidney", of all people, who along with Spenser belonged to a society that advocated the ethnic cleansing of Gaels; Philip's father, Henry, was one of the first cleaning agents sent over here. Evoking Sidney is simply rubbing our noses in it and *The Examiner* finds it "glorious." What country am I living in?

We have the legendary Cathal McCabe here, who in some kind of poetic stupor imagines himself to be living in a Gaeltacht and speaking Irish; no, not actually speaking Irish, mind you, but imagining it. Imagine:

> Lived in another language,
> In Teelin, Fahan, Port na Blagh,
> A fisherman busy by a pier
> Day in, day out, *gach lá, gach lá.*

Needless to say, it's the anglicized form of Gaeltacht place names that are given in the poem. No poets from the real Gaeltacht need apply, such as Seán Ó Curraoin, Dairena Ní Chinnéide, Proinsias Mac a' Bhaird, or Áine Uí Fhoghlú, but let's give Cathal McCabe a few inches for his virtual Gaeltacht.

Francis Ledwidge is described here in the style of the previously alluded-to *Daily Telegraph*: "Ledwidge saw action at Gallipoli and in the Balkans before being killed by a shell on 31 July, 1917, near Ypres." It's as if MacMonagle were writing for an English readership. Let's be careful not to mention the fact that Ledwidge was a member of the Gaelic League. It's doubtful if 1916 would ever have happened at all without Conradh na Gaeilge, but these matters do not concern our anthologist.

Apart from a poem by Colette Bryce and Alan Gillis, MacMonagle's view of the Troubles, as revealed by his selection, is one-sided and jaundiced. I didn't expect Bobby Sands, but surely even an extract from Kinsella's "troubled" *oeuvre* would have balanced things a little:

> I went with Anger at my heel
> Through Bogside of the bitter zeal
> – Jesus pity! – on a day
> Of cold and drizzle and decay.
> A month had passed. Yet there remained
> A murder smell that stung and stained.
> On flats and alleys – over all –
> It hung; on battered roof and wall,
> On wreck and rubbish scattered thick,

On sullen steps and pitted brick.
And when I came where thirteen died
It shrivelled up my heart. I sighed
And looked about that brutal place
Of rage and terror and disgrace.
Then my moistened lips grew dry.
I had heard an answering sigh!
There in a ghostly pool of blood
A crumpled phantom hugged the mud:
"Once there lived a hooligan.
A pig came up, and away he ran.
Here lies one in blood and bones,
Who lost his life for throwing stones."

No. We'll have none of that here, please. Kinsella did not wish to appear in this anthology. I wonder why? How many others poets would have withdrawn had they known the nature of the beast? OK. No "Butcher's Dozen" here, so make room for this four-lined squib from Desmond Egan:

THE NORTHERN IRELAND QUESTION

Two wee girls
Were playing tig near a car ...

How many counties would you say
Are worth their scattered fingers?

I am not saying that we shouldn't have poems such as John O'Donnell's on the Omagh bombing, or the bombing of the Europa Hotel, subject of a poem by Sinéad Morrissey. Dermot Healy is also outraged by the bombings. But since so many of the poems here depict the Republic as a failed state, what about the failed wee statelet up north? Where are the insightful poems that explain the ongoing saga of the North from the side of those who felt they could do nothing but resort to violence? Where are the poems about state terrorism?

In "July Twelfth" Macdara Woods expresses the horror which makes every civilized being recoil from extreme violence:

In
Ballymoney
In the night
Three children
Firebombed
Burnt to death …

Yes, yes, yes, but where are the poems from the other side of the barricades?
I'm old enough to remember when Republicans weren't allowed to give
their side of the story, their version of history, when they were all muzzled.

For me, the best poem about the Troubles was written in English by an
Irish-language poet, Gearóid Mac Lochlainn. It's not in this book. Here is
the ending of "Bus":

… And then I'm thinkin
That maybe he even thinks I'm one of them
Cos I say fuck all and keep a low profile
And why wouldn't ya?
It's not like I wanna socialise with my prod neighbours
They might burn me out
Except they're all middle class
And don't do that type of thing
Up there …

But they'd probably shop ya to the dole
For bein a poor fenian
Ya know

But anyway, he's walkin right up to me
And he's gonna speak to me …
And I'm wonderin what's goin on, like
And he stops and asks me for a light
And so I fumble about and dig out the lighter
And it's like a wee bit windy, so I try to light the lighter
And I hold up the flame, and it goes out
And then I say sorry and light it again
And it's still windy
So he cups his hands over the top of mine

And makes a wee windshield for the flame, see
And he lights his feg
And he thanks me

And he walks on down the road
And then the next bus comes
And I get on the bus
And I'm sittin on the bus
And I'm thinkin this was all really strange
I'm thinkin that he touched me
He touched me
Like his hands touched mine
When I gave him the light, see

And I'm rollin down the Ormeau Road on the bus
And I'm thinking it's the first time
I've ever been touched by a Protestant

And I'm feeling strange
About the whole thing
He touched my hands, you know …
He touched me.

The inclusion of Mac Lochlainn's poem would have given us a better feel for the Troubles than we get here. MacMonagle says about Ciaran Carson's "Belfast Confetti" that it's "an elegant metaphor for the chaos of the Troubles"; Longley's "Ceasefire", as opposed to the Mac Lochlainn poem, requires a Classical education to get the references (let's not forget that a demand for third-level education was one of the agendas of the civil-rights movement). Another Longley poem, "The Civil Servant", is easier to digest:

He was preparing an Ulster fry for breakfast
When someone walked into the kitchen and shot him …

This is Hellfast. In the words of Padraic Fiacc, in "Enemy Encounter": "You can't live here without being poisoned." Not one but two poems about the IRA from Paul Muldoon, "Ireland" and "Anseo."

A Classical education is not required to get the gist of the poem by

Frank McGuinness: "They kicked the shit out of me." OK. I think we get the picture by now. Self-hatred is the one and only legacy of colonialism we can rely on, if the author of *The Wretched of the Earth* (Fanon, Gallimard, 1961) is to be believed and self-hatred is the abiding flavor of this poisoned anthology.

———

> *Today I believe in the possibility of love; that is why I endeavor*
> *to trace its imperfections, its perversions.*
>
> (Frantz Fanon)

In Peter Fallon's "The State of the Nation", this is the poet's evaluation of readers of *An Phoblacht*:

> If their day comes
> The country's fucked.

And there you have it. Our poets have spoken. It would have been a completely different anthology, of course, if all our poets had spoken, such as those mentioned by Thomas Rain Crowe, the band of Irish-language poets missing in action. But, in case we get any notions about real inclusiveness, MacMonagle gives us another little titbit in "The Death of Irish", by Aidan Matthews, which would seem to justify linguistic apartheid. Sure if it's dead it's dead and why would we be resurrecting it?!

> The tide gone out for good,
> Thirty-one words for seaweed whiten on the foreshore.

Sir Philp Sidney and Sir Edmund Spencer can rest peacefully in their graves.

Translated, from the Irish, by the author.

A poet, short-story writer and translator, Gabriel Rosenstock was born in 1949 in Kilfinane, Co Limerick and is a graduate of University College, Cork. One of the INNTI *poets that transformed Irish-language poetry in the 1970s, he writes primarily in Irish and is the author or translator of over 150 books. His most recent collection of poetry is* Bliain an Bhandé *(Year of the Goddess, The Dedalus Press, 2007).*

THE ETHNIC BASIS OF IRISH POETRY

Chris Agee

Uniquely entitled.

―

Some Preliminaries

I begin with a series of preliminary observations.

1) The term *Irish* in "Irish poetry" and "Irish poet" is meaningful in a complex way, and not merely self-evident, factual, conventional, arbitrary, formulaic, or uncontested. While it may operate like a *brand*, this particular national-cultural literary label is far from a straightforward, well-defined or transparent *branding exercise*.

2) There is plenty of literary, critical, cultural and anecdotal evidence suggesting that the criterion (or "category-fence") for being deemed an "Irish poet", or for work to belong to "Irish poetry" is, surprisingly, not guaranteed by Irish citizenship (or in the context of birth or residence in the North, British citizenship). Instead, a series of interrelated ethnic and cultural markers have consistently trumped the alternative civic basis for Irish literature. In this, its autochthonous bias, Irish literary practice diverges sharply and obviously, and in a quite retrograde fashion, from national classifications in the literary worlds of Great Britain and the United States.

3) My own empirical experience as foreign-born poet (and Irish citizen) living in Ireland for almost all my adult life is obviously relevant to this Irish "category-fence." In citing this experience alongside that of other writers, however, I am not making any comparisons of a critical or artistic nature, but merely proffering my own personal insights within a line of argument that relates purely to the sociology of literature, subset poetry.

4) Viewing any art through the prism of sociological perspectives carries an anti-imaginative, reductionist risk. But it is precisely due to the opposite desire to uphold the claims of a uniform poetic standard regardless of implicitly exclusivist criteria, involving a narrower

definition of imagined community, that I believe it is worth challenging the ethnic basis of Irish poetry in the first place.

5) For a prime item on the critical-cultural agenda relating to Irish poetry is, all too often, its own essentialist exceptionality. As Peter Sirr has memorably remarked:

> But … a large part of me thinks that the whole notion of Irish poetry is fairly boring, a kind of branding exercise for a product few, if put to it, could really define. The currents of poetic influence flow across continents and languages and few poets would seek to confine themselves within national boundaries, or to measure themselves against a set of "national" criteria. The dismaying parochiality of so much of Irish critical and cultural discourse – not least the flawed concept of "Irish Studies" – shouldn't blind us to the internationalism that is the lifeblood of poetry. Those who assume the exceptionality of Irish poetry will witter on about the lines of influence from Yeats to Heaney to Muldoon and ignore the fact that Montale, Pessoa, Celan, Bonnefoy, Lowell, Murray and a host of other unacknowledged legislators have long since gatecrashed the party.

6) Whether the basis of Irish poetry is deemed ultimately to have an ethnic or civic basis, both approaches share this in common: the fundamental criterion underpinning each reflects a differing conception of *significant connection to Ireland*. *Significant connection*, then, is the core meaning of each approach. In this light, a new civic basis for Irish literature does not replace the old ethnic basis, but merely supplements it with new understandings of significant connection. It extends the category-fence of *Irish* in a concentric fashion in a way that mirrors the new, actually-existing multicultural Ireland. In contrast, the ethnic basis of Irish poetry remains wedded to a classic nation-state essentialism whose "imagined community" cannot accommodate, intellectually or culturally, the actual human face of globalized migration.

Two Questions

First question: *what is Irish poetry?* Irish poetry, mirroring the new multicultural reality, can now easily be conceptualized as "one grammar, with four inflections": (i) the "central grammar" (or core inflection) written by Irish people on the island of Ireland; (ii) the "northern inflection", always in danger of a Czech-Slovak secession; (iii) the "diasporic or commuter inflection", emigrant Irish poets overseas, in North America and elsewhere, with now-hybrid identities; (iv) the "naturalized/Hibernicized immigrant inflection", non-native-born Irish citizens and other immigrant poets, including ones from "the other island" and the Irish diaspora; (v) the originating "inflection *as Gaeilge*", including the influence of bilingualism and the psychic partition of the "dual tradition" in Irish poetry.

Second question: *what is an Irish poet?* In a nutshell, then, this comes down to the question of whether civic or ethnic nationalism is used as the foundational criterion; whether, that is, it is a matter of Irish citizenship (or British as well, in the context of the North), or some other (often unreflective) essentialist ethnic marker such as ancestry, name, birthplace, accent, early upbringing, education and so forth. In the United States, Charles Simic (from Serbia, with a marked Balkan accent) is universally considered an "American poet"; in Britain, Salman Rushdie (a British citizen, from India) is universally considered a "British novelist." In Ireland, it's clear that the same courtesy is not *widely* extended in literary, critical, and popular circles; a variety of unreflective essentialist criteria still mostly trump a foundational civic criterion of Irish citizenship and personal-social-geographical relationship; the old confessional, essentialist Ireland (i.e., the dual monoliths, North and South) is even now still bound up with the definitions of Irish literature, subset poetry.

All this raises an important (if implicit) civic-cultural question: the equal treatment – all things being equal, critically and artistically – between "native-born Irish citizens" (or Northern-born British citizens, for that matter) and "non-native-born Irish citizens" (such as myself) in any understanding of "Irish poetry" or "Irish poet." (Citizenship, more than permanent residence, is the trailblazing issue for immigrants – so I will stick to this revealing contrast between the native-born and non-native-born citizen.)

It's no longer acceptable, really, to assume that Irish poetry (in the North, no less than the South) consists only of the native-born roster.

Imagine the outcry in the Britain *of the other island* if any resident British citizen, and poet, was excluded from "British poetry" merely on the grounds that he/she was born or raised in a Commonwealth country! Yet this is precisely what happens in Irish literature, poetry in particular – there is a dogged and entrenched assumption that "Irish poet" implies native-born ethnicity rather than a civic (hence multicultural) identity, i.e., that this literary label, or *brand*, is an ethnic rather than constitutional marker: a bloodline rather a civic loyalty. Really not acceptable: this literary bias roughly analogous to unreflective discrimination.

And my line of reflection here is especially pertinent to a *republic*, a *res publica*, "a public affair", rule not by *a* people, but *the* people – since it goes without saying that all its citizens must, by definition, be treated equally, the non-native-born *no less* than the native-born – indeed, such *egalité*, such *fraternité*, is the fundamental meaning, the very *raison d'être* of a republic, our Irish one included. And so the literary label or cultural brand must follow the constitutional reality, for anyone who believes in that republic.

Ethnicity and Exclusion

My trope for Irish poetry as a core grammar with four distinct inflections is clearly easier said than accepted, still less internalized. Few would find anything challenging about a single Irish poetry with strong Northern, overseas and Irish-language dimensions. It is clearly the idea of a further immigrant Irish dimension that mounts some key challenges to certain mainstream assumptions about Irish poetry. I imagine many in the Irish literary world would accept this immigrant dimension in principle, but baulk in practice. That, anyway, is my perception after 36 years on the island.

The problem seems to begin when the actual foreign-born poet turns up on the actual Irish poetic doorstep. At that point, the assumed ethnic basis of Irish writing often kicks in, along with not a little self-interest.

Are you still unconvinced that the wider sociology of immigrant and host does not translate easily into the Irish literary scene?

In a brief but fascinating article in a recent issue of *Poetry Ireland News*, the Irish poet Celeste Augé describes her experience of the critical application of what I am calling the ethnic basis of Irish poetry. Apparently, one Irish reviewer of her first collection (which I haven't read) deemed her to be a non-Irish poet whose first language was French. She is in fact an Irish citizen whose only language is English. Her mother is Irish, her father French Canadian, and the family emigrated to Ireland when she was 14 – hardly an age when cultural identity is fixed in stone, if it ever is.

It is worth quoting this article because it illustrates succinctly my further point: the incoherence of Irish literary essentialism. Augé comes up with the wonderfully precise phrase "other *non-Irish, Irish people*", which captures exactly the difference between Irishness as a civic identity (Irishness like Britishness, as it were) and Irishness as a narrower ethnic category-fence (Irishness like the three other national identities of Great Britain, as it were), whilst at the same time underscoring, implicitly, the fundamental cultural equality of these two definitions. It is a small phrase, and a small comma, with a big future:

> Having a reviewer decide my cultural and linguistic identity ... has made me wonder about other non-Irish, Irish people, living and working here, contributing to the wider literary and cultural scene ... Have they been accepted as writers by their country first, before launching out into the wider world? And by "their country", I mean the country they live in, pay taxes in, drink in, sleep in, raise their children in, rather than the country of their birth.
>
> And to go deep into the idea of bloodlines and language-lines, how Irish do you have to be, to be considered an Irish writer? Does the poetry business in Ireland have standard criteria for assessment? Would an Irish grandmother do, as it does for the national soccer team and the Irish passport office? Or would a surname *as Gaeilge* suffice?
>
> Can a cultural hegemony such as Ireland – with its postcolonial history of forcefully and rigidly declaring the parameters of its cultural and geographical identity, to the point where a proportion of its full-blooded Irish citizens feel themselves outside this boundary – make space for those who don't even have an Irish name, or accent, or even freckles to fall back on? How will poetry in Ireland, along with the reviews, discussion and criticism surrounding it, accommodate these fluctuating cultural boundaries? Further, will the many "Irish Studies" university programs, here and abroad, take on this broader definition of "Irish" in their literary analyses?

The dynamic of literary exclusion, the *ad absurdum* incoherence of essentialism, the decisive role of postcolonial history, with its hegemonic parameters of imagined community, the reinforcing role of Irish Studies and, by extension, the Irish diaspora – Augé's brief but cogent discursus does, indeed, suggest that the immigrant dimension will soon begin to mount a challenge to the boundaries of the essentialist mainstream of Irish poetry.

Gael and *gall*: the trope's as hackneyed as it is perennial, and now even vaguely comical, like Beckett's Nag and Nell. But it can have its uses in the contemporary context if it reminds us that Irish history has passed through many large-scale variants of native and newcomer, outsider and host. This folk memory is, of course, part of what Roy Foster has called "the Irish Story"; "Kelt, Briton, Roman, Dane and Scot / time and this island tied a crazy knot", as two lines by John Hewitt have it. But perhaps it is a story that many in the Irish literary world should update to the present.

Augé appears in the anthology *Landing Places: Immigrant Poets in Ireland*, published by the Dedalus Press earlier this year (2010). The volume brings together 66 foreign-born poets resident in Ireland, and was first launched by Hugo Hamilton at the Dublin Book Festival. I suspect that this anthology – albeit of a highly variable and uneven standard – will come to be seen as *the* cultural moment when the immigrant experience of the last decade or so in Ireland was clearly and self-consciously registered by Irish literary publishing. In that sense alone, the book must be judged significant. But I also think that the critical response of a number of native-born Irish poets will be felt, in retrospect, to be revealing of a cultural fault-line that the anthology now makes manifest.

In his memorable remarks, Hugo Hamilton – son of a German immigrant mother – agreed. Though I'm sure he was not blind to the spectrum of poetry here, he celebrated the value of large-scale immigrant experience to Ireland, whilst identifying several poems and poets striking by any critical standard. His remarks are shot through with discernments born of actual intimacy with immigrant, and emigrant, experience:

> Here in Ireland, we understand the emptiness of migrancy perhaps better than anyone else. … These poets have begun to rewrite our story, our Irishness, reprogramming our identity and our place in the world … [This story] says what we cannot say for ourselves without newcomer clarity. And perhaps this book marks a striking new phase of Irish culture … a blood transfusion. An irrigation …

Above all, Hamilton makes plain that the "imagined community" that is Ireland can no longer simply privilege an essentialist *retrospective*, or a troubled or prosperous *present*, but has become now, equally, indubitably, an *immigrant prospect* – that is to say, not simply "The Old Country", as Muldoon memorably mocked in a poem of that name, but a also new country, seen in an entirely new way. Countries of massive continuous immigration, or great diversity, like Canada, the US, Australia, the Latin American nations, or even Russia internally, have long incorporated such immigrant perspectives into their dominant national narrative. But for Ireland, of course, a small land dominated for the past century by two very narrow religio-cultural monoliths, this is a comparatively new outlook on a mass scale.

In contrast to Hamilton's generous discernments, the two major Irish reviews of *Landing Places*, both by well-known non-immigrant poets, seemed to damn with faint praise. In one, in *The Irish Times*, Justin Quinn, who has lived in the Czech Republic for many years, describes (twice) *all* the contributors to the anthology as "resident aliens." It is a strange phrase, more American than Irish, but also an *outrageously* incorrect one – for a proportion of the poets in this anthology are actually Irish or British citizens, *thus in no sense "alien"*, especially in the North.

Nothing could better illustrate essentialist complacency in the Irish literary world. An Irish citizen long resident *overseas* can call an Irish citizen *long resident in Ireland* "a resident alien" according, presumably, to a number of habitual ethnic markers or assumptions. Somehow the native-born poet assumes his *significant connection* to the island is essential and truly immutable, never to be matched by the Martian poet who lacks the *first narrative* of early upbringing, accent, ancestry *et cetera*, thereby overriding, implicitly, any equal claim to *significant connection* via the second narrative of an adult life.

This is precisely the type of diaspora nationalism, so promoted by President Robinson, that the Irish essayist Hubert Butler so disliked. Instead, Butler argued for the primacy of "our country and not our blood", and its concomitant principles of "national commitment" and "a secular constitution." He was of the view that the people of Ireland, whether native or foreign, were more important to the life of the island than those who were off it. As Neal Ascherson glosses in an essay on Butler:

Butler admired Wolfe Tone for his inclusive patriotism, open to all who lived in the land whether they were Catholic or Protestant,

Irish, Scottish or English, but not invoking the overseas diaspora. This especially appealed to Butler, who felt that "diaspora nationalism" was akin to racism.

Harry Clifton is one of the very few Irish poets consistently alert to the dangers of Irish poetic essentialism, North and South. It's not surprising, then, that a prescient quote of his turns up in the introduction to *Landing Places*:

> English departments of universities are waiting for the emergence
> – poetry first, then prose – of a new immigrant literature, the first
> of its kind in the state, the bittersweet fruits of the Chinese, East
> European and African experience on our soil.

It's also worth dwelling for a moment on two other instances of an exclusionary dynamic in the recent and current Irish literary world. It is now slipping from cultural memory, but in the immediate aftermath of independence, a number of so-called "Anglo-Irish" writers, most notably Elizabeth Bowen and Hubert Butler, were widely considered to be insufficiently "Irish." They fell foul of perceived colonialist background and/or identification and the new narrower, more confessional postcolonial "imagined community." That ethnic bar has now fallen; and if a bar can fall once, it can fall again.

Then there is the question of Irish writing *as Gaeilge*. Although the two literary languages are now probably on better and more equal terms than they have ever been, there is still the residual historical fraughtness of the "dual tradition." No one has yet been mad enough to suggest that *Gaeilge* is not part of Irish literature, but monoglot anglophone Irish poetry is always running the risk of underestimating the psychic distance felt by Irish-language writers towards a now-globalized English. Liam Ó Muirthile has described the literary predicament this way, in English: "If being a poet in Irish feels like living offshore on land, that feeling of offshoreness seems to be the undercurrent of a primary call: of journeying there to stay here."

Living offshore on land? Sound familiar? Well, it might, because it echoes those quotes by Hamilton, himself a native Irish speaker. The more one thinks about it, in fact, the more the immigrant literary experience has actual and potential parallels with writing in Irish. Many immigrants already exist in a bilingualism and even trilingualism, involving English as one of their langauges. I once met a 13-year-old Nigerian-born girl who attended a *gaelscoil* in Dublin and spoke fluent Irish. What would happen if she became a poet?

In his writings on the sociology of culture, Raymond Williams famously observed that any one culture is comprised of *residual*, *dominant* and *emergent* elements. He further noted that it was often the *residual* and *emergent* elements that proved most fertile within the whole culture. Applying this rich schema to Irish poetry is a rather revealing way of viewing the interrelation of a dominant anglophone tradition with its Irish-language and immigrant inflections.

Part of the importance and fertility of the old language lies, of course, in its very residuality, giving us access, as Eoghan Ó Tuairisc once put it, to "the rich Gaelic culture with over a thousand years of literary endeavour in its texture." Meanwhile, in Hamilton's phrase, the immigrant literary inflection opens the emergent possibility of "a striking new phase of Irish culture." If there can be a dual poetic tradition, why not a further dimension? Is it possible that a sort of triple tradition might emerge in Irish poetry over the next couple of decades? It is a tempting thought.

The Incoherence of Essentialism

The word "immigrant" in the subtitle of *Landing Places* is problematic, because immigration involves a continuum of experience, ranging from willing movement, to economic necessity, to persecution and asylum. It might be better to view some of the contributors to the anthology as "nationally ambiguous writers." Typically, the nationally ambiguous writer (historical and contemporary examples are legion) inhabits multiple literary identities and so often falls between two essentialist stools, not unlike the aforementioned "Anglo-Irish" writers of earlier generations.

Indeed, the more one looks, the more one finds such writers, particularly in the pre-national period, before the rise of the modern nation-state – a period which lasted much longer in Central and Eastern Europe, and the Balkans, than in Western Europe, owing to the three internal European empires that disintegrated in the aftermath of the Great War. These imperial polities, and the three ethno-national federations which in part succeeded them (Soviet Union, Yugoslavia and Czechoslovakia), were based on a different pattern of principles than the nation state, with corresponding differences in the role of ethnicity in "imagined community."

In Central Europe, classic examples of the nationally ambiguous writer include Franz Kafka (Czech and German, from Bohemia), Joseph Roth (Polish and Austrian, from Galicia) and Paul Celan (German and Romanian, from Bukovina). What they all share, besides Judaism and the culturally dominant German language, is a first narrative shaped by the doomed polity of Austria-Hungary, with its ancient and complex confluences of the multinational, the multi-ethnic and the multi-confessional. In a cognate fashion, the recent Nobel laureate, the novelist Herta Muller from the Saxon or German minority of Transylvania, once also part of Austria-Hungry, is another classic example of the nationally ambiguous writer.

We are more familiar with the nationally ambiguous writer in the Anglo-American tradition. Henry James and T.S. Eliot were naturalized British citizens, but also "Americans belonging to Europe." Elizabeth Bishop was both a Canadian and an American poet. Derek Walcott belongs to both West Indian and American writing.

Let's not forget, either, that small but outstanding contingent of Slavonic writers whose English work must belong to the Anglo or/and American tradition: Conrad, Nabokov, Brodsky, Isaiah Berlin.

So what is it about the Irish literary scene that seems to resist such multiple literary identities, such cultural elisions? Because, in fact, a number of Ireland's major writers have been, or are, nationally ambiguous.

It's just that the predominant postcolonial critical assumptions relating to Irish literature have been so resolutely essentialist, so hibernocentric, that such national literary ambiguity is not much pondered even if it is factually registered. Its a Catch-22: Irish literary essentialism must, perforce, see the Irish narrative of such a writer as the most meaningful, genuine or real dimension of said writer. And since this Irish critical *mentalité* cannot see even some of its own writers in a fully dual light, it finds it difficult – and this is the key dynamic – to accommodate the idea that writers from elsewhere might be accorded the same type of double light on native Irish ground.

Beckett, of course, is the great corrective. He wrote most of his major works in French, back-translating them into English. He lived a half century in France and, interestingly, when asked by the Swedish Academy to assign a country to his Nobel prize, he chose France, not Ireland. In France itself, there is no question of his status as a fully French writer, understood also as an Irish one, somewhat like Camus, who is seen as both French and Algerian.

Brian Moore left Northern Ireland when he was 27, became a Canadian citizen, and wrote and published his first novels there. In Canada, he remains, of course, a major Canadian novelist. Like the French, the Canadian literary world, itself bilingual and bifocal, appears able to entertain the basically simple premise that one writer can have two literary identities.

Although Muldoon is invariably treated by most Irish criticism as a purely Irish poet, he is now an American citizen and so routinely considered an American, or Irish-American, poet in the United States, appearing a clutch of times in the annual anthology *The Best of American Poetry*, and even editing it. He has a very major presence in the American literary world and his later work incorporates, of course, his life in North America.

I have no idea whether Tim Robinson is now an Irish as well as a British citizen, but his profound engagement with all aspects of life and language in the West would make it churlish not to consider him a deeply Irish writer. His work may be rooted in a classic tradition of British travel-writing, but he is also the perfect exemplar of how *significant civic connection* alone constitutes one major civic basis for Irish literature.

Andreas Vogel (from Germany) and Alex Humans (from Holland) have chosen to write in Irish. As Hamilton puts it, "the heritage of this country placed in the hands of immigrants for safe-keeping." On the basis of the language alone, how could they be considered anything but Irish writers?

So if citizenship is not used as the decisive criterion, of what, exactly, does the narrower ethnic basis of Irish poetry consist? Mention has already been made of ancestry, physical traits, name, birthplace, accent, early upbringing, and education. To these must he added, very importantly, the *easy* acceptance of one's self-designation as *Irish*. Joined to citizenship, early upbringing, accent, and education are clearly the most decisive. One or more of these three can then be reinforced by one or more of the other markers, the assembled (though highly variable) ensemble making self-designation sociologically self-evident.

I am not disputing the centrality or even primacy of the first narrative, but the second narrative has its claims, too. Some mischievous person might ask: what's the difference, exactly, in *significant connection*?

Finally, what have I just described?

For me, the image of a kind of ethno-literary closed shop is not too far off the mark. A closed shop is a workplace that requires union membership. Its purpose is to reserve, control, and assign work. If *literary space* is substituted for *work* in this equation, then something like the ethnic basis of Irish poetry comes into view. Whilst I am sure that many of its native-born members do not think much about the cultural process of their automatic membership, I am just as certain that many other Irish writers, critics, academics, journalists, festival programmers, *et cetera* know exactly how the cultural set-up works. That these essentialist markers are, *au fond*, arbitrary, unreflective, discriminatory, and/or incoherent is simply the price to be paid for protecting one version of Irish cultural space.

The essentialist Irish literary tendency is, of course, still heavily reinforced from overseas. To the east and west of Ireland, two huge cultural and economic structures, British publishing and American Irish Studies, are deeply implicated in reinforcing, by "Celticist" expectation and cultural unfamiliarity with the modern Ireland, older and now-unreflective definitions of *Irish poetry* and *Irish poet*. Is there any other group of national writers better served by two other nations, or with a more evolved sense of outside entitlement, though little reciprocated to their own cultural "outsiders?"

To conclude: the final (and, I believe, now inevitable) switch to "the civic basis of Irish literature" opens the way to a political implication. It is time to underscore that native-born and foreign-born citizens are fully equal in any definition of Irish literature and culture. The old confessional, essentialist, monoethnic, post-imperial Ireland is self-evidently over – and multicultural Ireland is, as it were, the *new* republicanism, the *new* Yeatsian project, North *and* South.

This essay was first presented on 15 September 2010 at the British and Irish Contemporary Poetry Conference, hosted by the Seamus Heaney Centre for Poetry, Queen's University Belfast.

Chris Agee is the Editor of this journal. His third collection of poems, Next to Nothing *(Salt, 2009) was shortlisted for the 2010 Ted Hughes Award for New Work in Poetry. He is currently completing a fourth collection of poems, as well as editing* Balkan Essays, *the sixth volume of prose by Hubert Butler (1900–1991). He divides his time between Belfast and Glasgow, where he is Visiting Scholar at the University of Strathclyde.*

Subscribe online at www.irishpages.org